Ethics

Discovering Right and Wrong

Ethics
Discovering Right and Wrong
Third Edition

LOUIS P. POJMAN

UNITED STATES MILITARY ACADEMY

Wadsworth Publishing Company
I(T)P® An International Thomson Publishing Company

Belmont, CA • Albany, NY • Boston • Cincinnati • Johannesburg • London • Madrid • Melbourne
Mexico City • New York • Pacific Grove, CA • Scottsdale, AZ • Singapore • Tokyo • Toronto

Philosophy Editor: Peter Adams
Assistant Editor: Kerri Abdinoor
Marketing Manager: Dave Garrison
Production Editor: Kate Barrett
Print Buyer: Stacey J. Weinberger
Copy Editor: Douglas Becker
Cover Designer: Laurie Anderson
Compositor: Linda Weidemann/Wolf Creek Press
Printer: Banta Book Group

The painting on the cover, The Death of Socrates *by Jacques Louis David, shows Socrates carrying out his own execution by taking the poison hemlock as described in Plato's dialogue* Crito *in 399* B.C. *Socrates had been unjustly condemned to death by an Athenian court for corrupting the youth and not honoring the Athenian deities. Offered a way to escape by his friends, he reasons that it would be immoral to accept their offer. Being the first person in recorded history to put philosophy to work in the area of morals, Socrates is called the "Father of Ethics." The Metropolitan Museum of Art, Catharine Lorillard Wolfe Collection, Wolfe Fund, 1931. Copyright © 1980 The Metropolitan Museum of Art.*

Printed in The United States of America
1 2 3 4 5 6 7 8 9 10

For more information, contact Wadsworth Publishing Company, 10 Davis Drive, Belmont, CA 94002, or electronically at http://www.wadsworth.com

International Thomson Publishing Europe
Berkshire House
168-173 High Holborn
London, WC1V 7AA, United Kingdom

International Thomson Editores
Seneca, 53
Colonia Polanco
11560 México D.F. México

Nelson ITP, Australia
102 Dodds Street
South Melbourne
Victoria 3205 Australia

International Thomson Publishing Asia
60 Albert Street #15-01
Albert Complex
Singapore 189969

Nelson Canada
1120 Birchmount Road
Scarborough, Ontario
Canada M1K 5G4

International Thomson Publishing Southern Africa
Building 18, Constantia Square
138 Sixteenth Road, P.O. Box 2459
Halfway House, 1685 South Africa

International Thomson Publishing Japan
Hirakawa-cho Kyowa Building, 3F
2-2-1 Hirakawa-cho
Chiyoda-ku
Tokyo 102, Japan

Library of Congress Cataloging-in-Publication Data

Pojman, Louis P.
    Ethics: discovering right and wrong / Louis P. Pojman. — 3rd ed.
        p.   cm.
    Includes bibliographical references and index.
    ISBN 0-534-55181-5
    1. Ethics.   I. Title
BJ1012.P65   1998
170—dc21   98-23849

Contents

Preface

In all the world and in all of life there is nothing more important to determine than what is right. Whatever the matter which lies before us calling for consideration, whatever the question asked us or the problem to be solved, there is some settlement of it which will meet the situation and is to be sought. . . . Wherever there is a decision to be made or any deliberation is in point, there is a right determination of the matter in hand which is to be found and adhered to, and other possible commitments which would be wrong and are to be avoided.

C. I. LEWIS, *THE GROUND AND NATURE OF RIGHT,*
COLUMBIA UNIVERSITY PRESS, 1955, P. 27

WHY STUDY ETHICS?

What is it to live a morally good life? Why is morality important? Are moral principles valid only as they depend on cultural approval or are there universal moral truths? How should I live my life? Are there intrinsic values? Which is the best moral theory? Can we derive moral values from facts? Why should I be moral? Is there a right answer to every problem in life? What is the relationship of religion to morality?

These sorts of questions have concerned me for several years, and I believe that they should concern all thoughtful individuals. Many people in our society, including university students, are confused about morality. On the one hand, many claim (as judged from questionnaires and in-class conversations) that they are moral relativists (which they suppose promotes tolerance). But (as judged from their answers to different questions) these same people believe in absolute religious authority in faith and morals or answer "no" to questions such as "Is it ever morally permissible to have an abortion—except to save a woman's life?" and "Is capital punishment ever morally justified?" They often uncritically hold either deontological, utilitarian, or egoist positions without being aware of the problems inherent in those positions. In sum, such people are very far from having an articulate moral theory of their own to match their understanding of literature, science, math, or even basketball. Yet morality is more important than any of these subjects, for it goes to the heart of what it means to live in the right way.

I am convinced that the subject of ethics is of paramount importance to us at the end of the 20th century. With the onset of pluralism and the loss of confidence in traditional authorities, a rational approach to ethics is vital if we are to survive and flourish. I disagree with many ethicists, including G. E. Moore in *Principia Ethica* (1903) and C. D. Broad in *Five Types of Ethical Theory* (1930), who dismiss ethics as merely theoretical and as having no practical relevance.

On the contrary, ethical theory has enormous practical benefits. It can free us from prejudice and dogmatism. It sets forth comprehensive systems from which to orient our individual judgments. It carves up the moral landscape so that we can sort out the issues in order to think more clearly and confidently about moral problems. It helps us clarify in our minds just how our principles and values relate to one another, and, most of all, it gives us some guidance in how to live.

ABOUT THIS BOOK

Having taught ethical theory for several years, I felt the need for a textbook that challenged the student to develop his or her own moral theory, that emphasized the importance of the enterprise and could serve as a guide for intelligent young people. The available textbooks were either too light, sweeping over important distinctions, or too heavy, getting bogged down in needless formalization, or too narrow, omitting a serious discussion of the virtues or the relationship between ethics and religion or the nature of values.

This book is intended for undergraduates in ethics courses. I have tried to write in an interesting, conversational manner, raising the key theoretical questions and analyzing them fairly closely without using unnecessary jargon. I have opened some chapters or included in the chapter discussion or in the sections entitled "For Further Reflection" at the end of each chapter examples of moral problems in order that students might have material to which to apply the theoretical discussion. It will be even better if students think up examples from their own lives.

This book is comprehensive, covering the major issues in contemporary moral theory and including a discussion of classical as well as contemporary renditions of the problems. It has an outline similar to that of my anthology, *Ethics: Classical and Contemporary Readings,* Third Edition (Wadsworth, 1998) and may be used as a companion to and commentary on that work. But the user of this text is free to change the order of presentation. For example, many teachers, including myself at times, like to deal with the relation of religion to morality, including the divine command theory, early on in the course. Nothing will be lost by going directly from Chapter 1 ("Introduction") to Chapter 10 ("Religion and Ethics"). Chapter 5 ("Values") is related to Chapter 9 ("Why Should I Be Moral?"), so they may be read in sequence.

I strive to be fair to opposing sides of every question, but whenever I do offer my own solutions to problems (in a single-author text this is virtually inevitable), I do so in the spirit of fallibility and openness to correction, leaving the reader to form his or her own judgment on the matter. Philosophers will note that the title of this book reflects a fundamental disagreement with J. L. Mackie, who entitled his influential work on ethics *Ethics: Inventing Right and Wrong,* whose work is discussed in Chapters 3 and 12. The late John Mackie, from whom I learned a great deal, was my esteemed teacher at Oxford University, but I think that his starting point is misleading. Ethics, although it contains an element of human creativity and inventiveness, is even more clearly a discovery, something which is not of our own making but constitutes the blueprint for individual happiness and social harmony. Hence the subtitle of this book: *Discovering Right and Wrong.*

The reader will note that I raise more questions than I answer. I do this in part because what is important in philosophy is for the individual to work out his or her own solutions to problems and in part because I am unsure of many of the solutions myself. Study questions and a short, usable bibliography ("For Further Reading") accompany each chapter. A glossary appears at the end of the book.

In this third edition I have revised most of the chapters, added more study questions, and added a chapter on moral realism (Chapter 12), including a discussion of Mackie's error theory and Gilbert Harman's moral nihilism.

ACKNOWLEDGMENTS

Michael Beaty, Jonathan Harrison, Bill Lawhead, Robert Louden, Laura Purdy, Roger Rigterink, Bruce Russell, Walter Schaller, Robert Audi, and Bob Westmoreland were very helpful in offering trenchant criticisms on several chapters of this book. The students in my ethical theory classes at the University of Mississippi made a challenging sounding board for many of my arguments. Deserving of special mention are John Ates, Chris Bradford, Laura Burrell, Scott Morris, and Clayton Overton. Ronald F. Duska, Rosemont College; Peter List, Oregon State University; Peter Vallentyne, Virginia Commonwealth University; and Stephen Griffith, Lycoming College, reviewed the manuscript for the first edition of this work. Arthur Kuflik, University of Vermont; Fred Schueler, University of New Mexico; R. Duane Thompson, Indiana Wesleyan University; and David A. White, Marquette University, reviewed the manuscript for the second edition. Peter Boltuc, St. Olaf College; R. L. Borton, Orange Coast Community College; Ronald Cox, San Antonio College; Jamie Dreier, Brown University; Ed Langerack, St. Olaf College; Robert Mellert, Brookdale Community College; Mark Michael, Austin Peay State University; Ken Schenck, Indiana Wesleyan University; Ed Sherline, University of Wyoming; and Gordon Whiting, Brigham Young University, reviewed this work for the third edition. Each of the reviewers greatly enhanced the finished text.

I am grateful to Peter Adams for his strong support of this third edition. Kate Barrett did an excellent job of putting this work into its final form. I'm grateful to Douglas Becker for his helpful copyediting of the manuscript and to Ruth Stevens for proofreading this work. Most of all, I am indebted to my wife, Trudy, for living a morally inspiring life. Without her love and devotion, my life would be less joyous and this book would not have been written. To her this book is dedicated.

—LOUIS P. POJMAN

A Word to the Student: Why Study Moral Philosophy?

Ethics, or moral philosophy, is one branch of philosophy. What is philosophy? It is an enterprise that begins with wonder at the marvels and mysteries of the world, that pursues a rational investigation of those marvels and mysteries, seeking wisdom and truth, and that results in a life lived in passionate moral and intellectual integrity. Believing that "the unexamined life is not worth living," philosophy leaves no facet of life untouched by its inquiry. It aims for a clear, critical, comprehensive conception of reality.

The hallmark of philosophy is rational argument. Philosophers clarify concepts and analyze and test propositions and beliefs, but their major task is to analyze and construct arguments. Philosophical reasoning is closely allied with scientific reasoning, in that both build hypotheses and look for evidence to test those hypotheses with the hope of coming closer to the truth. However, scientific experiments take place in laboratories and have testing procedures to record objective or empirically verifiable results. The laboratory of the philosopher is the domain of ideas—the mind, where imaginative thought-experiments take place; the study, where ideas are written down and examined; and wherever conversation or debate about the perennial questions takes place, where thesis and counterexample and counterthesis are considered.

Let us apply this to ethics. Ethics is that branch of philosophy that deals with how we ought to live, with the idea of the Good, and with such concepts as "right" and "wrong." As such, it is a *practical* discipline. There are two parts to the study of ethics: the theoretical and the applied. The theoretical aspect, "ethical theory," deals with comprehensive theories about the good life and moral obligation. It analyzes and constructs grand systems of thought in order to explain and orient agents to the moral life. Included in this domain is a close analysis of concepts such as "right," "wrong," "permissible," and the like. The applied aspect, "applied ethics," deals with moral problems, including questions about the morality of abortion, premarital sex, capital punishment, euthanasia, and civil disobedience. Ethical theory and applied ethics are closely related: theory without application is sterile and useless, but action without a theoretical perspective is blind. There will be an enormous difference in the quality of discussions about abortion, punishment, sexual morality, and euthanasia when those discussions are informed by ethical theory as compared to when they are not. More light and less heat will be the likely outcome.

With the onset of pluralism and the loss of confidence in traditional authorities, a rational approach to ethics is vital for us to survive and thrive. Ethical theory may rid us of facile dogmatism and emotionalism—where shouting matches replace arguments—and liberate us from what Bernard Williams refers to as "vulgar relativism." Ethical theory clarifies relevant concepts, constructs and evaluates arguments, and guides us in living our lives. It is important that the educated person be able to discuss ethical situations with precision and subtlety.

Ethics is not only of instrumental value; it is valuable in its own right. It is satisfying to have knowledge of important matters for its own sake, and it is important to understand the nature and scope of moral theory for its own sake. We are rational beings who cannot help but want to understand the nature of the good life and all that it implies. You may become disturbed by the variety of theories discussed in this book, which seem mutually exclusive and so produce confusion when you desire guidance. But an appreciation of the complexity of ethics is valuable in offsetting our tendency toward dogmatism and provincialism. It is also a challenge to use your reason to endorse or produce the best system or combination of systems possible.

I have written this book as a quest for truth and understanding, hoping to create excitement about the value of ethics. It is a subject that I love, for it is about how we are to live, about the best kind of life. I hope that you will come to share my enthusiasm for the subject and to develop your own ideas in the process.

I would be delighted to hear your thoughts or questions on the ideas in this book, including any suggestions for ways to improve the work. Feel free to write to me at the following address:

Louis P. Pojman
United States Military Academy
West Point, NY, 10996

1

Introduction:
What Is Ethics?

We are discussing no small matter, but how we ought to live.

SOCRATES, IN PLATO'S REPUBLIC

Some years ago, the nation was stunned by a report from Kew Gardens, Queens, in New York City. A young woman, Kitty Genovese, was brutally stabbed in her neighborhood late at night during three separate attacks while thirty-eight respectable, law-abiding citizens watched and listened. Her neighbors looked on from their bedroom windows for some thirty-five minutes as the assailant beat her, stabbed her, left her, and returned to repeat the attack two more times until she died. No one lifted a phone to call the police; no one shouted at the criminal, let alone went to Genovese's aid. Finally, a seventy-year-old woman called the police. It took them two minutes to arrive, but by that time Genovese was dead. Only one other woman came out to testify before the ambulance came, which was an hour later. Then residents from the whole neighborhood poured out of their apartments. When asked why they hadn't done anything, they gave answers ranging from "I don't know" and "I was tired" to "Frankly, we were afraid."[1]

Who are our neighbors? What should these respectable citizens have done? What would you have done? If, with little inconvenience to yourself, you could save someone's life or save someone from harm, would you be partly responsible for any harm done to that person if you chose not to act? Are such acts of omission morally blameworthy? How much risk should we undergo to help someone in danger? What kinds of generalizations can we make from this episode about contemporary culture in America? What does the crime rate in our cities tell us about the moral climate of our society? Is the Genovese murder an anomaly, or is it quite indicative of a deeply disturbing trend?

What is it to be a moral person? What is the nature of morality? Why do we need morality? What function does it play? What is the good, and how shall I know it? Are moral principles absolute, or are they simply relative to social groups or individual decision? Is morality, like beauty, in the eye of the beholder? Is it always in my interest to be moral? Or is it sometimes in my best interest to act immorally? How do we justify our moral beliefs? What is the basis of morality? Which ethical theory best justifies and explains the moral life? What relationship does morality have with religion, law, and etiquette?

These are some of the questions we shall be looking at in this book. We want to understand the foundation and structure of morality. We want to know how we should live.

The terms "moral" and "ethics" come from Latin and Greek, respectively ("mores" and "ethos"), deriving their meaning from the idea of "custom." Although philosophers sometimes use these terms interchangeably, many philosophers distinguish among *morality, moral philosophy,* and *ethics.* I generally use *morality* to refer to certain customs, precepts, and practices of people and cultures. This is sometimes called *positive morality* or *descriptive morality* (since it describes actual beliefs and customs). I use *moral philosophy* to refer to philosophical or theoretical reflection on morality. Specific moral theories issuing from such philosophical reflection I call *ethical theories,* in line with a common practice. I use *ethics* to refer to the whole domain of morality and moral philosophy, since these two areas have many features in common. For example, both areas concern values, virtues, and principles and practices, though in different ways.

Moral philosophy refers to the systematic endeavor to understand moral concepts and justify moral principles and theories. It undertakes to analyze concepts and terms such as "right," "wrong," "permissible," "ought," "good," and "evil" in their moral contexts. Moral philosophy seeks to establish principles of right behavior that may serve as action guides for individuals and groups. It investigates which values and virtues are paramount to a worthwhile life or society. It builds and scrutinizes arguments in ethical theories and seeks to discover valid principles (e.g., "Never kill innocent human beings") and the relationship between valid principles (e.g., "Does saving a life in some situations constitute a valid reason for breaking a promise?").

MORALITY AS COMPARED
WITH OTHER NORMATIVE SUBJECTS

Moral precepts concern norms; roughly speaking, they concern not what is, but what ought to be. How should I live my life? What is the right thing to do in this situation? Should I always tell the truth? Do I have a duty to report a coworker whom I have seen cheating our company? Should I tell my friend that his spouse is having an affair? Is premarital sex morally permissible? Ought a woman ever to have an abortion? Morality has a distinct action-guiding, or *normative,* aspect,[2] which it shares with other practical institutions, such as religion, law, and etiquette.

Moral behavior, as defined by a given religion, is usually believed essential to that religion's practice. But neither the practices nor precepts of morality should be identified with religion. The practice of morality need not be motivated by religious considerations. And moral precepts need not be grounded in revelation or divine authority—as religious teachings invariably are. The most salient characteristic of ethics—by which I mean both philosophical morality (or *morality,* as I will simply refer to it) and moral philosophy—is its grounding in reason and human experience.

To use a spatial metaphor, secular ethics is horizontal, lacking a vertical or transcendental dimension. Religious ethics, being grounded in revelation or divine authority, has that vertical dimension, though religious ethics generally uses reason to supplement or complement revelation. These two differing orientations often generate different moral principles and standards of evaluation, but they need not do so. Some versions of religious ethics, which posit God's revelation of the moral law in nature or conscience, hold that reason can discover what is right or wrong even apart from divine revelation. We will discuss this subject in Chapters 3 (under natural law) and 10.

Morality is also closely related to law, and some people equate the two practices. Many laws are instituted in order to promote well-being, resolve conflicts of interest, and promote social harmony, just as morality does, but ethics may judge that some laws are immoral without denying that they are valid *laws.* For example, laws may permit slavery, spousal abuse, racial discrimination, or sexual discrimination, but these are immoral practices. A Catholic or antiabortion advocate may believe that the laws permitting abortion are immoral.

In a 1989 PBS television series, "Ethics in America," James Neal, a trial lawyer, was asked what he would do if he discovered that his client had committed a murder some years earlier for which another man had been convicted and would soon be executed.[3] Neal said that he had a legal obligation to keep this information confidential and that, if he divulged it, he would be disbarred. It is arguable that he has a moral obligation that overrides his legal obligation and demands that he act to save the innocent man from execution.

Furthermore, some aspects of morality are not covered by law. For example, although it is generally agreed that lying is usually immoral, there is no general law against it (except under special conditions, such as committing perjury or falsifying income tax returns). Sometimes college newspapers publish advertisements by vendors who offer "research assistance," despite knowing in advance that these vendors will aid and abet plagiarism. Publishing such ads is legal, but its moral correctness is doubtful. The thirty-eight people who watched the attacks on Kitty Genovese and did nothing to intervene broke no New York law, but they were very likely morally culpable for their inaction.[4]

There is one other major difference between law and morality. In 1351, King Edward of England promulgated a law against treason that made it a crime merely to think homicidal thoughts about the king. But, alas, the law could not be enforced, for no tribunal can search the heart and fathom the intentions of the mind. It is true that *intention,* such as malice aforethought, plays a role in determining the legal character of an act, once the act has been committed. But preemptive punishment for people who are presumed to have bad intentions is illegal. If malicious intentions ("mens rea," in law) were illegal, wouldn't we all deserve imprisonment? Even if one could detect others' intentions, when should the punishment be administered? As soon as the offender has the intention? But how do we know that the offender won't change his or her mind? Furthermore, isn't there a continuum between imagining some harm to X, wishing a harm to X, desiring a harm to X, and intending a harm to X?

Although it is impractical to have laws against bad intentions, these intentions are still bad, still morally wrong. Suppose I buy a gun with the intention of killing Uncle Charlie in order to inherit his wealth, but I never get a chance to fire it (for example, suppose Uncle Charlie moves to Australia). Although I have not committed a crime, I have committed a moral wrong.

Finally, law differs from morality in that there are physical and financial sanctions[5] (e.g., imprisonment and fines) enforcing the law but only the sanction of conscience and reputation enforcing morality.

Morality also differs from etiquette, which concerns form and style rather than the essence of social existence. Etiquette determines what is polite behavior rather than what is *right* behavior in a deeper sense. It represents society's decision as to how we are to dress, greet one another, eat, celebrate festivals, dispose of the dead, express gratitude and appreciation, and, in general, carry out social transactions. Whether people greet each other with a handshake, a bow, a hug, or a kiss on the cheek depends on their social system. People in Russia wear their wedding ring on the third finger of the right hand, whereas we wear it on the left hand. People in England hold their fork in the left hand, whereas people in other countries hold it in the right hand or whichever hand they prefer. People in India typically eat without a fork at all, using the forefingers of the right hand to convey food from the plate to the mouth. Whether we uncover our heads in holy places (as males do in Christian churches) or cover them (as females do in Catholic churches and males do in synagogues), none of these rituals has any moral superiority. Polite manners grace our social existence, but they are not what social existence is about. They help social transactions to flow smoothly but are not the substance of those transactions.

At the same time, it can be immoral to disregard or flout etiquette. Whether to shake hands when greeting a person for the first time or put one's hands together in front as one bows, as people in India do, is a matter of cultural decision. But once the custom is adopted, the practice takes on the importance of a moral rule, subsumed under the wider principle of Show Respect to People. Similarly, there is no moral necessity to wear clothes, but we have adopted the custom partly to keep warm in colder climates and partly to be modest. But there is nothing wrong with nudists who decide to live together in nudist colonies. However, for people to go nude outside of nudist colonies, say, in classrooms, stores, and along the road may well be so offensive that it is morally insensitive. Recently, there was a scandal on the beaches of south India, where American tourists swam in bikinis, shocking the more modest Indians. There was nothing immoral in itself about wearing bikinis, but given the cultural context, the Americans willfully violated etiquette and were guilty of moral impropriety.

Although Americans pride themselves on tolerance, pluralism, and awareness of other cultures, custom and etiquette can be—even among people from similar backgrounds—a bone of contention. A friend of mine, John, tells of an experience early in his marriage. He and his wife, Gwen, were hosting their first Thanksgiving meal. He had been used to small celebrations with his immediate family, whereas his wife had been used to grand celebrations. He writes, "I had been asked to carve, something I had never done before, but I was willing. I put on an apron, entered the kitchen, and attacked the bird with as much artistry as I could muster. And what reward did I get? [My wife] burst into tears. In *her* family the turkey is brought to the table, laid before the [father], grace is said, and *then* he carves! 'So I fail patriarchy,' I hollered later. 'What do you expect?'"[6]

Law, etiquette, and religion are all important institutions, but each has limitations. A limitation of law is that you can't have a law against every social malady, nor can you enforce every desirable rule. A limitation of etiquette is that it doesn't get to the heart of what is vitally important for personal and social existence. Whether or not one eats with one's fingers pales in significance when compared with the importance of being honest or trustworthy or just. Etiquette is a cultural invention, but morality claims to be a discovery. A limitation of religious injunction is that it rests on authority, and we may lack certainty or agreement about the authority's credentials or how the authority would rule in ambiguous or new cases. Since religion is founded not on reason but on revelation, you cannot use reason to convince someone from another religion that your view is the right one. I hasten to add that, when fundamental moral principles cause moral differences, philosophical reasoning is unlikely to settle the matter. Often, however, our moral differences have their roots in worldviews, not moral principles. For example, a pro-life and pro-choice advocate may agree that it is wrong to kill an innocent person, but they differ about the facts. The pro-life advocate's religion may state that a fetus has an eternal soul and thus a right to life, whereas the pro-choice advocate may believe that no one has a soul and only self-conscious, rational beings have a right to life.

The following table characterizes the relationship among ethics, religion, law, and etiquette:

Subject	Normative Disjuncts	Sanctions
Ethics	Right and wrong, as defined by conscience or reason	Conscience—praise and blame; reputation
Religion	Right and wrong (sin), generally as defined by religious authority	Conscience—eternal reward and punishment, due to a supernatural agent or force
Law	Legal and illegal, as defined by a judicial body	Punishments determined by the legislative body
Etiquette	Proper and improper, as defined by the culture	Social disapprobation and approbation

In summary, morality differs from law and etiquette by going deep into the essence of our social existence. It differs from religion by seeking reasons, rather than authority, to justify its principles. The central purpose of moral philosophy is to secure valid principles of conduct and values that can guide human actions and produce good character. As such, it is the most important activity we know, for it concerns how we are to live.

TRAITS OF MORAL PRINCIPLES

A central feature of morality is the moral principle. We have already noted that moral principles are practical action guides, but we must say more about the traits of such principles. Although there is no universal agreement on the traits a moral principle must have, there is a wide consensus about five traits:

1. Prescriptivity
2. Universalizability
3. Overridingness
4. Publicity
5. Practicability

Prescriptivity

Prescriptivity refers to the practical, or action-guiding, nature of morality. Moral principles are generally put forth as injunctions or imperatives (e.g., "Do not kill," "Do no unnecessary harm," and "Love your neighbor"). They are intended for use, to advise people and influence action. Prescriptivity shares this trait with all normative discourse. Retroactively, this trait is used to appraise behavior, assign praise and blame, and produce feelings of satisfaction or guilt. We will discuss this further in Chapter 9.

Universalizability

Moral principles must apply to all who are in the relevantly similar situation. If one judges that act X is right for a certain person P, then it is right for anyone relevantly similar to P. This trait is exemplified in the Golden Rule, "Do unto others what you would have them do unto you (if you were in their shoes)," and in the formal Principle of Justice:

> It cannot be right for A to treat B in a manner in which it would be wrong for B to treat A, merely on the ground that they are two different individuals, and without there being any difference between the natures or circumstances of the two which can be stated as a reasonable ground for difference of treatment.[7]

Universalizability applies to all evaluative judgments. If I say that X is a good Y, then I am logically committed to judge that anything relevantly similar to X is a good Y. This trait is an extension of the principle of consistency: One ought to be consistent about one's value judgments, including one's moral judgments. We will look further at this trait in Chapters 7 and 9.

Overridingness

Moral principles have hegemonic authority. They are not the only principles, but they take precedence over other considerations, including aesthetic, prudential, and legal ones. The artist Paul Gauguin may have been aesthetically justified in abandoning his family in order to devote his life to painting beautiful Pacific island pictures, but morally, or all things considered, he probably was not justified. It may be prudent to lie to save my reputation, but it probably is morally wrong to do so, in which case I should tell the truth. When the law becomes egregiously immoral, it may be my moral duty to exercise civil disobedience. There is a general moral duty to obey the law, since the law serves an overall moral purpose, and this overall purpose may give us moral reasons to obey laws that may not be moral or ideal. But there may come a time when the injustice of a bad law is intolerable and hence calls for illegal but moral defiance (such as the antebellum laws in the South requiring citizens to return slaves to their owners).[8] Religion is a special case: Many philosophers argue that a religious person may be morally justified in following a perceived command from God that overrides a normal moral rule. John's pacifist religious beliefs may cause him to renege on an obligation to fight for his country. Religious morality is morality, and ethics recognizes its legitimacy. We will say more about this in Chapter 10.

Publicity

Moral principles must be made public in order to guide our actions. Because we use principles to prescribe behavior, give advice, and assign praise and blame, it would be self-defeating to keep them a secret. Occasionally, a utilitarian argues that it would be better if some people didn't know or didn't try to follow the correct principles, but even those people would have a higher-order principle—or some reason for this exception—that subsumes such special cases. We will discuss this in Chapter 6.

Practicability

A moral theory must be workable; its rules must not lay a heavy burden on agents. The philosopher John Rawls speaks of the "strains of commitment"[9] that overly idealistic principles may cause in average moral agents. It might be desirable for morality to enjoin more altruism, but the result of such principles could be moral despair, deep or undue moral guilt, and ineffective action. Practicability may cause the difference between ethical standards over time and place. For instance, there is a discrepancy between Old Testament and New Testament ethics on such topics as divorce and the treatment of one's enemy. Jesus explained both these discrepancies. He said that, because of society's hardness of heart, God permitted divorce in pre-Christian times. Jesus also said that, in the future, it would be a valid principle to love one's enemies and pray for them, and he enjoined his disciples to begin living by this ideal morality. Most ethical systems take human limitations into consideration.

Since moral philosophers disagree somewhat about the above traits, discussing these traits fully would lead to a great deal of qualification. However, the present discussion should give you an idea of the general features of moral principles.

DOMAINS OF ETHICAL ASSESSMENT

At this point, it might seem that ethics concerns itself entirely with rules of conduct that are based solely on evaluating acts. However, the situation is more complicated than that. Most ethical analysis falls into one, or some, of the following domains:

Domain	Evaluative Terms
1. Action (the act)	Right, wrong, obligatory, optional
2. Consequences	Good, bad, indifferent
3. Character	Virtuous, vicious, neutral
4. Motive	Good will, evil will, neutral

Let us examine each of these domains.

Types of Action

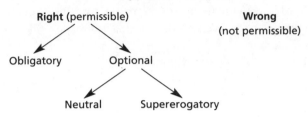

The most common distinction may be the classification of actions as right and wrong, but the term "right" is ambiguous. Sometimes it means "obligatory" (as in "the right act"), but sometimes it means permissible (as in "a right act" or "It's all right to do that"). Usually, philosophers define *right* as permissible, including in that category what is obligatory:

i. A *right act* is an act that is permissible for you to do. It may be either (a) optional or (b) obligatory.

    a. An *optional act* is an act that is neither obligatory nor wrong to do. It is not your duty to do it, nor is it your duty not to do it. Neither doing it nor not doing it would be wrong.

    b. An *obligatory act* is one that morality requires you to do; it is not permissible for you to refrain from doing it.

ii. A *wrong act* is an act you have an obligation, or a duty, to refrain from doing: It is an act you ought not to do; it is not permissible to do it.

Let us briefly illustrate these concepts. The act of lying is generally seen as wrong (prohibited), whereas telling the truth is generally seen as obligatory. But some acts do not seem either obligatory or wrong. Whether you take a course in art history or English literature or whether you write a letter with a pencil or pen seem morally neutral. Either is permissible. Whether you listen to pop music or classical music is not usually considered morally significant. Listening to both is allowed, and neither is obligatory. Whether you marry or remain single is of great moral significance (it is, after all, an important decision about how to live your life). The decision you reach, however, is usually considered morally neutral or optional. Under most circumstances, to marry (or not to marry) is considered neither obligatory nor wrong, but permissible. Within the range of permissible acts is the notion of *supererogatory* or highly altruistic acts. These acts are neither required nor obligatory, but they exceed what morality requires, going "beyond the call of duty." You may be obliged to give a donation to help people in dire need, but you are probably not obliged to sell your car, let alone become destitute, in order to help them.

Theories that emphasize the nature of the act are called *deontological* (from the Greek word for duty). These theories hold that something is inherently right or good about such acts as truth-telling and promise-keeping and inherently wrong or bad about such acts as lying and promise-breaking. Illustrations of deontological ethics include the Ten Commandments (in Exodus 20); natural law ethics, such as in Roman Catholicism; and Immanuel Kant's theory of the Categorical Imperative.

Immanuel Kant (1724–1804) argued that two kinds of commands or imperatives exist: *hypothetical* and *categorical*. Hypothetical imperatives are conditional, having the form "If you want X, do act A!" For example, if you want to pass this course, do your homework and study this book! Categorical imperatives, on the other hand, are not conditional, but universal and rationally necessary. Kant's primary version of the Categorical Imperative (he actually offered three versions that he thought were equivalent) states: "Act only on that maxim whereby you can at the same time will that it would become a universal law." Examples are "Never break your promise" and "Never commit suicide." Contemporary Kantians often interpret the Categorical Imperative as yielding objective, though not absolute principles. That is, although in general it is wrong to break promises or commit suicide, sometimes such principles may be overridden by other moral principles. Here is where consequences enter the picture (we will study Kant's theory in Chapter 7).

Consequences

We said above that lying is generally seen as wrong, and truthfulness is generally seen as right. But consider this situation. In your home, you are hiding an innocent woman named Laura, who is fleeing gangsters. Gangland Gus knocks on your door and asks you whether Laura is in your house. What should you do? Should you tell the truth or lie? Those who say that morality pertains to the consequences of actions would prescribe lying as the morally right thing to do. Those who say that morality is independent of the consequences when there is a clear and absolute rule of action would prescribe keeping silent or telling the truth. When no other rule is at stake, of course, the rule-oriented ethicist will allow the foreseeable consequences to determine a course of action. Theories that focus primarily on consequences in determining moral rightness and wrongness are called teleological ethical theories (from the Greek "telos," meaning goal-directed). The most famous of these theories is utilitarianism, set forth by Jeremy Bentham (1748–1832) and John Stuart Mill (1806–1873), which enjoins us to do what is likeliest to have the best consequences: do the act that will produce the greatest happiness for the greatest number. We will study utilitarianism in Chapter 6.

Character

Whereas some ethical theories emphasize principles of action in themselves, and some emphasize principles involving the consequences of action, other theories, such as Aristotle's ethics, emphasize character or virtue. According to Aristotle, it is most important to develop virtuous character, for if and only if we have good people can we ensure habitual right action. Although it may be helpful to have action-guiding rules, it is vital to empower character to do good. Many people know that cheating, gossiping, or overindulging in food or alcohol is wrong, but they are incapable of doing what is right. The virtuous person may not consciously follow the moral law when he or she does what is right and good. Although the virtues are not central to other types of moral theories, most moral theories consider the virtues important. Most reasonable people, whatever their notions about ethics, would judge that the witnesses of the Genovese murder lacked good character. Different moral systems emphasize different virtues and to different degrees. In Chapter 8 we will study the place of virtue.

Motive

Virtually all ethical systems, but especially Kant's system, accept the relevance of *motive*. For a full assessment of any action, it is important to take the agent's intention into account. Two acts may be identical, but one may be judged morally culpable and the other excusable. Consider John's pushing Joan off a ledge, causing her to break her leg. In situation (A), he is angry and intends to harm her, but in situation (B) he sees a knife flying in her direction and intends to save her life. In (A), he clearly did the wrong thing, whereas in (B) he did the right thing. On the other hand, two acts may have opposite results, but the action may be judged equally good on the basis of intention. For example, two soldiers may try to cross the enemy lines to communicate with an allied force, but one soldier gets captured through no fault of his own, and the other succeeds. A full moral description of any act will take motive into account as a relevant factor.

WHY DO WE NEED MORALITY?

Hobbes's Account

Why do we need morality? What is its nature and purpose? What does it do for us that no other social arrangement does? There are many philosophical replies to these questions, but a classic reply is from the English philosopher Thomas Hobbes (1588–1679) in his book *Leviathan* (1651). Hobbes believed that human beings always act out of perceived self-interest, that is, they invariably seek gratification and avoid harm. His argument goes like this. Nature has made us basically equal in physical and mental abilities, so that, even though one person may be somewhat stronger or smarter than another, each has the ability to harm, even kill, the other, if not alone, then in confederacy with others. Furthermore, we all want to attain our goals, such as having sufficient food, shelter, security, power, wealth, and other scarce resources. These two facts, equality of ability to harm and desire to satisfy our goals, lead to an unstable state:

> From this equality of ability arises equality of hope in the attaining of our ends. And therefore if any two people desire the same thing, which nevertheless they cannot both enjoy, they become enemies; and in the way to their end, which is principally their own preservation and sometimes their enjoyment only, endeavor to destroy, or subdue one another. And from hence it comes to pass, that where an invader hath no more to fear, than another man's single power; if one plant, sow, build, or possess a convenient seat, others may probably be expected to come prepared with forces united, to dispossess, and deprive him, not only of the fruit of his labor, but also of his life or liberty. And the invader again is in the like danger of another.

Given this state of insecurity, people have reason to fear one another. Hobbes calls this a "state of nature," in which there are no common ways of life, no enforced laws or moral rules, and no justice or injustice, for these concepts do not apply. There are no reliable expectations about other people's behavior—except that they will follow their own inclinations and perceived interests, tending to be arbitrary, violent, and capricious:

> Hereby it is manifest, that during the time men live without a common power to keep them all in awe, they are in that condition which is called war; and such a war, as is for *every man, against every man*. For war consists not in battle only or in the act of fighting; but in a tract of time, wherein the will to contend in battle is sufficiently known: and

therefore the notion of *time,* is to be considered in the nature of war; as it is in the nature of weather. For as the nature of foul weather lies not in the shower or two of rain, but in an inclination thereto of many days together; so the nature of war consists not in actual fighting, but in the known disposition thereto, during all the time there is no disposition to the contrary.

Hobbes described the consequence of the state of nature, this war of all against all, as follows:

In such a condition, there is no place for industry; because the fruit thereof is uncertain: and consequently no cultivating of the earth; no navigation, nor use of the comfortable buildings; no instruments of moving, and removing, such things as require much force; no knowledge of the face of the earth; no account of time; no arts; no literature; no society; and which is worst of all, continual fear, and danger of violent death; and the life of man solitary, poor, nasty, brutish and short.

But this state of nature, or more exactly, state of anarchy and chaos, is in no one's interest. We can all do better if we compromise, give up some of our natural liberty—to do as we please—so that we will all be more likely to get what we want: security, happiness, power, prosperity, and peace. So, rational egoists that we are, according to Hobbes, we give up some of our liberty and agree to a *social contract* or *covenant*. It sets a ruler and rules over us, which we are to obey, since the rules are enforced by a mighty ruler, the state, the *Leviathan*. Only within this contract does morality arise and do justice and injustice come into being. Where there is no enforceable law, there is neither right nor wrong, justice nor injustice.

So morality is a form of social control. We all opt for an enforceable set of rules such that if almost all of us obey them almost all the time, almost all of us will be better off almost all the time. A select few people, conceivably, may actually be better off in the state of nature, but the vast majority will be better off in a situation of security and mutual cooperation. Some people may cheat and thus renege on the social contract, but so long as the majority honors the contract most of the time, we will all flourish.

Hobbes didn't claim that a pure state of nature ever existed or that humanity ever really formally entered into such a contract, though he notes that such a state actually exists among nations, so a "cold war" keeps us all in fear. Rather, Hobbes was explaining the function of morality. He was answering the question, "Why do we need morality?" Why? Because without it existence would be an unbearable hell in which life is "solitary, poor, nasty, brutish and short."

William Golding's classic novel *Lord of the Flies* brilliantly portrays the Hobbesian account of morality.

A Reflection on *Lord of the Flies*

Which is better—to have rules and agree, or to hunt and kill?[10]

In the last section, we asked, "Why exactly do we need moral codes?" What function do they play in our lives and in society in general? Rather than continue my discursive essay on the benefits of morality, let me draw your attention to a book every young person has read or should have read: William Golding's classic novel *Lord of the Flies* (1954). This modern moral allegory may provide a clue about the nature and purpose of morality.

A group of boys aged six to twelve from an English private school, cast adrift on an uninhabited Pacific island, create their own social system. For a while, the constraints of civilized society prevent total chaos. All the older boys recognize the necessity of substantive and procedural rules. Only he who has the white conch, the symbol of authority, may speak during an assembly. They choose the leader democratically and invest him with limited powers. Even the evil Roger, while taunting little Henry by throwing stones near him, manages to keep the stones from harming the child.

> Here, invisible yet strong, was the taboo of the old life. Round the squatting child was the protection of parents and school and policemen and the law. Roger's arm was conditioned by a civilization that knew nothing of him and was in ruins. (p. 78)

After some initial euphoria in being liberated from the adult world of constraints and entering an exciting world of fun in the sun, the children come up against the usual banes of social existence: competition for power and status, neglect of social responsibility, failure of public policy, and escalating violence. Two boys, Ralph and Jack, vie for leadership, and a bitter rivalry emerges between them. As a compromise, a division of labor ensues in which Jack's choirboy hunters refuse to help the others in constructing shelters. Freeloading soon becomes common, as most of the children leave their tasks to play on the beach. Neglect of duty results in failure to be rescued by a passing airplane. The unbridled lust for excitement leads to the great orgiastic pig kills and finally, at its nadir, to the thirst for human blood.

Civilization's power is weak and vulnerable to atavistic, volcanic passions. The sensitive Simon, the symbol of religious consciousness (like Simon Peter, the first disciple of Jesus), who prophesies that Ralph will be saved and is the first to discover and fight against the "ancient, inescapable recognition" of the beast in us, is slaughtered by the group in a wild frenzy. Only Piggy and Ralph, mere observers of the orgiastic homicide, feel vicarious pangs of guilt at this atrocity.

The incarnation of philosophy and culture—poor, fat, nearsighted Piggy, with his broken spectacles and asthma—becomes ever more pathetic as the chaos increases. He reaches the nadir of his ridiculous position after the rebels, led by Jack, steal his spectacles in order to harness the sun's rays for starting fires. After Ralph, the emblem of not-too-bright but morally good civilized leadership, fails to persuade Jack to return the glasses, Piggy asserts his moral right to them:

> You're stronger than I am and you haven't got asthma. You can see.... But I don't ask for my glasses back, not as a favour. I don't ask you to be a sport...not because you're strong, but because what's right's right. Give me my glasses,...You got to. (p. 211)

Piggy might as well have addressed the fire itself, for in this state of moral anarchy moral discourse is a foreign tongue that only incites the worst elements to greater immorality. Roger, perched on a cliff above, responds to moral reasoning by dislodging a huge rock that hits Piggy and flings him to his death forty feet below.

The title "Lord of the Flies" comes from a translation of the Greek "Beelzebub," which is a name for the devil. Golding shows that we need no external devil to bring about evil, but that we have found the devil and, in the words of Pogo, "he is us." Ubiquitous, ever waiting for a moment to strike, the devil emerges from the depths of the subconscious whenever there is a conflict of interest or a moment of moral lassitude. As E. L. Epstein says, "The tenets of civilization, the moral and social codes, the Ego, the intelligence itself, form only a veneer over this white-hot power, this uncontrollable force, 'the fury and the mire of human veins.'"[11]

Beelzebub's ascendancy proceeds through fear, hysteria, violence, and death. A delegation starts out hunting pigs for meat. Then they find themselves enjoying the kill. To drown the incipient shame over blood-thirstiness and take on a persona more compatible with their deed, the children paint themselves with colored mud. Their lusting for the kill takes on all the powerful overtones of an orgiastic sexual ritual, so that, being liberated from their social selves, they kill without remorse whomever gets in their way. The deaths of Simon and Piggy (the symbols of the religious and the philosophical, the two great fences blocking the descent to hell) and the final orgiastic hunt with the "spear sharpened at both ends" signal for Ralph the depths of evil in the human heart.

Ironically, it is the British navy that finally comes to the rescue and saves Ralph (civilization) just when all seems lost. But the symbol of the navy is a Janus-faced omen. On the one hand, it symbolizes that a military defense is, unfortunately, sometimes needed to save civilization from the barbarians (Hitler's Nazis or Jack and Roger's allies), but on the other hand it symbolizes the quest for blood and vengeance latent in contemporary civilization. The children's world is really only a stage lower than the adult world whence they come, and that shallow adult civilization could very well regress to tooth and claw if it were scratched too sharply. The children were saved by the adults, but who will save the adults who put so much emphasis on military enterprises and weapons systems—in the euphemistic name of "defense"? To quote E. L. Epstein:

> The officer, having interrupted a man-hunt, prepares to take the children off the island in a cruiser which will presently be hunting its enemy in the same implacable way. And who will rescue the adult and his cruiser?[12]

The fundamental ambiguity of human existence is visible in every section of the book, poignantly mirroring the human condition. Even Piggy's spectacles, the sole example of modern technology on the island, become a bane for the island as Jack uses them to ignite a forest fire that will smoke out their prey, Ralph, and burn down the entire forest and destroy the island's animal life. It is a symbol both of our penchant for misusing technology to vitiate the environment and our ability to create weapons that will lead to global suicide.

THE PURPOSES OF MORALITY

What is the role of morality in human existence? What are little boys and girls and big men and women made of that requires ethical consciousness? Ralph answers these questions at the end of the tale.

> And in the middle of [the children], with filthy body, matted hair, and unwiped nose, Ralph wept for the end of innocence, the darkness of man's heart, and the fall through the air of the true, wise friend called Piggy. (p. 248)

In this wise modern moral allegory, we catch a glimpse of some of morality's purposes. Rules formed over the ages and internalized within us hold us back and, hopefully, defeat "The Lord of the Flies" in society, whether he be inherent in us individually or an emergent property of corporate existence. The moral code restrains the Rogers of society from doing evil until untoward social conditions open up the sluice gates of sadism and random violence. Morality is the force that enables Piggy and Ralph to maintain a modicum of order within their dwindling society, first motivating them to compromise with Jack and then keeping things in a wider perspective.

In Golding's allegory, morality is "honored more in the breach than in the observance,"[13] for we see the consequences of not having rules, principles, and virtuous character. As Piggy says, "Which is better—to have rules and agree, or to hunt and kill [each other]?" Morality consists of a set of rules such that, if nearly everyone follows them, then nearly everyone will flourish. These rules restrict our freedom but only in order to promote greater freedom and well-being. More specifically, morality seems to have these five purposes:

1. To keep society from falling apart
2. To ameliorate human suffering
3. To promote human flourishing
4. To resolve conflicts of interest in just and orderly ways
5. To assign praise and blame, reward and punishment, and guilt

Let us elaborate these purposes. Imagine what society would be like if everyone or nearly everyone did whatever he or she pleased without obeying moral rules. I would promise to help you with your philosophy homework tomorrow if you fix my car today. You believe me. So you fix my car, but you are deeply angry when I laugh at you tomorrow as I drive away to the beach instead of helping you with your homework. Or you loan me money, but I run off with it. Or I lie to you or harm you when it is in my interest or even kill you when I feel the urge.

Parents would abandon children, and spouses would betray each other whenever it was convenient. Under such circumstances, society would break down. No one would have an incentive to help anyone else, because reciprocity (a moral principle) was not recognized. Great suffering would go largely unameliorated, and, certainly, people would not be very happy. We would not flourish or reach our highest potential.

I recently visited the former Soviet republics, Kazakhstan and Russia, which are undergoing a difficult transition from communism to democracy. In this transition (hopefully, it will turn out favorably), with the state's power considerably withdrawn, crime is increasing, and distrust is prevalent. At night, trying to navigate my way up the staircases in the apartment building where I was staying, I was in complete darkness. I asked why there were no lightbulbs in the stairwells, only to be told that the residents stole them, believing that, if they did not take them, then their neighbors would. Absent a dominant authority, the social contract has eroded, and everyone must struggle alone in the darkness.

We need moral rules to guide our actions in ways that light up our paths and prevent and reduce suffering, enhance human well-being (and animal well-being, for that matter), resolve our conflicts of interests according to recognizably fair rules, and assign responsibility for actions, so that we can praise, blame, reward, and punish people according to how their actions reflect moral principles.

Even though these five purposes are related, they are not identical, and different moral theories emphasize different purposes in different ways. Utilitarianism fastens upon human flourishing and the amelioration of suffering, whereas contractual systems rooted in rational self-interest accent the resolution of conflicts of interest. A complete moral theory would include a place for each of these purposes. The goal of such a theory is to internalize in each moral person's life the rules that promote these purposes, thus producing the virtuous person, someone who is "a jewel that shines in [morality's] own light," to paraphrase Kant. The goal of morality is to create happy and virtuous people, the kind that create flourishing communities. That's why it is the most important subject on earth.

Conclusion

Let us return to questions I asked at the beginning of this chapter. You should be able to answer each of them.

What is the nature of morality, and why do we need it? Morality concerns discovering the rules that promote the human good, as elaborated in the five purposes discussed above. Without morality, we cannot promote that good.

What is the good, and how shall I know it? The good in question is the human good, specified as happiness, reaching one's potential, and so forth. Whatever we decide on that fulfills human needs and helps us develop our deepest potential is the good that morality promotes.

Are moral principles absolute, or are they simply relative to social groups or individual decision? It would seem that moral principles have universal and objective validity, since similar rules are needed in all cultures to promote human flourishing. So moral rules are not justified by cultural acceptance and are not relative. But neither are they absolute, if "absolute" means that one can never break or override them. Most moral rules can be overridden by other moral rules in certain contexts. For example, it is sometimes justified to lie in order to save an innocent life.

Is it in my interest to be moral? Yes in general and in the long run, for morality is exactly the set of rules that are most likely to help (nearly) all of us if nearly all of us follow them nearly all of the time. The good is good for you—at least most of the time. Furthermore, if we believe in the superior importance of morality, then we will bring children up so that they will be unhappy when they break the moral code. They will feel guilt. In this sense, the commitment to morality and its internalization nearly guarantee that, if you break the moral rules, you will suffer—both because of external sanctions and internal sanctions (moral guilt).

What is the relationship between morality and religion? Religion relies more on revelation, and morality relies more on reason, on rational reflection. But religion can provide added incentive for the moral life, offering the individual a relationship with God, who sees and will judge all our actions.

What is the relationship between morality and law? Morality and law should be very close, and morality should be the basis of the law, but there can be both unjust laws and immoral acts that cannot be legally enforced. The law is shallower than morality and has a harder time judging human motives and intentions. You can be morally evil, intending to do evil things, but so long as you don't do them, you are legally innocent.

What is the relationship between morality and etiquette? Etiquette consists in the customs of a culture, but they are typically morally neutral in that the culture could flourish with a different code of etiquette. In our culture, we eat with knives and forks, but a culture that eats with chopsticks or fingers is no less moral.

To go any further, we must examine the very status of moral principles. Are they wholly relative to culture—socially approved habits—or do some of them enjoy universal validity regardless of whether societies recognize them? We turn to this problem in Chapter 2.

NOTES

1. Martin Gansberg, "38 Who Saw Murder Didn't Call Police," *The New York Times,* March 27, 1964.

2. The term "normative" means seeking to make certain types of behavior a norm, or a standard, in a society.

Webster's Collegiate Dictionary defines it as "of, or relating or conforming to, or prescribing norms or standards."

3. "Ethics in America," PBS, 1989, produced by Fred Friendly.

4. In Anglo–American law, there is no general duty to rescue a person in need. In 1908, James Barr Ames proposed that a person should be required to "save another from impending death or great bodily harm, when he might do so with little or no inconvenience to himself." The proposal was defeated, as its opponents argued: Would a rich person to whom $20 meant very little be legally obliged to save the life of a hungry child in a foreign land? The rule was seen as confusing charity with law. Only Vermont and Minnesota have Good Samaritan laws, requiring that one come to the aid of a person in grave physical harm, but only to the extent that the aid "can be rendered without danger or peril to himself or without interference with important duties owed to others."

5. A *sanction* is a mechanism for social control, used to enforce society's standards. External sanctions may consist in rewards or punishment, praise or blame, approbation or disapprobation. The chief internal sanction is *conscience*. Sigmund Freud defined conscience as "the inner perception of objections to definite impulses that exist in us; and the emphasis is put upon the fact that this rejection does not have to depend on anything else, that it is sure of itself" [*Totem and Taboo*, in *The Basic Writings of Sigmund Freud*, trans. A. A. Brill (Modern Library, 1938), pp. 859f].

6. John Buehrens and Forrester Church, *Our Chosen Faith* (Beacon Press, 1989), p. 140.

7. Henry Sidgwick, *The Methods of Ethics*, 7th ed. (Macmillan, 1907), p. 380. More recently, some moral philosophers have denied that universalizability is a necessary condition for moral action. See, for example, Lawrence Blum, *Friendship, Altruism, and Morality* (Routledge & Kegan Paul, 1980).

8. Of the five listed characteristics of morality, this is the most controversial. Samuel Sheffler, in *Human Morality* (Oxford University Press, 1992), has questioned it, and John Kekes, in "On There Being Some Limits to Morality" [*Social Philosophy and Policy* 9(2) (1992)], argues that nonmoral considerations sometimes override moral ones. Although problems exist with this trait, it cannot be entirely given up without reducing morality to prudence. We will examine this point further in Chapter 10.

9. John Rawls, *A Theory of Justice* (Harvard University Press, 1971), pp. 176, 423. Samuel Scheffler similarly argues that, although conflicts between morality and self-interest arise, morality is essentially a *humane* and reasonable phenomenon [*Human Morality* (Oxford University Press, 1992)].

10. Piggy, the moral philosopher, in William Golding's *Lord of the Flies* (G. P. Putnam's, 1959), p. 222. All references are to this work.

11. E. L. Epstein, "Notes on *Lord of the Flies*," in *Lord of the Flies*, p. 252.

12. E. L. Epstein, "Notes," p. 251.

13. William Shakespeare, *Hamlet*.

FOR FURTHER REFLECTION

1. As the illustration from Golding's *Lord of the Flies* shows, we may come to understand and appreciate the need for and purposes of morality by looking at situations in which morality is absent or evil is present. Name some literature, social studies, or social experience in which this is further illustrated.

2. Illustrate the difference between a moral principle, a legal rule, a principle of etiquette, an aesthetic judgment, and a religious principle. Are these

sometimes related? Can something be so aesthetically repulsive that we conclude it is morally wrong? For example, our laws prohibit public nudity, and many people find public nudity revolting or deeply offensive, but is it necessarily morally wrong?

3. In a moral dilemma, no matter what action you take, some evil will result, or two accepted moral principles will meaningfully conflict. Moral dilemmas produce most of the hard cases in applying ethical theory. Here are a few dilemmas for you to discuss:

a. In William Styron's book *Sophie's Choice,* Sophie, a prisoner in a Nazi concentration camp, is told to choose which of her two children the Nazi commander will execute. If she refuses to choose between them, he will kill both. If she chooses one, the other will live. What should she do?

b. You are driving a trolley down the track, when suddenly the brakes fail and you cannot stop the trolley at the red light. Ahead of you are ten men working on the track, whom you will kill if you do nothing. Fortunately, there is a side spur you can turn onto and thus spare the men. But, unfortunately, if you do turn onto it, you will kill a child who is playing there. So if you do nothing, ten men will die because of the brake failure; but if you act voluntarily, you will kill the child. What should you do? (Judith Jarvis Thomson first proposed this example.)

c. You have discovered that your parents have embezzled a large sum of money from the corporation they work for. You have spoken to them about this, and they have denied it, but you know that they are lying. If you report them, they will go to jail, and their lives will be ruined. If you don't report them, the owners of the business will be financially ruined. How do you handle this situation?

d. You have discovered that your best friend's husband is having an affair.

Should you tell her and risk ruining her marriage, should you approach her husband, or should you do nothing? Do you have a moral duty at all here? Suppose you decide to talk to him first, and he denies the affair. You are convinced that he is lying. What should you do?

e. You and twenty friends are spelunking in a coastal cave when Freddy gets caught in the cave's mouth. The tide is rising, and soon all of you will drown (except Freddy, whose head is outside the cave) if Freddy isn't dislodged from the cave's mouth. Fortuitously, you have a stick of dynamite with you. Your options are to blow Freddy from his place or drown along with nineteen friends. What should you do?

4. On the cover of this book is Louis David's famous painting of Socrates bidding farewell to his disciples and friends in 399 B.C. Socrates has been unjustly condemned to death by the citizens of Athens. While Socrates is in jail awaiting execution, his friend Crito offers him a safe way of escaping. Crito argues that Socrates has an obligation to his friends and family to accept this opportunity, but Socrates argues that it is wrong to break the law in order to save oneself. Who is right? Read Plato's dialogue *Crito* to get the details of the arguments. This is probably the first case in history in which the issue of civil disobedience is discussed. Is civil disobedience ever morally justified? If so, when and under what conditions?

5. Tom Jones, an up-and-coming young businessman, is walking to work on a bridge over a river when he sees a small girl fall into the river. She begins to scream for help. Tom is a good swimmer and knows he can save her life, but if he does so, he will miss a meeting that is important to his career. In addition, the water is cold, and Tom doesn't want to ruin his new suit. He doesn't want to jump in, and reasons that it's not his fault that the

girl fell into the river. Does he have a duty to jump in despite his objections? Why or why not? What would you say if Tom accidentally pushes the girl into the river? Or purposely pushes her into the river?

6. The late French existentialist Jean-Paul Sartre (1905–1980) related the following dilemma. During World War II, when the German army occupied France, a student came to Sartre asking for moral advice. The boy's father was a Nazi collaborator, but the German army had killed the boy's older brother a few years earlier. The boy wanted to avenge his brother's death and help free his country. However, his mother, now estranged from her collaborationist husband, lived alone with this boy, who was her only consolation. Sartre wrote:

> The boy was faced with the choice of leaving for England and joining the Free French Forces—that is, leaving his mother behind—or remaining with his mother and helping her to carry on. He was fully aware that the woman lived only for him and that his going off—and perhaps his death—would plunge her into despair. He was also aware that every act that he did for his mother's sake was a sure thing, in the sense that it was helping her to carry on, whereas every effort he made toward going off and fighting was an uncertain move which might run aground and prove completely useless.
>
> As a result, he was faced with two very difficult kinds of action: one, concrete, immediate, but concerning only one individual; the other concerned an incomparably vaster group, a national collectivity, but for that very reason was dubious, and might be interrupted en route. And, at the same time, he was wavering between two kinds of ethics. On the one hand, an ethics of sympathy, of personal devotion; on the other, a broader

ethics, but one whose efficacy was more dubious. He had to choose between the two. [Jean-Paul Sartre, *Existentialism and Human Emotions,* trans. Bernard Fechtman and Hazel Barnes (Philosophical Library, 1957), pp. 24–25.].

a. What should Sartre have advised the student to do? What was the correct advice?

b. Is there a correct solution to the student's dilemma? Is one option the right one and the other the wrong one? Explain your response.

c. It is sometimes said that men and women tend to view morality from different perspectives, men being more rule-governed and emphasizing global duties, and women being more nurturing and emphasizing caring and sympathy. In the student's dilemma, then, women would generally advise staying home with the mother, whereas men would generally advise fighting for the cause of freedom. Do you agree with this analysis?

7. Where does etiquette leave off and ethics begin? When does rudeness cease to be simply bad manners and become bad morals? Is it immoral not to say "Thank you" for a medium-sized favor? Is it immoral not to be grateful for a service rendered? Consider the following contemporary problem. It has become accepted practice to use the disjunctive "he or she" instead of simply the old generic "he," in an attempt to be more gender-inclusive. Recently, an acquaintance of mine asked his editor (at a major publishing company) "Why can't I use the generic 'man' and 'he' instead of the cumbersome 'human beings' and 'he and she'?" The editor replied that using the old forms would not be allowed, for the more inclusive language was "morally correct." My acquaintance replied, "It may be courteous, but I don't see anything intrinsically moral about the issue." What do you think?

8. In 1881, the French painter Paul Gauguin (1848–1903) gave up his job as a banker and abandoned his wife and children in order to pursue a career as an artist. He moved to Martinique and later to Tahiti, eventually becoming one of the most famous postimpressionist artists in the world. Did Gauguin do what was morally permissible?

Our moral judgment would seem to condemn him. He had a special duty to his wife and children that obligated him to care for them. Success in art is no justification for abandoning these primary duties. Moral duties, we generally believe, override all other reasons for action, especially aesthetic ones.

Some 2,450 years earlier, an Indian prince, Siddhartha Gautama (560–480 B.C.), appalled by the tremendous and pervasive suffering in the world, abandoned his wife and child in order to lead the life of an ascetic monk. Six years later, while sitting under the Bo-tree, he attained enlightenment and became known as the Buddha. In deserting his wife and child, did Siddhartha do what was morally right?

I have never heard anyone criticize Siddhartha for that act. People seem to think that his religious quest justified his act. Is this true? Note that Siddhartha was not a theist. He sought liberation (*moksa*) from suffering; he did not seek the will of God. Does this make a difference?

What is the moral difference between Paul Gauguin and Siddhartha Buddha?

9. Think of some difficult moral issues and keep them in mind as you work through the rest of this book, asking yourself how the various theories would treat these issues.

FOR FURTHER READING

Baier, Kurt. *The Moral Point of View.* Cornell University Press, 1958. An abridged 1965 edition of this fine work is available in paperback from Random House. The work sees morality primarily in terms of social control.

Brandt, Richard. *Ethical Theory: The Problems of Normative and Critical Ethics.* Prentice-Hall, 1959. A thorough and thoughtful treatment of ethical theory.

Frankena, William K. *Ethics,* 2nd ed. Prentice-Hall, 1973.

Gert, Bernard. *Morality: A New Justification of the Moral Rules,* 2nd ed. Oxford University Press, 1988. A clear and comprehensive discussion of the nature of morality.

MacIntyre, Alasdair. *A Short History of Ethics.* Macmillan, 1966. A lucid, if uneven, survey of the history of Western ethics.

Mackie, J. L. *Ethics: Inventing Right and Wrong.* Penguin, 1976. This book takes a very different view of ethics from my own.

Pojman, Louis, ed. *Ethical Theory: Classical and Contemporary Readings,* 3rd ed. Wadsworth, 1998. Contains readings for each section of this book.

Scheffler, Samuel. *Human Morality.* Oxford University Press, 1992. A defense of a "moderate" view of morality between the "extremes." According to the latter, either morality generally requires sacrificing one's self-interest or morality never conflicts with self-interest. Scheffler argues that, although conflicts between morality and self-interest sometimes arise, morality is essentially reasonable.

Singer, Peter. *The Expanding Circle: Ethics and Sociobiology.* Oxford University Press, 1983. A fascinating attempt to relate ethics to sociobiology.

Taylor, Paul. *Principles of Ethics.*
Wadsworth, 1975. This work covers
many of the same topics as my book,
usually from a different perspective.
His discussion of the principle of universalizability (pp. 95–105) is especially useful.

Taylor, Richard. *Good and Evil.* Prome-
theus, 1970. A lively, easy-to-read
work that considers morality's main
role to be the resolution of conflicts of
interest.

Turnbull, Colin. *The Mountain People.*
Simon & Schuster, 1972. An excellent
anthropological study of a people
living on the edge of morality.

Warnock, G. J. *The Object of Morality.*
Methuen, 1971. A clearly written,
well-argued analysis of the nature of
morality.

Wilson, James Q. *The Moral Sense.* The Free
Press, 1993. A leading social scientist
argues for the existence of a universal
moral sense. Well worth reading.

2

Ethical Relativism: Who's to Judge What's Right and Wrong?

Ethical relativism is the doctrine that the moral rightness and wrongness of actions varies from society to society and that there are no absolute universal moral standards binding on all men at all times. Accordingly, it holds that whether or not it is right for an individual to act in a certain way depends on or is relative to the society to which he belongs.

JOHN LADD, *ETHICAL RELATIVISM*

In the 19th century Christian missionaries sometimes used coercion to change the customs of pagan tribal people in parts of Africa and the Pacific Islands. Appalled by the customs of public nakedness, polygamy, working on the sabbath, and infanticide, they paternalistically went about reforming the "poor pagans." They clothed them, separated wives from their husbands in order to create monogamous households, made the Sabbath a day of rest, and ended infanticide. In the process they sometimes created social malaise, causing the estranged women to despair and their children to be orphaned. The natives often did not understand the new religion, but accepted it in deference to the white man's power. The white people had guns and medicine.

Since the 19th century we've made progress in understanding cultural diversity, and now realize that social dissonance caused by "do-gooders" was a bad thing. In the last century or so, anthropology has exposed our penchant for ethnocentrism, the prejudicial view that interprets all of reality through the eyes of one's own cultural beliefs and values. We have come to see enormous variety in social practices throughout the world.

For instance, Eskimos allow their elderly to die by starvation, whereas we believe that this is morally wrong. The Spartans of ancient Greece and the Dobu of New Guinea believe that stealing is morally right; but we believe it is wrong. Many cultures, past and present, have practiced or still practice infanticide. A tribe in East Africa once threw deformed infants to the hippopotamus, but our society condemns such acts. Sexual practices vary over time and clime. Some cultures permit homosexual behavior, whereas others condemn it. Some cultures, including Moslem societies, practice polygamy, while Christian cultures view it as immoral. Anthropologist Ruth Benedict describes a tribe in Melanesia that views cooperation and kindness as vices, and anthropologist Colin Turnbull has documented that the Ik in northern Uganda have no sense of duty toward their children or parents. There are societies that make it a duty for children to kill their aging parents (sometimes by strangling).

The ancient Greek historian Herodotus (485–430 B.C.) told the story of how Darius, the king of Persia, once brought together some Callatians (Asian tribal people) and some Greeks. He asked the Callations how they disposed of their deceased parents. They explained that they ate the bodies. The Greeks, who cremate their parents, were horrified at such barbarous behavior and begged Darius to cease from such irreverent discourse. Herodotus concluded that "Custom is the king o'er all."[1]

Today we condemn ethnocentrism as a variety of prejudice tantamount to racism and sexism. What is right in one culture may be wrong in another, what is good east of the river may be bad west of the same river, what is virtue in one nation may be seen as a vice in another, so it behooves us not to judge others but to be tolerant of diversity.

This rejection of ethnocentrism in the West has contributed to a general shift in public opinion about morality, so that for a growing number of Westerners, consciousness-raising about the validity of other ways of life has led to a gradual erosion of belief in moral objectivism, the view that there are universal moral principles, valid for all people and climes. For example, in polls taken in my ethics and introduction to philosophy classes over the past several years (in three different universities in three areas of the country) students affirmed by a two to one ratio, a version of moral relativism over moral absolutism with barely three percent seeing something in between these two polar opposites. Of course, I'm not suggesting that all these students have a clear understanding of what relativism entails, for many of those who say they are ethical relativists also state on the same questionnaire that "abortion, except to save a woman's life, is always wrong," that "capital punishment is always morally wrong," or that "suicide is never morally permissible." The apparent contradictions signal some confusion on the matter.

In this chapter, we examine the central notions of ethical relativism and look at the implications that seem to follow from it. In Chapter 3, we set forth the outlines of two forms of objectivism, which hold that moral principles have a universal validity that is not dependent on cultural or individual approval.

AN ANALYSIS OF RELATIVISM

Ethical relativism holds that there are no universally valid moral principles, but rather that all moral principles are valid relative to culture or individual choice. It is to be distinguished from *moral skepticism*—the view that there are no valid moral principles at all (or at least we cannot know whether there are any)—and from all forms of *moral objectivism* or *absolutism*. John Ladd's statement at the beginning of this chapter, which we repeat here, is a typical characterization of the theory:

> Ethical relativism is the doctrine that the moral rightness and wrongness of actions varies from society and that there are no absolute universal moral standards binding on all men at all times. Accordingly, it holds that whether or not it is right for an individual to act in a certain way depends on or is relative to the society to which he belongs.[2]

If we analyze this passage, we derive the following argument:

1. What is considered morally right and wrong varies from society to society, so that there are no universal moral standards held by all societies.

2. Whether or not it is right for an individual to act in a certain way depends on or is relative to the society to which he or she belongs.

3. Therefore, there are no *absolute* or objective moral standards that apply to all people everywhere and at all times.

The Diversity Thesis

The first thesis, which may be called the *diversity thesis* and identified with *cultural relativism,* is simply an anthropological thesis that acknowledges that moral rules differ from society to society. As we illustrated earlier in this chapter, there is enormous variety in what may count as a moral principle in a given society. The human condition is malleable in the extreme, allowing any number of folkways or moral codes. As Ruth Benedict has written:

> The cultural pattern of any civilization makes use of a certain segment of the great arc of potential human purposes and motivations, just as we have seen...that any culture makes use of certain selected material techniques or cultural traits. The great arc along which all the possible human behaviors are distributed is far too immense and too full of contradictions for any one culture to utilize even any considerable portion of it. Selection is the first requirement.[3]

It may or may not be the case that there is not a single moral principle held in common by every society, but if there are any, they seem to be few, at best. Certainly, it would be very hard to derive one single "true" morality on the basis of observation of various societies' moral standards.

The Dependency Thesis

The second thesis, the *dependency thesis,* asserts that individual acts are right or wrong depending on the nature of the society in which they occur. Morality does not exist in a vacuum; rather, what is considered morally right or wrong must be seen in a context, depending on the goals, wants, beliefs, history, and environment of the society in question. As William Graham Sumner says,

> We learn the [morals] as unconsciously as we learn to walk and hear and breathe, and [we] never know any reason why the [morals] are what they are. The justification of them is that when we wake to consciousness of life we find them facts which already hold us in the bonds of tradition, custom, and habit.[4]

Trying to see things from an independent, noncultural point of view would be like taking out our eyes in order to examine their contours and qualities. We are simply culturally determined beings.

We could, of course, distinguish both a weak and a strong thesis of dependency. The nonrelativist can accept a certain relativity in the way moral principles are *applied* in various cultures, depending on beliefs, history, and environment. For example, Asians show respect by covering the head and uncovering the feet, whereas Occidentals do the opposite. Though both adhere to a principle of respect for deserving people, they apply the principle differently. But the ethical relativist must maintain a stronger thesis, one that insists that the very validity of the principles is a product of the culture and that different cultures will invent different valid principles. The ethical relativist maintains that even beyond the environmental factors and differences in beliefs, there are fundamental disagreements among societies.

In a sense, we all live in radically different worlds. Each person has a different set of beliefs and experiences, a particular perspective that colors all of his or her perceptions. Do the farmer, the real estate dealer, and the artist looking at the same spatiotemporal field actually see the same thing? Not likely. Their different orientations, values, and expectations govern their perceptions, so that different aspects of the field are highlighted and some features are missed. Even as our individual values arise from personal experience, so social values are grounded in the particular history of the community. Morality, then, is just the set of common rules, habits, and customs that have won social approval over time, so that they seem part of the nature of things, like facts. There is nothing mysterious or transcendent about these codes of behavior. They are the outcomes of our social history.

There is something conventional about *any* morality, so that every morality really depends on a level of social acceptance. Not only do various societies adhere to different moral systems, but the very same society could (and often does) change its moral views over time and place. For example, in the southern United States slavery is now viewed as immoral, whereas just over 100 years ago, it was not. We have greatly altered our views on abortion, divorce, and sexuality as well.

The conclusion—that there are no absolute or objective moral standards binding on all people—follows from the first two propositions. Cultural relativism (the diversity thesis) plus the dependency thesis yields ethical relativism in its classic form. If there are different moral principles from culture to culture and if all morality is rooted in culture, then it follows that there are no universal moral principles valid for all cultures and all people at all times.

SUBJECTIVE ETHICAL RELATIVISM

(SUBJECTIVISM)

Some people think that this conclusion is still too tame, and they maintain that morality depends not on the society but rather on the individual. As my students sometimes maintain, "Morality is in the eye of the beholder."

They treat morality like taste or aesthetic judgments, which are person-relative. Ernest Hemingway wrote:

> So far, about morals, I know only that what is moral is what you feel
> good after and what is immoral is what you feel bad after and judged
> by these moral standards, which I do not defend, the bullfight is very
> moral to me because I feel very fine while it is going on and have a
> feeling of life and death and mortality and immortality, and after it is
> over I feel very sad but very fine.[5]

This form of moral subjectivism has the sorry consequence that it makes morality a very useless concept, for, on its premises, little or no interpersonal criticism or judgment is logically possible. Hemingway may feel good about killing bulls in a bullfight, whereas Saint Francis or Mother Teresa would no doubt feel the opposite. No argument about the matter is possible. Suppose that you are repulsed by observing John torturing a child. You cannot condemn him if one of his principles is "torture little children for the fun of it." The only basis for judging him wrong might be that he was a *hypocrite* who condemned others for torturing. However, one of his or Hemingway's principles could be that hypocrisy is morally permissible (he "feels very fine" about it), so that it would be impossible for him to do wrong. For Hemingway, hypocrisy and nonhypocrisy are both morally permissible (except, perhaps, when he doesn't feel very fine about it).

On the basis of subjectivism, Adolf Hitler and the serial murderer Ted Bundy could be considered as moral as Gandhi, so long as each lived by his own standards, whatever those might be. Witness the following paraphrase of a tape-recorded conversation between Ted Bundy and one of his victims, in which Bundy justifies his murder:

> Then I learned that all moral judgments are "value judgments," that
> all value judgments are subjective, and that none can be proved to be
> either 'right' or 'wrong.' I even read somewhere that the Chief Justice
> of the United States had written that the American Constitution ex-
> pressed nothing more than collective value judgments. Believe it or
> not, I figured out for myself—what apparently the Chief Justice
> couldn't figure out for himself—that if the rationality of one value
> judgment was zero, multiplying it by millions would not make it one
> whit more rational. Nor is there any 'reason' to obey the law for any-
> one, like myself, who has the boldness and daring—the strength of
> character—to throw off its shackles.... I discovered that to become
> truly free, truly unfettered, I had to become truly uninhibited. And

I quickly discovered that the greatest obstacle to my freedom, the greatest block and limitation to it, consists in the insupportable 'value judgment' that I was bound to respect the rights of others. I asked myself, who were these 'others'? Other human beings, with human rights? Why is it more wrong to kill a human animal than any other animal, a pig or a sheep or a steer? Is your life more to you than a hog's life to a hog? Why should I be willing to sacrifice my pleasure more for the one than for the other? Surely, you would not, in this age of scientific enlightenment, declare that God or nature has marked some pleasures as 'moral' or 'good' and others as 'immoral' or 'bad'? In any case, let me assure you, my dear young lady, that there is absolutely no comparison between the pleasure I might take in eating ham and the pleasure I anticipate in raping and murdering you. That is the honest conclusion to which my education has led me—after the most conscientious examination of my spontaneous and uninhibited self.[6]

Notions of good and bad, or right and wrong, cease to have interpersonal evaluative meaning. We might be revulsed by Ted Bundy's views, but that is just a matter of taste.

In the opening days of my philosophy classes, I often find students vehemently defending subjective relativism—"Who are you to judge?" they ask. I then give them their first test. In the next class period, I return all the tests, marked "F," even though my comments show that most of them are a very high calibre. When the students express outrage at this (some have never before seen that letter on their papers and inquire about its meaning), I answer that I have accepted subjectivism for marking the exams. "But that's unjust!" they typically insist—and then they realize that they are no longer being merely subjectivist about ethics.

Absurd consequences follow from subjectivism. If it is correct, then morality reduces to aesthetic tastes about which there can be neither argument nor interpersonal judgment. Although many students say they espouse subjectivism, there is evidence that it conflicts with some of their other moral views. They typically condemn Hitler as an evil man for his genocidal policies. A contradiction seems to exist between subjectivism and the very concept of morality, which it is supposed to characterize, for morality has to do with *proper* resolution of interpersonal conflict and the amelioration of the human predicament (both deontological and teleological systems do this, but in different ways—see Chapters 6 and 7). Whatever else it does, morality has a minimal aim of preventing a Hobbesian state of nature (see Chapter 1), wherein life is "solitary, nasty, poor, brutish and short." But if so, then subjectivism is no help at all, for it rests neither on social agreement of principle (as the conventionalist maintains) nor on an objectively independent set of norms that bind all people for the common good. If there were only one person on earth, then there would be no occasion for morality, because there wouldn't be any interpersonal conflicts to resolve or others whose suffering he or she would have a duty to ameliorate. Subjectivism implicitly assumes something of this solipsism, an atomism in which isolated individuals make up separate universes.

Subjectivism treats individuals as billiard balls on a societal pool table where they meet only in radical collisions, each aimed at his or her own goal and striving to do the others in before they do him or her in. This atomistic view of personality is belied by the facts that we develop in families and mutually dependent communities in which we share a common language, common institutions, and similar rituals and habits, and that we often feel one another's joys and sorrows. As John Donne wrote, "No man is an island, entire of itself; every man is a piece of the continent."

Radical individualistic ethical relativism is incoherent. If so, it follows that the only plausible view of ethical relativism must be one that grounds morality in the group or culture. This form is called *conventionalism,* which we noted earlier and to which we now return.

CONVENTIONAL ETHICAL RELATIVISM
(CONVENTIONALISM)

Conventional ethical relativism, the view that there are no objective moral principles but that all valid moral principles are justified (or are made true) by virtue of their cultural acceptance, recognizes the social nature of morality. That is precisely its power and virtue. It does not seem subject to the same absurd consequences that plague subjectivism. Recognizing the importance of our social environment in generating customs and beliefs, many people suppose that ethical relativism is the correct metaethical theory. Furthermore, they are drawn to it for its liberal philosophical stance. It seems to be an enlightened response to the sin of ethnocentricity, and it seems to entail or strongly imply an attitude of tolerance towards other cultures. As the anthropologist Ruth Benedict says, in recognizing ethical relativity "We shall arrive at a more realistic social faith, accepting as grounds of hope and as new bases for tolerance the coexisting and equally valid patterns of life which mankind has created for itself from the raw materials of existence."[7] The most famous proponent of this position is the anthropologist Melville Herskovits, who argues even more explicitly than Benedict that ethical relativism entails intercultural tolerance:

1. If morality is relative to its culture, then there is no independent basis for criticizing the morality of any other culture but one's own.

2. If there is no independent way of criticizing any other culture, then we ought to be *tolerant* of the moralities of other cultures.

3. Morality is relative to its culture.

4. Therefore, we ought to be *tolerant* of the moralities of other cultures.[8]

Tolerance is certainly a virtue, but is this a good argument for it? I think not. If morality simply is relative to each culture, then if the culture in question has no principle of tolerance, its members have no obligation to be tolerant. Herskovits seems to be treating the *principle of tolerance* as the one exception to his relativism. He seems to be treating it as an absolute moral principle. But from a relativistic point of view, there is no more reason to be tolerant than to be intolerant, and neither stance is objectively morally better than the other.

Not only do relativists offer no basis for criticizing those who are intolerant, but also they cannot rationally criticize anyone who espouses what they might regard as a heinous principle. If, as seems to be the case, valid criticism supposes an objective or impartial standard, then relativists cannot morally criticize anyone outside their own culture. Adolf Hitler's genocidal actions, so long as they are culturally accepted, are as morally legitimate as Mother Teresa's works of mercy. If conventional relativism is accepted, then racism, genocide of unpopular minorities, oppression of the poor, slavery, and even the advocacy of war for its own sake are as moral as their opposites. And if a subculture decided that starting a nuclear war was somehow morally acceptable, we could not morally criticize these people. Any actual morality, whatever its content, is as valid as every other and more valid than ideal moralities—since no culture adheres to the latter.

There are other disturbing consequences of ethical relativism. It seems to entail that reformers are always (morally) wrong, since they go against the tide of cultural standards. Consider the following examples. William Wilberforce was wrong in the 18th century to oppose slavery. The British were immoral in opposing *suttee* in India (the burning of widows, which is now illegal there). The early Christians were wrong in refusing to serve in the Roman army or bow down to Caesar, since the majority in the Roman Empire believed that these two acts were moral duties. In fact, Jesus himself was immoral in breaking the law of his day by healing on the Sabbath day and by advocating the principles of the Sermon on the Mount, since it is clear that few in his time (or in ours) accepted them.

Yet we normally feel just the opposite, that the reformer is a courageous innovator who is right, who has the truth, who stands against the mindless majority. Sometimes the individual must stand alone with the truth, risking social censure and persecution. In Ibsen's *Enemy of the People,* after Dr. Stockman loses the battle to declare his town's profitable, but polluted, tourist spa unsanitary, he says, "The most dangerous enemy of the truth and freedom among us—is the compact majority. Yes, the damned, compact and liberal majority. The majority has *might*—unfortunately—but *right* it is not. Right—are I and a few others." Yet if relativism is correct, the opposite is necessarily the case. Truth is with the crowd and error with the individual.

Similarly, conventional ethical relativism entails disturbing judgments about the law. Our normal view is that we have a prima facie duty to obey the law, because law, in general, promotes the human good. According to most objective systems, this obligation is not absolute but relative to the particular law's relation to a wider moral order. Civil disobedience is warranted in some cases wherein the law seems to seriously conflict with morality. However, if moral relativism is true, then neither law nor civil disobedience has a firm foundation. On the one hand, from the side of the society at large, civil disobedience will be morally wrong, so long as the majority culture agrees with the law in question. On the other hand, if you belong to the relevant subculture that doesn't recognize the particular law in question (because it is unjust from your point of view), then disobedience will be morally mandated. The Ku Klux Klan, which believes that Jews, Catholics, and Blacks are evil or undeserving of high regard, is, given conventionalism, morally permitted or required to break the laws that protect these endangered groups. Why should I obey a law that my group doesn't recognize as valid?

To sum up, unless we have an independent moral basis for law, it is hard to see why we have any general duty to obey it; and unless we recognize the priority of a universal moral law, we have no firm basis for justifying our acts of civil disobedience against "unjust laws." Both the validity of law and morally motivated disobedience of unjust laws are annulled in favor of a power struggle.

There is an even more basic problem with the notion that morality depends on cultural acceptance for its validity. The problem is that the notion of a *culture* or *society* is notoriously difficult to define. This is especially so in a pluralistic society like our own where the notion seems to be vague, with unclear boundary lines. One person may belong to several societies (subcultures) with different value emphases and arrangements of principles. A person may belong to the nation as a single society with certain values of patriotism, honor, courage, and laws (including some that are controversial but have majority acceptance, such as the current law on abortion). But he or she may also belong to a church that opposes some of the laws of the state. He or she may also be an integral member of a socially mixed community where different principles hold sway and may belong to clubs and a family where still other rules prevail. Relativism would seem to tell us that, if a person belongs to societies with conflicting moralities, then that person must be judged both wrong and not wrong whatever he or she does. For example, if Mary is a U.S. citizen and a member of the Roman Catholic Church, then she is wrong (qua Catholic) if she has an abortion and not wrong (qua citizen of the U.S.) if she acts against the Church's teaching on abortion. As a member of a racist university fraternity, KKK, John has no obligation to treat his fellow Black student as an equal, but as a member of the university community (which accepts the principle of equal rights), he does have the obligation; but as a member of the surrounding community (which may reject the principle of equal rights), he again has no such obligation; but then again, as a member of the nation at large (which accepts the principle), he is obligated to treat his fellow students with respect. What is the morally right thing for John to do? The question no longer makes much sense in this moral Babel. It has lost its action-guiding function.

Perhaps the relativist would adhere to a principle that says that, in such cases, the individual may choose which group to belong to as his or her primary group. If Mary has an abortion, she is choosing to belong to the general society relative to that principle. And John must likewise choose among groups. The trouble with this option is that it seems to lead back to counterintuitive results. If Murder Mike of Murder, Incorporated feels like killing Bank President Ortcutt and wants to feel good about it, he identifies with the Murder, Incorporated society rather than the general public morality. Does this justify the killing? In fact, couldn't one justify anything simply by forming a small subculture that approved of it? Ted Bundy would be morally pure in raping and killing innocents simply by virtue of forming a little coterie. How large must the group be in order to be a legitimate subculture or society? Does it need ten or fifteen people? How about just three? Come to think of it, why can't my burglary partner and I found our own society with a morality of its own? Of course, if my partner dies, I could still claim that I was acting from an originally social set of norms. But why can't I dispense with the interpersonal agreements altogether and invent my own morality—since morality, in this view, is only an invention anyway? Conventionalist relativism seems to reduce to subjectivism. And subjectivism leads, as we have seen, to moral solipsism, to the demise of morality altogether.

If one objects that this is an instance of the *slippery slope fallacy,*[9] then let that person give an alternative analysis of what constitutes a viable social basis for generating valid (or true) moral principles. Perhaps we might agree (for the sake of argument, at least) that the very nature of morality entails two people who are making an agreement. This move saves the conventionalist from moral solipsism, but it still permits almost any principle at all to count as moral. And what's more, one can throw out those principles and substitute their contraries for them as the need arises. If two or three people decide to make cheating on exams morally acceptable for themselves, via forming a fraternity, Cheaters Anonymous, at their university, then cheating becomes moral. Why not? Why not rape, as well?

However, I don't think you can stop the move from conventionalism to subjectivism. The essential force of the validity of the chosen moral principle is that it depends on *choice.* The conventionalist holds that it is the group's choice, but why should I accept the group's "silly choice," when my own is better (for me)? If this is all that morality comes to, then why not reject it altogether—even though, to escape sanctions, one might want to adhere to its directives when others are looking? Why should anyone give such august authority to a culture of society? I see no reason to recognize a culture's authority, unless that culture recognizes the authority of something that *legitimizes* the culture. It seems that we need something higher than culture by which to assess a culture.

A CRITIQUE OF ETHICAL RELATIVISM

However, though we may fear the demise of morality, as we have known it, this in itself may not be a good reason for rejecting relativism—that is, for judging it false. Alas, truth may not always be edifying. But the consequences of this position are sufficiently alarming to prompt us to look carefully for some weakness in the relativist's argument. So let us examine the premises and conclusion we derived earlier from Ladd's statement and consider them the three theses of relativism.

1. **The Diversity Thesis.** What is considered morally right and wrong varies from society to society, so there are no moral principles that all societies accept.

2. **The Dependency Thesis.** All moral principles derive their validity from cultural acceptance.

3. **Ethical Relativism.** Therefore, there are no universally valid moral principles, objective standards that apply to all people everywhere and at all times.

Does any one of these statements seem problematic? Let us consider the diversity thesis, which we have also called cultural relativism. Perhaps there is not as much diversity as anthropologists like Sumner and Benedict suppose. One can also see great similarities among the moral codes of various cultures. E. O. Wilson has identified over a score of common features,[10] and before him Clyde Kluckhohn noted some significant common ground:

> Every culture has a concept of murder, distinguishing this from execution, killing in war, and other "justifiable homicides." The notions of incest and other regulations upon sexual behavior, the prohibitions upon untruth under defined circumstances, of restitution and reciprocity, of mutual obligations between parents and children—these and many other moral concepts are altogether universal.[11]

Colin Turnbull's description of the sadistic, semidisplaced, disintegrating Ik in northern Uganda supports the view that a people without principles of kindness, loyalty, and cooperation will degenerate into a Hobbesian state of nature. But he has also produced evidence that, underneath the surface of this dying society, there is a deeper moral code from a time when the tribe flourished, which occasionally surfaces and shows its nobler face.

On the other hand, there is enormous cultural diversity, and many societies have radically different moral codes. Cultural relativism seems to be a fact, but, even if it is, it does not by itself establish the truth of ethical relativism. Cultural diversity in itself is neutral with respect to theories. The objectivist could concede complete cultural relativism but still defend a form of universalism; for he or she could argue that some cultures simply lack correct moral principles.[12]

On the other hand, a denial of complete cultural relativism (i.e., an admission of some universal principles) does not disprove ethical relativism. For even if we did find one or more universal principles, this would not prove that they had any objective status. We could still *imagine* a culture that was an exception to the rule and be unable to criticize it. So the first premise doesn't by itself imply ethical relativism, and its denial doesn't disprove ethical relativism.

We turn to the crucial dependency thesis. Morality does not occur in a vacuum, but rather what a society considers morally right or wrong must be seen in a context, depending on the goals, wants, beliefs, history, and environment of that society. We distinguished a *weak* and a *strong* thesis of dependency. The weak thesis says that the application of principles depends on the particular cultural predicament, whereas the strong thesis affirms that the principles themselves depend on that predicament. The nonrelativist can accept a certain relativity in the way moral principles are *applied* in various cultures, depending on beliefs, history, and environment. For example, a raw environment with scarce natural resources may justify the Eskimos' brand of euthanasia to the objectivist, who would consistently reject that practice if it occurred in another environment. One Sudanese tribe throws its deformed infants into the river because the tribe believes that such infants *belong* to the hippopotamus, the god of the river. We believe that these groups' belief in euthanasia and infanticide is false, but the point is that the same principles of respect for property and respect for human life operate in such contrary practices. The tribe differs with us only in belief, not in substantive moral principle. This is an illustration of how nonmoral beliefs (e.g., deformed infants belong to the hippopotamus), when applied to common moral principles (e.g., give to each his or her due), generate different actions in different cultures. In our own culture, the difference in the nonmoral belief about the status of a fetus generates opposite moral prescriptions. The major difference between pro-choicers and pro-lifers is not whether we should kill persons but whether fetuses are really persons. It is a debate about the facts of the matter, not the principle of killing innocent persons.

So the fact that moral principles are weakly dependent doesn't show that ethical relativism is valid. In spite of this weak dependency on nonmoral factors, there could still be a set of general moral norms applicable to all cultures and even recognized in most, which a culture could disregard only at its own expense.

Nevertheless, the relativists still have at least one more arrow in their quiver—the argument from the indeterminacy of translation. This theory, set forth by B. L. Whorf and W. V. Quine,[13] holds that languages are often so fundamentally different from each other that we cannot accurately translate concepts from one to another. Language groups mean different things by words. Quine holds that it may be impossible to know whether a native speaker who points toward a rabbit and says "gavagai" is using the word to signify "rabbit," or "rabbit part," or something else. This thesis holds that language is the essence of a culture and fundamentally shapes its reality, cutting the culture off from other languages and cultures. But experience seems to falsify this thesis. Although each culture does have a particular language with different meanings—indeed, each person has his or her own particular set of meanings—we do learn foreign languages and learn to translate across linguistic frameworks. For example, people from a myriad of language groups come to the United States and learn English and communicate perfectly well. Rather than causing a complete hiatus, the interplay between these other cultures and ours eventually enriches the English language with new concepts (for example, forte, foible, taboo, and coup de grace), even as English has enriched (or "corrupted," as the French might argue) other languages. Even if some indeterminacy of translation exists between language users, we should not infer from this that no translation or communication is possible. It seems reasonable to believe that general moral principles are precisely those things that can be communicated transculturally. The kind of common features that Kluckhohn and Wilson advance—duties of restitution and reciprocity, regulations on sexual behavior, obligations of parents to children, a no-unnecessary-harm principle, and a sense that the good people should flourish and the guilty people should suffer—these and other features constitute a common human experience, a common set of values within a common human predicament of struggling to survive and flourish in a world of scarce resources.[14] So it is possible to communicate cross-culturally and find that we agree on many of the important things in life. If this is so, then the indeterminacy-of-translation thesis, which relativism rests on, must itself be relativized to the point at which it is no objection to objective morality.

What the relativist needs is a strong thesis of dependency, that somehow all principles are essentially cultural inventions. But why should we choose to view morality this way? Is there anything to recommend the strong thesis of dependency over the weak thesis of dependency? The relativist may argue that, in fact, we lack an obvious impartial standard to judge from. "Who's to say which culture is right and which is wrong?" But this seems dubious. We can reason and perform thought experiments in order to make a case for one system over another. We may not be able to *know* with certainty that our moral beliefs are closer to the truth than those of another culture or those of others within our own culture, but we may be *justified* in believing this about our moral beliefs. If we can be closer to the truth about factual or scientific matters, why can't we be closer to the truth on moral matters? Why can't a culture simply be confused or wrong about its moral perceptions? Why can't we say that a culture like the Ik, which enjoys watching its own children fall into fires, is less moral in that regard than a culture that cherishes children and grants them protection and equal rights? To take such a stand is not ethnocentricism, for we are seeking to derive principles through critical reason, not simply uncritical acceptance of one's own mores.

Conclusion

Ethical relativism—the thesis that moral principles derive their validity from dependence on society or individual choice—seems plausible at first glance, but on close scrutiny it presents some severe problems. Subjectivism seems to boil down to anarchistic individualism, an essential denial of the interpersonal feature of the moral point of view, and conventionalism, which does contain an interpersonal perspective, fails to deal adequately with the problem of the reformer, the question of defining a culture, and the whole enterprise of moral criticism. Nevertheless, unless moral objectivism can make a positive case for its position, relativism may survive these criticisms.

NOTES

1. *History of Herodotus,* trans. George Rawlinson (Appleton, 1859), Bk. 3, Ch. 38.

2. John Ladd, *Ethical Relativism* (Wadsworth, 1973), p. 1.

3. Ruth Benedict, *Patterns of Culture* (New American Library, 1934), p. 257.

4. W. G. Sumner, *Folkways* (Ginn & Co., 1905), section 80, p. 76. Ruth Benedict indicates the depth of our cultural conditioning this way: "The very eyes with which we see the problem are conditioned by the long traditional habits of our own society." ["Anthropology and the Abnormal," *The Journal of General Psychology* (1934): 59–82.]

5. Ernest Hemingway, *Death in the Afternoon* (Scribners, 1932), p. 4.

6. This is a statement by Ted Bundy, paraphrased and rewritten by Harry V. Jaffa, *Homosexuality and the Natural Law* (The Claremont Institute of the Study of Statesmanship and Political Philosophy, 1990), pp. 3–4.

7. Ruth Benedict, *Patterns of Culture* (New American Library, 1934), p. 257.

8. Melville Herskovits, *Cultural Relativism* (Random House, 1972).

9. The fallacy of objecting to a proposition on the erroneous grounds that, if accepted, it will lead to a chain of states of affairs that are absurd or unacceptable.

10. E. O. Wilson, *On Human Nature* (Bantam Books, 1979), pp. 22–23.

11. Clyde Kluckhohn, "Ethical Relativity: Sic et Non" *Journal of Philosophy,* LII (1955).

12. Colin Turnbull, *The Mountain People* (Simon & Schuster, 1972).

13. See Benjamin Whorf, *Language, Thought and Reality* (MIT Press, 1956) and W. V. Quine, *Word and Object* (MIT Press, 1960) and *Ontological Relativity* (Columbia University Press, 1969).

14. See James Q. Wilson, *The Moral Sense* (Free Press, 1993), pp. 191–230.

FOR FURTHER REFLECTION

1. Go over John Ladd's definition of ethical relativism, quoted at the beginning of this chapter and discussed within it. Is it a good definition? Can you find a better definition of ethical relativism? Ask your friends what they think ethical relativism is and whether they accept it. You might put the question this way: "Are there any moral absolutes, or is morality completely relative?" Discuss your findings.

2. Examine the notion of subjective ethical relativism. It bases morality on radical individualism, that each person is the inventor of morality. "Morality is in the eye of the beholder." Consider this assumption of individualism. Could there be a morality for only one person? Imagine that only one person existed in the world (leave God out of the account). Suppose you were that person. Would you have any moral duties? Certainly there would be *prudential* duties—some ways of living would help you attain your goals—but would there be moral duties?

3. Now imagine a second person has come into your world—a fully developed, mature person with wants, needs, hopes, and fears. How does this change the nature of the situation of the solitary individual?

4. Here is a puzzle for subjectivist relativists: Consider a baby who gets hold of a knife and stabs its four-year-old sister. The baby doesn't know any better. We would suppose it is innocent. Tragic though this is, we would not hold the baby responsible for its deed. Now consider a father who stabs that same four-year-old girl. Suppose the father explains his act by saying, "I felt good exercising my power, and what feels good must be morally good." Does the fact that he thought his act was morally permissible really make it morally permissible? Discuss your answer.

5. Can you separate the anthropological claim (the diversity thesis—called "cultural relativism") that different cultures have different moral principles from the judgment that *therefore* they are all equally good ("ethical relativism")? Are there independent criteria by which we can say that some cultures are "better" than others?

6. Ruth Benedict has written that our culture is "but one entry in a long series of possible adjustments" and that "the very eyes with which we see the problem are conditioned by the long traditional habits of our own society." What are the implications of these statements? Is she correct? How would an objectivist respond to these claims?

7. Let's repeat the illustration from the Greek historian Herodotus discussed early in this chapter: The Persian King Darius asked some Greeks what he should pay them to eat the bodies of their fathers when they died. They replied that no sum of money would tempt them to do such a terrible deed. Whereupon Darius sent for people of the Callatian tribe, who eat their dead fathers, and asked them, in the presence of the Greeks, what he should give them to burn the bodies of their fathers at their decease, as the Greeks do. The Callatians were horrified at the thought and bid him desist in such terrible talk. So Herodotus concluded, "Custom is the King o'er all." Is this a good illustration of the truth of ethical relativism? Why or why not?

8. Consider the following argument, which I call *the reductio ad absurdum of ethical relativism,* which attempts to demonstrate that ethical relativism is an incoherent, hence false theory. Suppose we define ethics as "the principles necessary for promoting the social good—principles which, if almost everyone follows them almost all the time, will make almost everyone

better off almost all the time." That is, ethics is social and not purely individualistic. So the only possible form of ethical relativism is conventional. Then let the following abbreviations stand for theories:

CER = conventional ethical relativism

SER = subjective ethical relativism

OE = objective ethics

EN = ethical nihilism (ethics is a myth—it doesn't exist.)

We construct the following argument:

1. Suppose CER is true (culture is the sole validator of ethical principles).

2. We can logically reduce CER to SER.

3. SER is the very annihilation of ethics (by definition).

4. The opposite of ER is OE.

5. Therefore, either EN or OE is true.

6. Probably EN is false (there is no reason to believe it).

7. Therefore probably OE is true (the best reasons we have point to the reality of OE).

Examine the premises. Do you find any of them questionable or false? Premise 2 is very important. I argued in this chapter that, since a culture consists of a set of beliefs and practices, there is no reason to prohibit a culture from consisting of only one person. By definition, ethics is social, so premise 3 seems correct. Evaluate this argument.

FOR FURTHER READING

Brink, David. *Moral Realism and the Foundation of Ethics.* Cambridge University Press, 1989.

Fishkin, James. *Beyond Subjective Morality.* Yale University Press, 1984.

Harman, Gilbert, and Judith Jarvis Thomson. *Moral Relativism and Moral Objectivity.* Blackwell, 1996.

Harman, Gilbert. "What is Moral Relativism?" in *Values and Morals,* eds. A. I. Goldman and J. Kim. D. Reidel, 1978.

Ladd, John, ed. *Ethical Relativism.* Wadsworth, 1973.

Lyons, David. "Ethical Relativism and the Problem of Incoherence," *Ethics:* 86. Reprinted in *Relativism,* eds. Jack Meiland and Michael Krausz. University of Notre Dame, 1982.

Mackie, J. L. *Ethics: Inventing Right and Wrong.* Penguin, 1976.

Pojman, Louis P. "Gilbert Harman's Internalist Moral Relativism," *The Modern Schoolman* (vol. LXVIII) (November 1990).

Stace, W. T. *The Concept of Morals.* Macmillan, 1937.

Sumner, William Graham. *Folkways.* Ginn & Co., 1906.

Taylor, Paul. *Principles of Ethics.* Wadsworth, 1975. Ch. 2.

Wellman, Carl. "The Ethical Implications of Cultural Relativity," *Journal of Philosophy,* LX (1963).

Westermarck, Edward. *Ethical Relativity.* Humanities Press, 1960.

Williams, Bernard. *Morality.* Harper Torchbooks, 1972.

Wong, David. *Moral Relativity.* University of California Press, 1985.

3

The Case for
Moral Objectivism

There is a great uniformity among the actions of men, in all nations and ages,
and that human nature remains still the same, in its principles and operations.
The same events follow from the same causes. Ambition, avarice, self-love, vanity,
friendship, generosity, public spirit; these passions, mixed in various degrees, and
distributed through society, have been, from the beginning of the world, and still
are, the source of all the actions and enterprises which have ever been observed
among mankind. . . . [History's] chief use is only to discover the constant and
universal principles of human nature, by showing men in all varieties of circum-
stances and situations, and furnishing us with materials, from which we may
form our observations, and become acquainted with the regular springs of human
action and behavior.

DAVID HUME, *ESSAYS, MORAL, POLITICAL AND LITERARY*

In the last chapter, we examined moral relativism, the thesis that moral
principles gain their validity only via approval by the culture or the individual, and concluded that it was plagued with severe problems. But showing that relativism is loaded with liabilities is one thing; showing that moral
principles have objective validity, independent of cultural acceptance, is
quite another. If the objectivists are to make their case, they must offer a
better explanation of cultural diversity and of why we should nevertheless

adhere to moral objectivism. One kind of explanation is to appeal to a divine law and to human sin, which causes deviation from that law. Although I think that human greed, selfishness, pride, self-deception, and other maladies have a great deal to do with moral differences and that religion may lend great support to morality (see the discussion in Chapter 10), I don't think that a religious justification is necessary to establish the validity of moral principles. Another kind of explanation is to appeal to the doctrine of *natural law,* which holds that morality is a function of human nature, meaning that reason can discover valid moral principles by looking at the nature of humanity and society. I will examine this position and distinguish a strong, or absolutist, version from a moderate, or nonabsolutist, version of natural law. I will defend this latter view, which may be called *modest objectivism,* first by appealing to our intuitions and second by giving a naturalist account of morality that transcends individual cultures.

First, let's distinguish between moral *absolutism* and moral *objectivism.* The *absolutist* believes there are nonoverridable moral principles that one ought never violate. The moral norms are *exceptionless.* Kant's system is a good example of this (see Chapter 7). One ought never break a promise, no matter what. *Act utilitarianism* also seems absolutist, for the principle "Do that act that has the most promise of yielding the most utility" is nonoverridable. In this chapter, we will examine the strong view of natural law, which is also absolutist.

The *objectivist,* on the other hand, shares with the absolutist the notion that moral principles have universal, objective validity but denies that moral norms are necessarily exceptionless. The objectivist could believe that, although moral principles override all other considerations (see Chapter 1), no moral duty has absolute weight or strict priority; each moral principle must be weighed against other moral principles. There are many types of objectivism, ranging from the position that there are some absolutes and some nonabsolute objective principles to the position that there are no absolutes, some nonabsolute objective principles, and some principles that are valid through a society's acceptance.

We turn first to the absolutist position, natural law ethics.

NATURAL LAW

The idea of natural law first appears among the Stoics (first century B.C.), who believed that human beings have within them a divine spark (*logos spermatikos*—"the rational seed or sperm") that enables them to discover the essential eternal laws necessary for individual happiness and social harmony.[1] The whole universe is governed by laws that exhibit rationality. Nature in general and animals in particular obey these laws by necessity, but humans have choice. Humans obey these laws because they can perceive the laws' inner reasonableness. This notion enabled the Stoics to be *cosmopolitans* ("people of the cosmos") who imposed a universal standard of righteousness (*jus naturale*) on all societies, evaluating various positive laws (*jus gentium*—"laws of the nations") by this higher bar of reason.

Thomas Aquinas (1225–1274) combined the sense of cosmic natural law with Aristotle's view that human beings, like every other natural object, have a specific nature, purpose, and function. A knife's function is to cut sharply, a chair's function is to support the body in a certain position, and a house's function is to provide shelter from the elements. Humanity's essence or proper function is to live the life of reason. As Aristotle put it:

> Reason is the true self of every man, since it is the supreme and better part. It will be strange, then, if he should choose not his own life, but some other's.... What is naturally proper to every creature is the highest and pleasantest for him. And so, to man, this will be the life of Reason, since Reason is, in the highest sense, a man's self.[2]

Humanity's function is to exhibit rationality in all its forms: contemplation, deliberation, and action. For Aquinas, reason's deliberative processes discover the natural laws. They are universal rules, or "ordinances of reason for the common good, promulgated by him who has the care of the community":

> To the natural law belong those things to which a man is inclined naturally; and among these it is proper to man to be inclined to act according to reason.... Hence this is the first precept of law, that *good is to be done and promoted, and evil is to be avoided.* All other precepts of the natural law are based upon this; so that all the things which the practical reason naturally apprehends as man's good belong to the precepts of the natural law under the form of things to be done or avoided.
>
> Since, however, good has the nature of an end, and evil, the nature of the contrary, hence it is that all those things to which man has a natural inclination are naturally apprehended by reason as good, and consequently as objects of pursuit, and their contraries as evil, and objects of avoidance. Therefore, the order of the precepts of the natural law is according to the order of natural inclinations.[3]

Aquinas and other Christians who espoused natural law appealed to the Epistle to the Romans in the New Testament, where Paul wrote:

> When the Gentiles, who have not the [Jewish-revealed] law, do by nature what the law requires, they are a law to themselves, even though they do not have the law. They show that what the law requires is written on their hearts, while their conscience also bears witness and their conflicting thoughts accuse or perhaps excuse them.

The key ideas of the natural law tradition are the following:

1. Human beings have an essential rational nature established by God, who designed us to live and flourish in prescribed ways (from Aristotle and the Stoics).
2. Even without knowledge of God, reason, as the essence of our nature, can discover the laws necessary for human flourishing (from Aristotle; developed by Aquinas).
3. The natural laws are universal and unchangeable, and one should use them to judge individual societies and their positive laws. Positive (or actual) laws of societies that are not in line with the natural law are not truly laws but counterfeits (from the Stoics).

Moral laws have objective validity. Reason can sort out which inclinations are part of our true nature and how we are to relate them to one another. Aquinas listed the desires for life and procreation as fundamental values without which other values could not even get established. Knowledge and friendship (or sociability) are two other intrinsic values. These values are not good because we desire them; rather, we desire them because they are good—they are absolutely necessary for human flourishing.

Aquinas's position and the natural law tradition in general are absolutist. Humanity has an essentially rational nature, and reason can discover the right action in every situation by following an appropriate exceptionless principle. But sometimes we encounter moral conflicts, "dilemmas" in which we cannot do good without also bringing about evil consequences. To this end, the doctrine of *double effect* was devised—a doctrine that provides a neat algorithm for solving all moral disputes in which an act will have two effects, one good and the other bad. The doctrine says, roughly, that it is always wrong to do a bad act intentionally in order to bring about good consequences, but that it is sometimes permissible to do a good act despite knowing that it will bring about bad consequences. This doctrine consists in four conditions that must be satisfied before an act is morally permissible:

1. **The Nature-of-the-Act Condition:** The action must be either morally good or indifferent. Lying or intentionally killing an innocent person are never permissible.

2. **The Means-End Condition:** The bad effect must not be the means by which one achieves the good effect.

3. **The Right-Intention Condition:** The intention must be the achieving of only the good effect, with the bad effect being only an unintended side effect. If the bad effect is a means of obtaining the good effect, then the act is immoral. The bad effect may be foreseen but must not be intended.

4. **The Proportionality Condition:** The good effect must be at least equivalent in importance to the bad effect.

Let's illustrate this doctrine by applying it to a woman whose life is endangered by her pregnancy. Is it morally permissible for her to have an abortion in order to save her life? The doctrine of double effect says that an abortion is not permissible. Since abortion kills an innocent human being, and since intentionally killing innocent human beings is always wrong, it is always wrong to have an abortion—even to save the woman's life. Abortion also fails condition 2 (the means–end condition). Killing the innocent in order to bring about a good effect is never justified, not even to save a whole city—or the world. As the Stoics said, "Let justice be done, though the heavens fall." However, if the woman's uterus happens to be cancerous, then she may have a hysterectomy, which will result in the death of the fetus. This is because the act of removing a cancerous uterus is morally good (thus passing condition 1). The act of performing a hysterectomy also passes condition 3, since the death of the fetus is the unintended (though foreseen) effect of the hysterectomy. Condition 2 is passed, since the death of the fetus isn't the means of saving the woman's life—the hysterectomy is. Condition 4 is passed, since saving the woman's life is a great good, at least as good as saving the fetus. In this case, given the doctrine of double effect, the woman is really lucky to have a cancerous uterus.

On the other hand, if the doctor could save the woman's life only by changing the composition of the amniotic fluid (say, with saline solution), which in turn would kill the fetus, then this would not be morally permissible. In this case, the same result occurs as in the hysterectomy, but killing the fetus is *intended* as the means of saving the woman's life.

The Roman Catholic Church uses this doctrine to prohibit not only most abortions but also the use of contraceptives. Since the procreation of life is good and the frustration of life is bad, and since the natural purpose of sexual intercourse is to produce new life, it is wrong to use devices that prevent intercourse from producing its natural result.

Consider another example. Suppose that Sally's father has planted a nuclear bomb that will detonate in a half hour. Sally is the only person who knows where he hid it, and she has promised him that she will not reveal the location to anyone. Although she regrets his act, as a devoted daughter she refuses to break her promise and give away the secret. However, if we do not discover where the bomb is and dismantle it within the next half hour, it will blow up a city and kill a million people. Suppose we can torture Sally in order to get this information from her. According to the doctrine of the double effect, is this permissible? No, for the end does not justify the means. Condition 2 is violated. We are using a bad act to bring about a good effect.

On the other hand, suppose someone has tampered with the wires of my television set in such a way that turning it on will send an electrical signal to the next town, where it will detonate a bomb. Suppose I know that this will happen. Is it morally wrong, according to the doctrine of the double effect, to turn on my television to watch an edifying program? Yes it is, since condition 4 is violated. The unintended evil outweighs the good.

But if we interpret the proportionality principle in this way, then a lot of other seemingly innocent or good actions would also violate it. Suppose that I am contemplating joining the true religion (I leave you to tell me which one that is) in order to save my eternal soul. However, I realize that, by doing so, I will create enormous resentment in my neighborhood over my act, resentment that will cause five neighbors to be damned. Or suppose that my marrying the woman of my heart's desire generates such despair in five other fellows (who, we may imagine, would be reasonably happy as bachelors as long as no one married her) that they all commit suicide. We may suppose that the despair I cause these five fellows will make their free will nonoperational. I understand ahead of time that my act will have this result. Is my act morally justified?

There is also a problem with distinguishing unforeseen from unintended consequences. Could I not redescribe abortion in which the woman's health or life is in danger as *intending* to improve the woman's health (or save her life) and only foreseeing that removing the fetus will result in its (unintended) death? Or could I not steal some food from the grocery store, intending to feed the poor and foreseeing that the grocer will be slightly poorer?

Of course, the doctrine of double effect must set limits to redescription; otherwise almost any act can be justified. Eric D'Arcy has attempted to set such limits. He quotes the jingle "Imperious Caesar, dead and turned to clay, might stop a hole to keep the wind away," but adds that it would be ridiculous to describe killing Caesar as intending to block a windy draft. His own solution to this problem is that "certain kinds of acts are of such significance that the terms which denote them may not, special contexts apart, be elided into terms which (a) denote their consequences, and (b) conceal, or even fail to reveal, the nature of the act itself."[4]

This explanation may lend plausibility to the doctrine of double effect, but it is not always possible to identify the exact nature of the act itself—it may have various interpretations. Furthermore, the absolutism of the doctrine will make it counterintuitive to many of us. It would seem to prohibit lying in order to save a life or breaking a promise in order to spare someone great suffering. Why should we accept a system that allows the destruction of many innocent people simply because we may have to override a normal moral precept? Aren't morals made for the human good? And doesn't the strong natural law tradition get things reversed—requiring that humans serve rules for the rules' own sake? Furthermore, there may be more than a single right answer to every moral dilemma. The doctrine of double effect gives us solutions to problems that seem to impose an artificial rigidity on human existence.

But there is one other difficulty with the absolute version of natural law: It is tied closely to a teleological view of human nature, a view that sees humanity, and each individual, as having a plan designed by God or a godlike nature, so that any deviation from the norm is morally wrong. Hence, since the plan of humanity includes procreation, and since sexuality is the means to that goal, only heterosexual intercourse (without artificial birth control devices) is morally permitted.

If Darwinian evolutionary theory is correct, there is no design. Human beings are animals who evolved from "lower" forms of life via the survival of the fittest. We are the product of chance in this struggle for existence. If this is so, then the ideas of a single human purpose and an absolute set of laws to serve that purpose are problematic. We may have many purposes, and our moral domain may include a certain relativity. For example, heterosexuality may serve one social purpose whereas homosexuality serves another, and both may be fulfilling for different types of individuals. Reason's task may not be to discover an essence of humanity or unchangeable laws, but, rather, simply to help us survive and fulfill our desires.

However, even if this nonreligious account of evolution is inaccurate, and there is a God who has guided evolution, it's still not obvious that the absolutist's way of looking at the world and morality is the best one available.

Although I must say more on this subject (see Chapter 10 for a discussion of the relationship of religion to ethics), I now want to propose a more modest version of an objectivist ethics, one that is consistent with evolutionary theory but could be seen as a nonabsolutist version of the natural law theory.

MODERATE OBJECTIVISM

If we give up the notion that a moral system must contain only absolute principles, duties that proceed out of a definite algorithm such as the doctrine of double effect, what can we put in its place?

The *moderate objectivist's* account of moral principles is what William Ross refers to as "prima facie principles"[5]—valid rules of action that one should generally adhere to but that, in cases of moral conflict, may be overridable by another moral principle. For example, even though a principle of justice may generally outweigh a principle of benevolence, there are times when one could do enormous good by sacrificing a small amount of justice; thus an objectivist would be inclined to act according to the principle of benevolence. There may be some absolute or nonoverridable principles, but there need not be any (or many) for objectivism to be true.[6] Renford Bambrough states this point nicely:

> To suggest that there is a *right* answer to a moral problem is at once to be accused of or credited with a belief in moral absolutes. But it is no more necessary to believe in moral absolutes in order to believe in moral objectivity than it is to believe in the existence of absolute space or absolute time in order to believe in the objectivity of temporal and spatial relations and of judgments about them.[7]

If we can establish or show that it is reasonable to believe that there is, in some ideal sense, at least one objective moral principle that is binding on all people everywhere, then we shall have shown that relativism probably is false and that a limited objectivism is true. Actually, I believe that many qualified general ethical principles are binding on all rational beings, but one principle will suffice to refute relativism:

A. It is morally wrong to torture people for the fun of it.

I claim that this principle is binding on all rational agents, so that if some agent, S, rejects A, we should not let that affect our intuition that A is a true principle; rather, we should try to explain S's behavior as perverse, ignorant, or irrational instead. For example, suppose Adolf Hitler doesn't accept A. Should that affect our confidence in the truth of A? Is it not more reasonable to infer that Hitler is morally deficient, morally blind, ignorant, or irrational than to suppose that his noncompliance is evidence against the truth of A?

Suppose further that there is a tribe of "Hitlerites" somewhere who enjoy torturing people. Their whole culture accepts torturing others for the fun of it. Suppose that Mother Teresa or Mahatma Gandhi tries unsuccessfully to convince these sadists that they should stop torturing people altogether, and the sadists respond by torturing her or him. Should this affect our confidence in A? Would it not be more reasonable to look for some explanation of Hitlerite behavior? For example, we might hypothesize that this tribe lacks the developed sense of sympathetic imagination that is necessary for the moral life. Or we might theorize that this tribe is on a lower evolutionary level than most *Homo sapiens*. Or we might simply conclude that the tribe is closer to a Hobbesian state of nature than most societies, and as such probably would not survive very long—or if it did, the lives of its people would be largely "solitary, poor, nasty, brutish and short," as in the Ik culture in northern Uganda, where the core morality has partly broken down.

But we need not know the correct answer as to why the tribe is in such bad shape in order to maintain our confidence in A as a moral principle. If A is a basic or core belief for us, then we will be more likely to doubt the Hitlerites' sanity or ability to think morally than to doubt the validity of A.

We can perhaps produce other candidates for membership in our minimally basic objective moral set:

1. Do not kill innocent people.

2. Do not cause unnecessary pain or suffering.

3. Do not steal or cheat.

4. Keep your promises and honor your contracts.

5. Do not deprive another person of his or her freedom.

6. Do justice, treating equals equally and unequals unequally.

7. Reciprocate: Show gratitude for services rendered.

8. Tell the truth or, at least, do not lie.

9. Help other people, at least when the cost to oneself is minimal.

10. Obey just laws.

These ten principles are examples of the *core morality*, principles necessary for the good life. They are not arbitrary, for we can give reasons that explain why they are necessary to social cohesion and human flourishing. Principles like the Golden Rule, not killing innocent people, treating equals equally, truth-telling, promise-keeping, and the like are central to the fluid progression of social interaction and the resolution of conflicts that ethics bears on (at least minimal morality does, even though there may be more to morality than simply these kinds of concerns). For example, language itself depends on a general and implicit commitment to the principle of truth-telling. Accuracy of expression is a primitive form of truthfulness. Hence, every time we use words correctly we are telling the truth. Without this behavior, language wouldn't be possible. Likewise, without the recognition of a rule of promise-keeping, contracts are of no avail, and cooperation is less likely. And without the protection of life and liberty, we could not secure our other goals.

A moral code or theory would be adequate if it contained a requisite set of these objective principles or the core morality, but there could be more than one adequate moral code or theory that contained different rankings of these principles and other principles consistent with *core morality*. That is, there may be a certain relativity to secondary principles (whether to opt for monogamy rather than polygamy, whether to include a principle of high altruism in the set of moral duties, whether to allocate more resources to medical care than to environmental concerns, whether to institute a law requiring motorists to drive on the left side of the road or the right side of the road, and so forth), but in every morality a certain core will remain, though we apply it somewhat differently because of differences in environment, belief, tradition, and the like.

The core moral rules are analogous to the set of vitamins necessary for a healthy diet. We need an adequate amount of each vitamin—some humans need more of one than another—but in prescribing a nutritional diet we needn't set forth recipes, specific foods, place settings, or culinary habits. Gourmets will meet the requirements differently than ascetics and vegetarians, but all may obtain the basic nutrients without rigid regimentation or an absolute set of recipes.

In more positive terms, an objectivist who bases his or her moral system on a common human nature with common needs and desires might argue for objectivism somewhat in this manner:

1. Human nature is relatively similar in essential respects, having a common set of needs and interests.

2. Moral principles are functions of human needs and interests, instituted by reason in order to promote the most significant needs and interests of rational beings (and perhaps of others).

3. Some moral principles will meet human needs and promote human interests better than other principles will.

4. Principles that will meet essential human needs and promote the most significant human interests in optimal ways can be said to be objectively valid moral principles.

5. Therefore, since there is a common human nature, there is an objectively valid set of moral principles, applicable to all humanity.

This argument assumes that there is a common human nature. In a sense, I accept a *strong dependency thesis*—morality *depends* on human nature and the needs and interests of humans in general, but not on any specific cultural choice. There is only one large human framework to which moral principles are relative.[8] The quotation from Hume at the beginning of this chapter points to such a conclusion. But the relativist sometimes objects that there is no such thing as human nature. Although I think we do have a common human nature (rooted perhaps in our animality and ability to reason and use language), suppose we concede the point for the sake of argument. We would then content ourselves with a less controversial first premise, stating that some principles will tend to promote the most significant interests of persons. The revised argument would go like this:

1. Objectively valid moral principles are such that adherence to them meets the needs of and promotes the most significant interests of persons.

2. Some principles are such that adherence to them meets the needs of and promotes the most significant interests of persons.

3. Therefore, there are some objectively valid moral principles.

Either argument would satisfy objectivism, but the former makes it clearer that our common human nature generates the common principles.[9] However, as I mentioned, some philosophers might not accept the concept of a common human nature, in which case we may use the second version of the argument. It has the advantage that, even if it turned out that we did have somewhat different natures or that other creatures in the universe had somewhat different natures, some of the basic moral principles would still survive.

If this argument succeeds, then there are ideal moralities (and not simply adequate ones). Of course, there could still be more than one ideal morality, which presumably an ideal observer would choose under optimal conditions. The ideal observer may conclude that, out of an infinite set of moralities, two, three, or more moralities would tie for first place. One would expect these to be similar, but there is every reason to believe that all of these would contain the set of core principles.

Of course, we don't know what an ideal observer would choose, but we can imagine that such an observer would choose under conditions of maximal knowledge about the consequences of action types and impartiality, second-order qualities that ensure that agents have the best chance of making the best decisions. If this is so, then the more we learn to judge impartially and the more we know about possible forms of life, the better chance we have to approximate an ideal moral system. And if ideal moral systems with an objective core and other objective components can be approximated, then ethical relativism is certainly false. We can confidently dismiss it as an aberration and get on with the job of working out better moral systems.

Let me make the same point by appealing to your intuitions by relating a dream I had as a child. Deeply afraid that I would go to hell when I died, I would regularly have nightmares of hell. One night I dreamed that I had died and gone to the dark kingdom of hell. I viewed the damned writhing in misery, contorting their faces and howling like wounded dogs. Why were they writhing? What was their punishment? Well, they had eternal back itches that ebbed and flowed. But they couldn't scratch their backs, for their arms were paralyzed in a frontal position, so they writhed with itchiness throughout eternity. But just as I began to feel my own back itch, I was suddenly transported to heaven. What do you think I saw in the kingdom of the blessed? People with eternal back itches who couldn't scratch their own backs. But they were all smiling instead of writhing. Why? Because everyone had stretched his or her arms out to scratch someone else's back, and, so arranged in one big circle, they turned a hell into a heaven of ecstasy.

If we can imagine some states of affairs or cultures that are better than others in a way that depends on human action, we can ask what character traits make them so. In my dream, people in heaven, but not in hell, cooperated to ameliorate suffering and produce happiness and pleasure. These are very primitive goods, not sufficient for a full-blown morality, but they give us a hint as to the objectivity of morality. Moral goodness has something to do with the amelioration of suffering, the resolution of conflict, and the promotion of human flourishing, as I pointed out in Chapter 1. If a blissful heaven is rationally preferable, really better than the eternal itchiness of hell, then whatever makes it so is constitutively related to moral rightness.

AN EXPLANATION OF THE ATTRACTION OF
ETHICAL RELATIVISM

If one can make a reasonable case for a modest objectivism, why is there such a strong inclination toward ethical relativism? I think there are five reasons, which haven't been adequately emphasized. The first reason is that the options are usually presented as though absolutism and relativism were the only alternatives, so conventionalism wins out against an implausible competitor. My student questionnaire reads: "Are there any ethical absolutes—moral duties binding on all persons at all times—or are moral duties relative to culture? Is there any alternative to these two positions?" Less than 5 percent of my students suggest a third position, and very few of these identify objectivism. Granted, it takes a little philosophical sophistication to make the crucial distinctions, and it is precisely for the lack of this sophistication or reflection that relativism has achieved its enormous prestige. But, as Ross and others have shown, and as I have argued in this chapter, one can have an objective morality without being absolutist.

The second reason for the inclination toward ethical relativism is similar to the first. Some philosophers and thoughtful people confuse objectivism with *realism,* the view that moral truths make up an independent reality, as scientific truths do. Plato is perhaps the classic realist; he believed in a separate and transcendental sphere of reality ("the really real") wherein ideal forms exist that all the things in our world more or less copy. Moral ideals and principles would have their existence in this sphere of reality. Most contemporary moral realists hold less extravagant views, but they believe, nevertheless, in an independent status for moral truths. Moral principles are synthetic a priori truths or necessary truths, valid for all possible worlds. But moral objectivists need not be realists. They may affirm the validity of moral principles only on the basis of common human nature and intersubjective agreement among people in favorable conditions.

A leading relativist, my teacher, J. L. Mackie, while attacking moral objectivism, admits that there is a great deal of intersubjectivity in ethics: "There could be agreement in valuing even if valuing is just something people do, even if this activity is not further validated. Subjective agreement would give intersubjective values, but intersubjectivity is not objectivity."[10] But Mackie fails to note that there are two kinds of intersubjectivity and that one of them gives all that the objectivist wants for a moral theory. Consider the following situations of intersubjective agreement:

A1. All the children in first grade at school S would agree that playing in the mud is preferable to learning arithmetic.

A2. All the youth in the district would rather take drugs than go to school.

A3. All the people in Jonestown, Guyana, agree that Reverend Jones is a prophet from God and love him dearly.

A4. Almost all the people in community C voted for Bill Clinton.

B1. All the thirsty desire water to quench their thirst.

B2. All humans (and animals) prefer pleasure to pain.

B3. Almost all people agree that living in society is more satisfying than living alone as hermits.

The naturalist contrasts these two sets of intersubjective agreements (A1–A4 and B1–B3) and says that the first set is accidental, not part of what it means to be a person, whereas the agreements in the second set are basic to being a person, basic to our nature. Agreement on the essence of morality, the core set, is the kind of intersubjective agreement that is more like the second set, not the first set. It is part of the essence of humans in community, part of what it means to flourish as a person, to agree with and adhere to the moral code. I will discuss Mackie's views and this kind of subjectivism in Chapter 12.

The third reason is that our recent sensitivity to cultural relativism and the evils of ethnocentrism, which have plagued Europeans' and Americans' relations with people of other cultures, has made us conscious of the frailty of many aspects of our moral repertoire, so that there is a tendency to wonder, "Who's to judge what's really right and wrong?" However, the move from a reasonable cultural relativism, which rightly causes us to rethink our moral systems, to an ethical relativism, which causes us to give up the heart of morality altogether, exemplifies the fallacy of confusing factual or descriptive statements with normative ones. Cultural relativism doesn't entail ethical relativism. The very reason that we are against ethnocentrism constitutes the basis for our favoring an objective moral system: Impartial reason draws us to it.

We may well agree that cultures differ and that we ought to be cautious in condemning what we don't understand, but this in no way must imply that there are not better and worse ways of living. We can understand and excuse, to some degree at least, those who differ from our best notions of morality, without abdicating the notion that cultures that lack principles of justice, promise-keeping, or protection of the innocent are morally poorer for these omissions.

The fourth reason, which has driven some to moral nihilism and others to relativism, is the decline of religion in Western society. As one of Dostoevsky's characters said, "If God is dead, all things are permitted." People who have lost religious faith feel a deep vacuum and understandably confuse it with a moral vacuum, or they finally become resigned to a form of secular conventionalism. Such people reason that, if there is no God to guarantee the validity of the moral order, then there must be no universal moral order—just radical cultural diversity and death at the end. I have tried to argue that, even without God, objective moral principles are valid. The relationship of religion to morality will be discussed at length in Chapter 10.

The fifth reason, one that is influential with philosophers overly impressed with *metaethics,* is that many philosophers believe it is important to begin the study of ethics with a morally neutral definition. *Webster's Collegiate Dictionary,* tenth edition, defines *ethics* as "the principles of conduct governing an individual or a group." No judgment is made from the outset about the content of those principles, and since the diversity thesis is plausible, one can be led to think that a certain relativism follows.

Although this definition may be a fair one for sociology or anthropology, it is inadequate for philosophy. There is a narrower, more substantive definition of *ethics* that has to do with the good, with human flourishing (and, I believe, with animal flourishing as well). And this flourishing involves the amelioration of suffering, the resolution of conflicts of interest, and the promotion of happiness. Given this content-laden conception of morality, we can explain why we are loathe to call Hitler's actions or the torturing of little children morally right, regardless of whether a majority approves of such actions.

Conclusion

I have presented arguments for an objective morality—both the strong natural law version and the moderate objectivist (or moderate natural law) version. If either of these is correct, then society will not long survive, and individuals will not flourish, without adherence to a core set of moral principles. Reason can discover the correct principles, and it is in our interest to promote them.

Let us return, finally, to the question asked at the beginning of Chapter 2: "Who's to judge what's right and wrong?" The reply is, "We are—every rational being on earth." And we are to judge on the basis of the best reasoning we can bring forth, in dialogue with one another, and with sympathy and understanding.

NOTES

1. Arthur Kuflik, in his review of this book, has pointed out that one can find the idea of natural law in the early chapters of Genesis and in the Talmud. Kuflik writes:

   As long as we are looking for *early* manifestations of natural law thinking (and not insisting on a wholly non-theistic model for natural law), we can find very important elements of natural law thinking in the first chapters of *Genesis:* (1) when God approaches Cain about the whereabouts of Abel, Cain doesn't simply say he killed him (something he might well have said without guilt or fear if he had no sense of having behaved wrongly). On the contrary, Cain is afraid to answer God truthfully and he is awkwardly defensive in his denial that he knows what happened to Abel. But recall that God had not previously laid down any law against murder nor made any explicit pronouncement on the wrongness of murder. Despite this, God punishes Cain. Cain and Abel were the third and fourth human beings ever to walk the earth—universal human proto-types—living long before the revelations on Mount Sinai of an elaborate Divine Law. Hence implicit in this story is the idea that murder is a basic, naturally recognizable wrong that can be justly punished with *or without* a preexisting humanly legislated or Divinely stated prohibition; (2) when God sets out to destroy all the people on earth except Noah and his family—because the earth was "filled with violence"—the implication seems to be not only that those other people should have lived *much* less violent lives than they did, but that they should have, and could have, realized the badness of their ways; also (3) in Deuteronomy 30:11–14, Moses, speaking on behalf of God, claims that the commandment which God had commanded the people that day [to do what is good and refrain from what is

   evil] is not "far off"—"it is not in the heavens that you should say, who will go up and bring it down to us" but is "near to you . . . in your mouth and in your heart." Kuflik also points out that the Talmudic rabbis worked a theory called "the seven laws of the sons of Noah" that contained rules of conduct "that all the peoples of the world (descended after all from Noah) should be able to recognize and live by, even though they were not audience to an explicit Divine Revelation such as took place at Mount Sinai."

2. Aristotle, *Nicomachean Ethics,* trans. W.P. Ross (Oxford University Press, 1925), Book X, p. 7.

3. Thomas Aquinas, *Summa Theologica.* In *Basic Writings of St. Thomas Aquinas,* trans. Anton C. Pegis (Random House, 1945), question 94. All references to Aquinas are from this volume.

4. Eric D'Arcy, *Human Acts* (Oxford University Press, 1963), ch. 4. Quoted in J. Glover, *Causing Deaths and Saving Lives* (Penguin Books, 1977), p.91.

5. William Ross, *The Right and the Good* (Oxford University Press, 1932), pp. 18 f.

6. See Marcus Singer's "The Idea of a Rational Morality" (*Proceedings of the American Philosophical Association,* September 1986), in which he argues that such principles as "It is always wrong to lie for lying's sake" are absolutely wrong. "Given any moral rule to the effect that some kind of action is generally wrong, it follows that it is always wrong to do an act of that kind just for the sake of doing it" (p. 28). An unqualified general principle would be of the form "Always do X" or "In general, do X," but a qualified general principle would be of the form "In general, do X except under condition C" or "Except under condition C, always do X." Suitably conditioned objective principles might turn out to be qualified absolutes. I am sympathetic to this approach and

suspect that some absolutes are valid. Most objectively valid moral principles seem to be principles of prima facie duty rather than of absolute, unconditional duty.

7. Renford Bambrough, *Moral Skepticism and Moral Knowledge* (Routledge & Kegan Paul), p. 33.

8. In Gilbert Harman's essay "Moral Relativism," in Gilbert Harman and Judith Jarvis Thomson, *Moral Relativism and Moral Objectivity* (Blackwell, 1996), p. 5, he defines moral relativism as the claim that "There is no single true morality. There are many different moral frameworks, none of which is more correct than the others." I hold that morality has a function of serving the needs and interests of human beings, so that some frameworks do this better than others. Essentially, all adequate theories will contain the principles I have identified in this essay.

9. I owe the reformulation of the argument to Bruce Russell.

10. J. L. Mackie, *Ethics: Inventing Right and Wrong* (Penguin, 1977), p. 22. We will discuss Mackie's error theory of morality in Chapter 12.

FOR FURTHER REFLECTION

1. After reading this chapter, how would you respond to the following question: "Are there any moral absolutes, or is morality completely relative to social or subjective acceptance?"

2. Explain the difference between moral absolutism and moral objectivism. What are the best arguments for each position?

3. What is the natural law position on morality? How is it different from physical laws, the laws of nature? What are its strengths and weaknesses?

4. The doctrine of double effect is often used in Just War Theory. For example, it is permissible to bomb a munitions factory in the midst of a civilian population if doing so meets the relevant conditions, especially if the deaths of the civilians (noncombatants) are not intended but simply foreseen. How would the doctrine of double effect assess the dropping of atom bombs on Hiroshima and Nagasaki in August 1945, bringing about the end of World War II?

5. H. L. A. Hart relates a case in which a man was trapped in the cabin of a blazing truck. The man begged a bystander to shoot him in order to save him from the suffering he was undergoing. What would the doctrine of double effect prescribe in this case? What do you think would be the right thing to do?

6. Examine the following quotation by David Hume on the essential uniformity of human nature. Do you agree with Hume? If so, can such information be the basis of an objective morality? Explain your answer.

It is universally acknowledged, that there is a great uniformity among the actions of men, in all nations and ages, and that human nature remains still the same, in its principles and operations. The same events follow from the same causes. Ambition, avarice, self-love, vanity, friendship, generosity, public spirit; these passions, mixed in various degrees, and distributed through society, have been, from the beginning of the world, and still are, the source of all the actions and enterprises which have ever been observed among mankind. Would you know the sentiments, inclinations, and course of life of the Greeks and Romans? Study well the temper and actions of the French and English:

you cannot be much mistaken in transferring to the former most of the observations which you have made with regard to the latter. Mankind are so much the same, in all times and places, that history informs us of nothing new or strange in that particular. Its chief use is only to discover the constant and universal principles of human nature, by showing men in all varieties of circumstances and situations, and furnishing us with materials, from which we may form our observations, and become acquainted with the regular springs of human action and behavior. These records of wars, intrigues, factions, and revolutions, are so many collections of experiments by which the politician or moral philosopher fixes the principles of his science; in the same manner as the physician or natural philosopher

becomes acquainted with the nature of plants, minerals, and other external objects, by the experiments which he forms concerning them. Nor are the earth, water, and other elements examined by Aristotle and Hippocrates, more like to those which at present lie under our observation, than the men, described by Polybius and Tacitus, are to those who now govern the world. [*Essays, Moral, Political and Literary* (Longman, Green, 1875)].

7. Do you agree that ethical relativism is a very attractive position in today's society, especially at college campuses? Why do you think this is so?

8. Ask two friends or fellow students whether they believe in ethical relativism or some form of objectivism. What reasons do they give for their positions?

FOR FURTHER READING

Bambrough, Renford. *Moral Skepticism and Moral Knowledge*. Routledge & Kegan Paul, 1979.

Brink, David. *Moral Realism and the Foundation of Ethics.* Cambridge University Press, 1989. A cogent defense of objectivism.

Finnis, John. *Natural Law and Natural Rights.* Oxford University Press, 1980. A contemporary defense of natural law.

Finnis, John. *Moral Absolutes: Tradition, Revision, and Truth*. Catholic University of America Press, 1991. A revisionist interpretation of natural law.

Gert, Bernard. *Morality: A New Justification of the Moral Rules.* Oxford University

Press, 1988. A defense of a minimal core morality.

Gewirth, Alan. *Reason and Morality.* University of Chicago Press, 1978. A defense of a strong objectivism.

Harman, Gilbert, and Judith Jarvis Thomson. *Moral Relativism and Moral Objectivity.* Blackwell, 1996. A sharp debate on relativism and objectivism.

Taylor, Paul. *Principles of Ethics.* Wadsworth, 1975. Chapter 2 contains a good discussion of moral objectivism.

Wilson, James Q. *The Moral Sense.* Free Press, 1993. A far-reaching, probing exploration of the thesis that human beings possess an inner moral sense, enabling them to discover moral truth.

4

Egoism, Self-Interest, and Altruism

Nice guys finish last.

LEO DUROCHER, FORMER MANAGER OF THE BROOKLYN DODGERS

The achievement of his own happiness is man's highest moral purpose.

AYN RAND, *THE VIRTUE OF SELFISHNESS*

AN OVERVIEW OF THE PROBLEM

Children are sometimes brought up to feel guilty for being concerned about their own good. They are taught that self-love is selfishness, a sinful attitude. To do things for oneself is evil. Indeed, I was brought up in a strict religious community in which children were made to feel they were sinful. The proper attitude toward oneself was one of humility ("Blessed are the poor in spirit, for theirs is the kingdom of heaven") and self-effacement ("Unless a person hate his own life, he cannot enter the kingdom of God").[1]

Sometimes such an upbringing results in self-hatred, low self-esteem, a lack of self-confidence, masochism, and pervasive, irrational guilt. Let's call this attitude the *morality of self-effacement*.

In Dostoevsky's *The Brothers Karamazov* Lise breaks her engagement with the saintly Alyosha, explaining to him that he is too gentle for her needs:

> I was just thinking for the thirtieth time what a good thing it is that I broke off our engagement and decided not to become your wife. You wouldn't be much of a husband, you know. . . . I want someone to marry me, tear me to pieces, betray me, and then desert me. I don't want to be happy.

Shortly afterwards we read:

> Lise unlocked the door, opened it a little, put her finger in the crack, and slammed the door as hard as she could. Ten seconds later she released her hand, went slowly to her chair, sat down, and looked intently at her blackened, swollen finger and the blood that was oozing out from under the nail. Her lips quivered. "I'm vile, vile, vile, a despicable creature."[2]

At the opposite extreme is the *morality of self-exaltation,* or the *morality of me-ism,* by which we are to love ourselves first. Ayn Rand's *The Virtue of Selfishness,* Robert Ringer's *Looking Out for Number One,* and David Seabury's *The Art of Selfishness* advise us to love ourselves first even if it means hurting others. Perhaps no one was more candid about the legitimacy of egoism than Friedrich Nietzsche (1844–1900), who taught that we should strive to satisfy our own will to power, even to the extent of exploiting and dominating others before they dominated us:

> What is strong wins. That is the universal law. To speak of right and wrong per se makes no sense at all. No act of violence, rape, exploitation, destruction, is intrinsically "unjust," since life itself is violent, rapacious, exploitative, and destructive and cannot be conceived otherwise.[3]

But Nietzsche's version of egoism is an extreme one. A less virulent form is found in Thomas Hobbes' (1588–1679) classic, *Leviathan* (1651). Hobbes believes egoism is the proper foundation for the moral and political life. Human nature is basically self-interested, so that it makes no sense to ask people to be altruistic. All apparently altruistic acts are, if you look deeply into the heart of people, merely disguised acts of selfishness. Nevertheless, Hobbes is no relativist. Out of enlightened egoism arise objective moral norms and a legitimate political system, the *Leviathan.*

Hobbes' argument goes like this: Suppose we existed outside of any society, without laws or agreed-upon morality, in a "state of nature." There are no common ways of life, no means of settling conflicts of interest except violence, no reliable expectations of how other people will behave—except that, as psychological egoists, they will follow their own inclinations and perceived interests, tending to act and react and overreact in fearful, capricious, and violent ways.

The result of life in the state of nature is chaotic anarchy. Reason advises us not to depend on anyone except ourselves, for others will let us down if it is in their interests to do so. I must always be on my guard, protecting my vital interests. But I see that others are thinking the same thing—perhaps they are ganging up on me. This increases my fear of others and leads in turn to preventive or preemptive aggression, which leads to "a war of all against all":

> During the time men live without a common Power to keep them all in awe they are in that condition called War; and such a war, as is of every man against every other man. . . . To this war every man against every man, this is consequent; that nothing can be Unjust. The notions of Right and Wrong, Justice and Injustice have no place.[4]

In such a state, life is "solitary, poor, nasty, brutish, and short."

But reason tells us that a war of all against all is really in no one's interest. It would be better for all of us, individually and collectively, if we adopted certain minimal rules that would override immediate self-interest whenever self-interest was a threat to others. So the notion of a mutually agreed-upon moral code arises from a situation of rational self-interest.

But, of course, the moral code will not work if only some obey it. They will be slaughtered like sheep before waiting wolves. Reason can only support morality when the presumption about other people's behavior is reversed. Hobbes thought that this could be achieved only by the creation of a *Leviathan,* an absolute ruler with absolute power to enforce his laws. But this is incorrect. The minimal moral society can be achieved by a people democratically if there are common rules or ways of life that are taught to all members of the society, inculcated in them early in life, and enforced by the group.

The members must be able to count on one another to obey these rules even when it is not in their immediate self-interest. Nonetheless, it is still rational to violate the rules whenever two conditions obtain: You calculate that you can get away with it, and your infraction will not seriously threaten the stability of the social system as a whole, sending you back toward the state of nature.

To prevent such violations Hobbes proposes a strong central government with a powerful police force and a sure and effective system of punishment. The threat of being caught and punished should function as a deterrent to crime. People must believe that offenses against the law are not in their overall interest. Is Hobbes correct in his account of human nature? Is he correct in his view that ethical egoism is the correct moral theory?

What is the place of self-regard, self-interest, or self-love in the moral life? Is everything we do really done out of the motive of self-interest, so that morality is necessarily egoistic? Is some form of egoism the best moral theory? Or is egoism really diametrically opposed to true morality? Is altruism possible, and, if so, is it rational? These are the questions we shall discuss in this chapter.

But before we can consider such questions, we need to make some careful distinctions and define our terms. First of all, there are at least four different types of egoism: psychological egoism, personal egoism, individual ethical egoism, and universal ethical egoism. These may be roughly defined in the following way:

1. **Psychological Egoism.** This is the doctrine that we always do that act that we perceive to be in our own best self-interest. That is, we have no choice but to be selfish. We cannot be motivated by anything other than what we believe will promote our interests. I always try to promote my self-interest and you always try to promote your self-interest.

2. **Personal Egoism.** This is the state of being selfish by choice. I simply always choose to serve my own best interest, regardless of what happens to anyone else. This is not a reflective judgment about what is right or wrong or what ought to be the case. As such it is not an ethical theory at all, but a phenomenal state of exclusive self-love. We might call this form of egoism "phenomenal *egotism*," or just plain selfishness.

3. **Individual Ethical Egoism.** This is the view that everyone *ought* to serve *my* best interest. Unlike personal egoism or phenomenal egotism, this doctrine prescribes that others serve me (the speaker). This claims to be a moral theory, obligating others to look after my interests before everything else. It also is a version of selfishness, a version that claims moral authority.

4. **Universal Ethical Egoism.** This is the view that everyone *ought* always to do those acts that will best serve his or her own best self-interest, even when it conflicts with the interests of others.

We turn now to an examination of each of these views, starting with psychological egoism.

PSYCHOLOGICAL EGOISM

Mr. Lincoln once remarked to a fellow-passenger on an old-time mud-coach that all men were prompted by selfishness in doing good. His fellow-passenger was antagonizing this position when they were passing over a corduroy bridge that spanned a slough. As they crossed this bridge they espied an old razorbacked sow on the bank making a terrible noise because her pigs had got into the slough and were in danger of drowning. As the old coach began to climb the hill, Mr. Lincoln called out, "Driver, can't you stop just a moment?" Then Mr. Lincoln jumped out, ran back and lifted the little pigs out of the mud and water and placed them on the bank. When he returned, his companion remarked: "Now Abe, where does selfishness come in on this little episode?" "Why, bless your soul, Ed, that was the very essence of selfishness. I should have had no peace of mind all day had I gone on and left that suffering old sow worrying over those pigs. I did it to get peace of mind, don't you see?"

[Quoted from the *Springfield Monitor,*
by F. C. Sharp in his *Ethics* (Appleton-Century, 1928), p. 28]

Psychological egoism (PE) purports to be a *description* of human nature. It claims that we cannot do other than act from self-interested motivation, so that *altruism*—the theory that we can and should sometimes act in favor of others' interests—is simply invalid because it's impossible. Since "ought" implies "can" (that is, we can never be under an obligation to do what is impossible), it follows that we cannot do anything but act on our own interests. Psychological egoism is not itself an ethical theory. It is a psychological theory about human nature or the nature of motivation, but as such it seems to imply ethical egoism, the doctrine that it is morally right always to seek one's own self-interest. The argument might be set down like this:

1. Everyone always seeks to maximize one's own self-interest. (PE)

2. If one cannot do an act, one has no obligation to do that act.

3. Altruistic acts involve putting other peoples' interests ahead of our own.

4. But altruism contradicts human nature (PE, or premise 1) and so is impossible.

5. Therefore, (by premises 2 and 4) altruistic acts are never morally obligatory. We have no duty to put another's interests ahead of our own.

It follows from this that the only obligations we can be said to have are those that maximize our own self-interest, as ethical egoism prescribes.

Let us begin our analysis by examining the following statement as an illustration of psychological egoism:

S. "Everyone is an egoist, for everyone always tries to do what will bring them satisfaction."

Is S true? What can be said in its favor?

Well, at first sight it seems ambiguous. On the one hand, it might mean:

S1. For any act A, everyone does A *in order* to obtain satisfaction.

Satisfaction is the goal. From this interpretation it may be inferred that everyone always acts in such a way as to maximize their self-interest (PE), self-interest being interpreted in terms of satisfaction of wants. But S could conceivably mean:

S2. Everyone does the act they most want to do, and as a *consequence* are satisfied by the success of carrying out the act.

The first interpretation implies psychological egoism, but the second does not.

Consider the first interpretation, which might be enlarged to read:

"We all want to be happy—to find satisfaction in life—and everything we do we consciously do toward that end."

Abe Lincoln, in the story quoted at the beginning of this section, claimed to help the piglets out of the slough to relieve his conscience, sheerly out of selfish motivation. As he says of his rescue of the piglets, "Why, bless your soul, Ed, that was the very essence of selfishness. I should have had no peace of mind all day had I gone on and left the suffering old sow worrying over those pigs. I did it to get peace of mind...."

Lincoln argues that there is no such thing as disinterested or altruistic action. Is he correct about this? Is everything we do done out of selfish motivation? Consider a variation on the Lincoln story: The situation is the same, only it is Ed who calls to the driver to halt and who spontaneously jumps out to save the piglets. He returns from the ordeal, pleased. Lincoln now greets him with these words; "Ed, you know that what you did was the very essence of selfishness. You couldn't have lived with yourself had you not tried to help those piglets." But Ed replies, "Abe, I wasn't aware of seeking my own happiness in trying to help those piglets. I did it because I believe that suffering should be alleviated. Of course, I feel satisfaction for having succeeded, but satisfaction is an automatic accompaniment of any successful action. Even if I had failed to help them, I would have felt a measure of satisfaction in that I succeeded in *trying* to help them."

Lincoln seems wrong and Ed seems right in his assessment of the relation of motivation to success. We do not always consciously seek our own satisfaction or happiness when we act. In fact, some people seem to seek their own unhappiness, as masochists and self-destructive people do, and we all sometimes seem to act spontaneously without consciously considering our happiness. Ed's position approximates the second interpretation of the motivation statement S:

S2. Everyone does the act they most want to do, and *as a consequence* are satisfied by the success of carrying out the act.

Actually, S2 doesn't seem quite right, for it is doubtful whether we always do what we most want to do. When I am on a diet, I most want to refrain from eating delicious chocolate cakes and rich ice cream, but I sometimes find myself yielding to the temptation. Alcoholics and addicts have even more poignant experiences of doing what they don't want to do. Such experiences of weakness of will count heavily against S2. Let us therefore attempt one more interpretation of S:

S3. Everyone always tries to do what one most wants to do, and as a consequence of success in carrying out the act experiences satisfaction.

S3 takes weakness of will into account and so seems closer to the truth. It also seems better for the following reason: We usually are not conscious of any concern for satisfaction when we seek some goal, but satisfaction seems to follow naturally on accomplishing any task. When I reach out to grab a child who is about to be hit by a car, pulling her back from danger, I feel satisfaction at my success, but I didn't save her in order to feel satisfied. To conclude that, because I feel satisfaction after saving her, I must have had satisfaction as my purpose is to confuse a consequent of an act with a purpose. This is as fallacious as reasoning that, because a car constantly consumes gasoline during driving, the purpose of such driving is to consume gasoline.

Suppose a super psychologist who could reliably predict outcomes told you that two courses of actions were open to you: (a) you would perform a perfect robbery, kill the bank president and the only person who knew your whereabouts, namely, your best friend or mother, and flee to Argentina to live a happy life; or (b) you would refrain from crime and live a simple but decent middle-class life as a teacher. Suppose further that he convinced you that option (a) would yield 1,000 units of happiness or satisfaction (call these units "hedons"), whereas option (b) would yield only 500 hedons. Which would you choose? If you would choose (b), then this is evidence that psychological egoism is false.

This seems to show that we act out of our overall value schemas and find satisfaction in achieving our goals, but that satisfaction is not the only goal. This is what John Stuart Mill meant when he said, "Better Socrates dissatisfied, than the pig satisfied." Likewise, "Better a discontented good person than a blissful bad person." Seeking satisfaction for its own sake and nothing else seems to merit Mill's pejorative "pig philosophy." We all want to be happy, but we don't want happiness at any price or to the exclusion of certain other values.

Moreover, happiness itself seems a peculiar kind of goal. As the *paradox of hedonism* asserts, the best way to get happiness is to forget it. That is, you'll have a higher probability of attaining happiness if you aim at accomplishing worthy goals that will indirectly bring about happiness:

I sought the bird of bliss, she flew away.

I sought my neighbor's good, bliss flew my way.

Happiness seems to be an elusive goal so long as we desire it alone and for its own sake. It is in the process of reaching other intrinsically worthy goals that happiness comes into being. Joel Feinberg puts the paradox of hedonism this way. Imagine a person, Jones, who is, first of all, devoid of intellectual curiosity. He has no desire to acquire any kind of knowledge for its own sake, and thus is utterly indifferent to questions of science, mathematics, and philosophy. Imagine further that the beauties of nature leave Jones cold: he is unimpressed by the autumn foliage, the snow-capped mountains, and the rolling oceans. Long walks in the country on spring mornings and skiing forays in the winter are to him equally a bore. Moreover, let us suppose that Jones can find no appeal in art. Novels are dull, poetry a pain, paintings nonsense and music just noise. Suppose further that Jones has neither the participant's nor the spectator's passion for baseball, football, tennis, or any other sport. Swimming to him is a cruel aquatic form of calisthenics, the sun only a cause of sunburn. Dancing is co-educational idiocy, conversation a waste of time, the other sex an unappealing mystery. Politics is a fraud, religion mere superstition; and the misery of millions of underprivileged human beings is nothing to be concerned with or excited about. Suppose finally that Jones has no talent for any kind of handicraft, industry, or commerce, and that he does not regret that fact.

What then is Jones interested in? He must desire something. To be sure, he does. Jones has an overwhelming passion for, a complete pre-occupation with, his own happiness. The one exclusive desire of his life is to be happy. It takes little imagination at this point to see that Jones's one desire is bound to be frustrated.[5]

The paradox of hedonism seems to suggest that psychological egoism has severe problems.

But suppose that the psychological egoist alters his interpretation of S to include subconscious motivations. The thesis now states that sometimes we are self-deceived about our motivation, but whenever we overcome self-deception and really look deep into our motivational schemes, we find an essential selfishness.

Is the self-deception argument sound? One problem with it is that it seems to be an unfalsifiable dogma, for what evidence could ever count against it? Suppose that you look within your motivational structure and do not find a predominant egoistic motive. What does the egoist say to this? The egoist responds that you just haven't looked deep enough. But how, you may wonder, do you know when you have looked deep enough? Egoist: When you discover the selfish motive.

Perhaps the self-deception argument is simply an outcome of dubious psychological theories. Or perhaps it is built on the doctrine of original sin or the Calvinist notion of the total depravity of human nature, in which case it is a theological doctrine, not a truth discoverable by empirical investigation. For example, if Lincoln's friend Ed introspects about his motivational scheme in pulling the piglets out of the slough and fails to find a selfish motive, Abe might respond, "Ed, I don't mean that the selfishness is always conscious. Self-deception is very deep in humans, so you just haven't looked deep enough."

This contention may show that we can never disprove psychological egoism. But it doesn't offer comfort to the egoist thesis either. Quite the contrary. If we look as deep as we can and still don't come up with a selfish motive, then we're justified in believing that not all action is motivated by agent-utility considerations. The burden of proof is on the egoist to convince us that we are still self-deceived. The egoist seems to be guilty of committing the fallacy of unwarranted generalization. Just because we are *sometimes* self-deceived about our motives, he reasons, we must *always* be deceived. But this doesn't follow at all.

Suppose that humans are predominantly psychological egoists, that we are very often motivated by self-regarding motives. This does not imply that we are entirely egoists, nor does it mean that we are necessarily selfish.

Merriam Webster's Collegiate Dictionary, tenth edition, defines *selfish* as "seeking or concentrating on one's own advantage, pleasure, or well-being without regard for others." But we may find our values such that we incorporate the good of others as part of our happiness. A friend's or a lover's happiness is so bound up with the good of the other that the two cannot be separated. So if psychological egoism is interpreted as selfishness, it is surely false. If it is simply a statement of how we are motivated, then it probably still is false. Something like it—predominant psychological egoism—may be true, but this does not rule out the possibility of disinterested action. We will examine the implications of predominant psychological egoism in the following section.

Let us now return to our original argument against the possibility of altruism, the view that we are able at times to act on other-regarding motives.

1. Everyone always seeks to maximize one's own self-interest. (PE)

2. If one cannot do an act, one has no obligation to do that act.

3. Altruistic acts involve putting other people's interests ahead of our own.

4. But altruism contradicts human nature (PE, or premise 1) and so is impossible.

5. Therefore, (by premises 2 and 4) altruistic acts are never morally obligatory. We have no duty to put another's interests ahead of our own.

We see that the first premise, if interpreted as selfishness, is false, for sometimes we do put other people's interests ahead of our own; thus the argument is unsound and does not show that altruism is impossible.

Whether altruism is a moral duty is another question, one we shall examine in the next two sections. We turn now to other forms of egoism.

ETHICAL EGOISM

In this section we will consider three other forms of egoism: personal egoism, individual ethical egoism, and universal ethical egoism. Personal egoism does not claim to be an ethical theory, though some people live by it. Individual ethical egoism and universal ethical egoism are ethical theories.

Personal egoism is not a description of human nature, but merely a description of a type of personality. It has no moral prescriptive force. It does not imply any of the other theories and is neutral between egoist and nonegoist ethical theories. Although psychological egoism is false, there seem to be many personal egoists. Personal egoism may be equated with selfishness, and it comes closest to *egotism,* the behavioral pattern in which one constantly draws attention to oneself. Egoists need not be egotists, but may be more subtle about their self-interestedness.

Individual ethical egoism is the view that everyone ought to serve *my* self-interest. That is, moral rightness is defined solely in terms of what is good for me, whether or not it is good for anyone else. Of course, each one of us could put his or her own name in the place of "me." Say, for example, that Aunt Ruth is a personal egoist. So all moral rightness defines itself in terms of what is good for Aunt Ruth. It would follow that whether or not a mother in India loves her child is morally irrelevant, for it has no effect on Aunt Ruth. Once Aunt Ruth is dead, morality is dead, for it has no object. Interestingly enough, while individual ethical egoism seems implausible, it may be the central position of many religious people who define ethics as "that which serves God's interests and pleases Him." Be that as it may, as far as mere mortals are concerned, individual ethical egoism seems a partial and absurd theory. What makes *you* so special that all of us are obligated to serve your interests as our primary concern?

Universal ethical egoism is the theory that everyone ought always to serve his or her own self-interest. That is, everyone ought to do what will maximize one's own expected utility or bring about one's own happiness, even when it means harming others. This has all the earmarks of a legitimate ethical theory. It is a universal theory, which individual ethical egoism is not. It is not egotistical; rather, it is prudential and favors long-term interests over short-term interests. In its most sophisticated form it urges everyone to *try* to win in the game of life, and it recognizes that in order to do this, some compromises are necessary. Indeed, the universal egoist will admit that to some extent we must all give up a certain freedom and cooperate with others to achieve our ends.

What are the arguments for ethical egoism? There are three that should be considered: (1) the economist argument; (2) the Ayn Rand argument for the virtue of selfishness; and (3) the Hobbesian argument. Let's examine each of these in turn.

The Economist Argument

Economists in the mold of Adam Smith often argue that individual self-interest in a competitive marketplace produces a state of optimal goodness for society at large, because the peculiar nature of self-interested competition causes each individual to produce a better product and sell it at a lower price than competitors. Thus, enlightened self-interest leads, as if by an invisible hand, to the best overall situation.

The Ayn Rand Argument for the Virtue of Selfishness

In her book *The Virtue of Selfishness,* Ayn Rand argues that selfishness is a virtue and altruism a vice, a totally destructive idea that leads to the undermining of individual worth. She defines *altruism* as the view that

> any action taken for the benefit of others is good, and any action taken for one's own benefit is evil. Thus, the *beneficiary* of an action is the only criterion of moral value—and so long as the beneficiary is anybody other than oneself, anything goes.[6]

As such, altruism is suicidal:

> If a man accepts the ethics of altruism, his first concern is not how to live his life, but how to sacrifice it. . . . Altruism erodes men's capacity to grasp the value of an individual life; it reveals a mind from which the reality of a human being has been wiped out.

Since finding happiness is the highest goal and good in life, altruism, which calls on us to sacrifice our happiness for the good of others, is contrary to our highest good. Her argument seems to go something like this:

1. The perfection of one's abilities in a state of happiness is the highest goal for humans. We have a moral duty to attempt to reach this goal.
2. The ethics of altruism prescribes that we sacrifice our interests and lives for the good of others.
3. Therefore the ethics of altruism is incompatible with the goal of happiness.
4. Ethical egoism prescribes that we seek our own happiness exclusively, and as such it is consistent with the happiness goal.
5. Therefore ethical egoism is the correct moral theory.

The Hobbesian Argument

According to some interpretations of Hobbes, we are not pure psychological egoists, but simply *predominantly* psychological egoists, having a powerful tendency in this direction.[7] Human action generally is predominantly motivated by self-interest. Since we cannot do otherwise without unreasonable effort, it follows that it is morally permissible to act entirely out of self-interest. However, enlightened common sense tells us that we should aim at fulfilling our long-term versus our short-term interests, and so we need to refrain from immediate gratification of our senses, from doing those things that would break down the social conditions that enable us to reach our goals. We should even, perhaps, generally obey the Golden Rule, "Do unto others as you would have them do unto you," for doing good unto others will help ensure that they do good unto us. However, sometimes we should cheat, when doing so will maximize agent utility, and sometimes we should harm others, when it is in our overall self-interest to do so.

Sometimes this version of egoism is based on the notion of agent-relative values. The theory states that all values are essentially owned by an agent and that each of us has our own hierarchy and specific set of values, so that each of us has different reasons for acting. There are no agent-neutral values that are identical in all persons. Naturally, we will have to cooperate with others in the pursuit of our projects, but ultimately we are alone in the world, the only persons who know exactly what our values are. Sometimes we may have to harm others in order to realize our projects.[8]

A CRITIQUE OF ETHICAL EGOISM

Essentially, the economist argument is not an argument for ethical egoism. It is really an argument for utilitarianism (see Chapter 6), which makes use of self-interest to attain (paradoxically) the good of all. The goal of this theory is social utility, but it places its faith in an invisible hand inherent in the free enterprise system that guides enlightened self-interest to reach that goal. We might say that it is a two-tier system: On the highest level it is utilitarian, but on a lower level of day-to-day action it is practical egoism.

Tier 2   General Goal: Social Utility

Tier 1   Individual Motivation: Egoistic

The economist argument via the two-tier system suggests that we not worry about the social good but only about our own good, and in that way we will attain the highest social good possible.

There may be some truth in such a two-tier system. But in the first place, it is unclear (at best) whether you can transpose the methods of economics (which are debatable) into the realm of personal relations. Personal relations may have a different logic than economic relations. The best way to maximize utility in an ethical sense may be to give one's life for others rather than kill another person, as an egoist might enjoin.

Secondly, it is not clear that classical laissez-faire capitalism works. Since the 1929 depression, most economists have altered their faith in classical capitalism, and most Western nations have supplemented capitalism with some governmental intervention. Likewise, though self-interest often leads to greater social utility, it may get out of hand and need to be supplemented by a concern for others. Just as classical capitalism has been altered to allow governmental intervention—resulting in a welfare system for the worst-off people, public education, social security, and medicare—an adequate moral system may need to draw attention to the needs of others and direct us to meeting those needs even when we do not consider it to be in our immediate self-interest.

The Ayn Rand argument for the virtue of selfishness appears to be flawed by the fallacy of a false dilemma. It simplistically assumes that absolute altruism and absolute egoism are the only alternatives. But this is an extreme view of the matter. There are plenty of options between these two positions. Even a predominant egoist would admit that (analogous to the paradox of hedonism) sometimes the best way to reach self-fulfillment is for us to forget about ourselves and strive to live for goals, causes, or other persons. Even if altruism is not required (as a duty), it may be permissible in many cases. Furthermore, self-interest may not be incompatible with other-regarding motivation. Even the Second Great Commandment set forth by Moses and Jesus states not that you must always sacrifice yourself for the other person, but that you ought to love your neighbor *as* yourself (Lev. 19:19; Matt. 23). Self-interest and self-love are morally good things, but not at the expense of other people's legitimate interests. When there is moral conflict of interests, a fair process of adjudication needs to take place.

Regarding the Hobbesian argument, which is the most plausible of the three arguments for ethical egoism, we can say that it seems to rest too heavily on psychological egoism. It assumes that we cannot do any better than be egoists, so we should be as enlightened about our egoism as possible. But if, as we argued earlier, psychological egoism is false, there is no reason to rule out the possibility of nonegoistic behavior. If Hobbesians qualify their position to embrace predominant psychological egoism—the theory that human nature causes us to be heavily biased toward our own self-interest over that of others' interest—then we need not of necessity become ethical egoists. However, the modified Hobbesian argument may make ethical egoism plausible.

Next we turn our attention to attempts to refute egoism in order to assess just how plausible it is as an ethical theory.

ATTEMPTED REFUTATIONS OF EGOISM

The Inconsistent Outcomes Argument

Brian Medlin argues that ethical egoism cannot be true because it fails to meet a necessary condition of morality, that of being a guide to action. He claims that it will be like advising people to do inconsistent things based on incompatible desires.[9] His argument goes like this:

1. Moral principles must be universal and categorical.
2. I must universalize my egoist desire to come out on top over Tom, Dick, and Harry.
3. But I must also prescribe Tom's egoist desire to come out on top over Dick, Harry, and me (and so on).
4. Therefore I have prescribed incompatible outcomes and have not provided a way of adjudicating conflicts of desire. In effect, I have said nothing.

The proper response to this is that of Jesse Kalin, who argues that we can separate our beliefs about ethical situations from our desires.[10] He likens the situation to a competitive sports event, in which you believe that your opponent has a right to try to win as much as you, but you desire that you, not he, will in fact win. An even better example is that of the chess game in which you recognize that your opponent ought to move her bishop to prepare for checkmate, but you hope she won't see the move. Belief that A ought to do Y does not commit you to wanting A to do Y.

The Publicity Argument

On the one hand, in order for something to be a moral theory it seems necessary that its moral principles be publicized. Unless principles are put forth as universal prescriptions that are accessible to the public, they cannot serve as guides to action or as aids in resolving conflicts of interest. But on the other hand, it is not in the egoist's self-interest to publicize them. Egoists would rather that the rest of us be altruists. (Why did Nietzsche and Rand write books announcing their positions? Were the royalties taken in by announcing ethical egoism worth the price of letting the cat out of the bag?)

Thus it would be self-defeating for the egoist to argue for her position, and even worse that she should convince others of it. But it is perfectly possible to have a private morality that does not resolve conflicts of interest. So the egoist should publicly advocate standard principles of traditional morality—so that society doesn't break down—while adhering to a private, nonstandard, solely self-regarding morality. So, if you're willing to pay the price, you can accept the solipsistic-directed norms of egoism.

If the egoist is prepared to pay the price, egoism could be a consistent system that has some limitations. Although the egoist can cooperate with others in limited ways and perhaps even have friends—so long as their interests don't conflict with his—he has to be very careful about preserving his isolation. The egoist can't give advice or argue about his position—not sincerely at least. He must act alone, atomistically or solipsistically in moral isolation, for to announce his adherence to the principle of egoism would be dangerous to his project. He can't teach his children the true morality or justify himself to others or forgive others.

The Paradox of Egoism

The situation may be even worse than the sophisticated, self-conscious egoist supposes. Could the egoist have friends? And if limited friendship is possible, could he or she ever be in love or experience deep friendship? Suppose the egoist discovers that in the pursuit of the happiness goal, deep friendship is in his best interest. Can he become a friend? What is necessary to deep friendship? A true friend is one who is not always pre-occupied about his own interest in the relationship but who forgets about himself altogether, at least sometimes, in order to serve or enhance the other person's interest. "Love seeketh not its own." It is an altruistic disposition, the very opposite of egoism. So the *paradox of egoism* is that in order to reach the goal of egoism one must give up egoism and become (to some extent) an altruist, the very antithesis of egoism.

The Argument from Counterintuitive Consequences

The final argument against ethical egoism is that it is an absolute ethics that not only permits egoistic behavior but demands it. Helping others at one's own expense is not only not required, it is morally wrong. Whenever I do not have good evidence that my helping you will end up to my advantage, I must refrain from helping you. If I can save the whole of Europe and Africa from destruction by pressing a button, then so long as there is nothing for me to gain by it, it is wrong for me to press that button. The Good Samaritan was, by this logic, morally wrong in helping the injured victim and not collecting payment for his troubles. It is certainly hard to see why the egoist should be concerned about environmental matters if he or she is profiting from polluting the environment. (For example, if the egoist gains 40 hedons in producing P, which produces pollution that in turn causes others 1,000 dolors—units of suffering—but suffers only 10 of those dolors himself, then by an agent-maximizing calculus he is morally obligated to produce P.) There is certainly no obligation to preserve scarce natural resources for future generations. "Why should I do anything for posterity?" the egoist asks. "What has posterity ever done for me?"

In conclusion, we see that ethical egoism has a number of serious problems. It cannot consistently publicize itself, nor often argue its case. It tends towards solipsism and the exclusion of many of the deepest human values, such as love and deep friendship. It violates the principle of fairness, and, most of all, it entails an absolute prohibition on altruistic behavior, which we intuitively sense as morally required (or, at least, permissible).

EVOLUTION AND ALTRUISM

If sheer unadulterated egoism is an inadequate moral theory, does that mean we ought to aim at complete altruism, total self-effacement for the sake of others? What is the role of self-love in morality? An interesting place to start answering these queries is with the new field of sociobiology, which theorizes that social structures and behavioral patterns, including morality, have a biological base, explained by evolutionary theory.

In the past, linking ethics to evolution meant justifying exploitation. Social Darwinism justified imperialism and the principle that "Might makes right" by saying that survival of the fittest is a law of nature. This philosophy lent itself to a promotion of ruthless egoism. This is nature's law, "nature red in tooth and claw." Against this view ethologists such as Robert Ardrey and Konrad Lorenz argued for a more benign view of the animal kingdom—one reminiscent of Rudyard Kipling's, in which the animal kingdom survives by cooperation, which is at least as important as competition. On Ardrey's and Lorenz's view it is the group or the species, not the individual, that is of primary importance.

With the development of sociobiology—in the work of E. O. Wilson but particularly the work of Robert Trivers, J. Maynard Smith, and Richard Dawkins—a theory has come to the fore that combines radical individualism with limited altruism. It is not the group or the species that is of evolutionary importance but the gene, or, more precisely, the gene type. Genes—the parts of the chromosomes that carry the blueprints for all our natural traits (e.g., height, hair color, skin color, intelligence)— copy themselves as they divide and multiply. At conception they combine with the genes of a member of the opposite sex to form a new individual.

In his fascinating sociobiological study, Richard Dawkins describes human behavior as determined evolutionarily by stable strategies set to replicate the gene.[11] This is not done consciously, of course, but by the invisible hand that drives consciousness. We are essentially gene machines.

Morality—that is, successful morality—can be seen as an evolutionary strategy for gene replication. Here's an example: Birds are afflicted with life-endangering parasites. Because they lack limbs to enable them to pick the parasites off their heads, they—like much of the animal kingdom—depend on the ritual of mutual grooming. It turns out that nature has evolved two basic types of birds in this regard: those who are disposed to groom anyone (the nonprejudiced type?), and those who refuse to groom anyone but who present themselves for grooming. The former type of bird Dawkins calls "Suckers" and the latter "Cheaters."

In a geographical area containing harmful parasites and where there are only Suckers or Cheaters, Suckers will do fairly well, but Cheaters will not survive, for want of cooperation. However, in a Sucker population in which a mutant Cheater arises, the Cheater will prosper, and the Cheater gene-type will multiply. As the Suckers are exploited, they will gradually die out. But if and when they become too few to groom the Cheaters, the Cheaters will start to die off too and eventually become extinct.

Why don't birds all die off, then? Well, somehow nature has come up with a third type, call them "Grudgers." Grudgers groom all and only those who reciprocate in grooming them. They groom each other and Suckers, but not Cheaters. In fact, once caught, a Cheater is marked forever. There is no forgiveness. It turns out then that unless there are a lot of Suckers around, Cheaters have a hard time of it—harder even than Suckers. However, it is the Grudgers that prosper. Unlike Suckers, they don't waste time messing with unappreciative Cheaters, so they are not exploited and have ample energy to gather food and build better nests for their loved ones.

J. L. Mackie argues that the real name for Suckers is "Christian," one who believes in complete altruism, even turning the other cheek to one's assailant and loving one's enemy. Cheaters are ruthless egoists who can survive only if there are enough naive altruists around. Whereas Grudgers are *reciprocal* altruists who have a rational morality based on cooperative self-interest, Suckers, such as Socrates and Jesus, advocate "turning the other cheek and repaying evil with good."[12] Instead of a Rule of Reciprocity, "I'll scratch your back if you'll scratch mine," the extreme altruist substitutes the Golden Rule, "If you want the other fellow to scratch your back, you scratch his—even if he won't reciprocate."

The moral of the story is this: Altruist morality (so interpreted) is only rational given the payoff of eternal life (with a scorekeeper, as Woody

Allen says). Take that away, and it looks like a Sucker system. What replaces the "Christian" vision of submission and saintliness is the reciprocal altruist with a tit-for-tat morality, someone who is willing to share with those willing to cooperate.

Mackie may caricature the position of the religious altruist, but he misses the subtleties of wisdom involved (Jesus said, "Be as wise as serpents but as harmless as doves"). Nevertheless, he does remind us that there is a difference between core morality and complete altruism. We have duties to cooperate and reciprocate, but no duty to serve those who manipulate us nor an obvious duty to sacrifice ourselves for people outside our domain of special responsibility. We have a special duty of high altruism toward those in the close circle of our concern, namely, our family and friends.

Conclusion

Martin Luther once said that humanity is like a man who, when mounting a horse, always falls off on the opposite side, especially when he tries to overcompensate for his previous exaggerations. So it is with ethical egoism. Trying to compensate for an irrational, guilt-ridden, Sucker altruism of the morality of self-effacement, it falls off the horse on the other side, embracing a Cheater's preoccupation with self-exaltation that robs the self of the deepest joys in life. Only the person who mounts properly, avoiding both extremes, is likely to ride the horse of happiness to its goal.

NOTES

1. Luke 14:26: "If any man come to me and hate not his father and his mother and his wife and children and brethren and sisters, yea and his own life also, he cannot be my disciple." Some interpretations of this difficult passage argue that Jesus is saying that *in comparison* to one's devotion to God, which should be absolute, other relationships should be quite secondary or nonabsolute.

2. Fyodor Dostoevsky, *The Brothers Karamazov,* trans. Andrew MacAndrews (Bantam Books, 1970), pp. 697, 703.

3. Friedrich Nietzsche, *Genealogy of Morals,* trans. Walter Kaufmann (Ran-

dom House, 1966), p. 208. Some may accuse Nietzsche of "nihilism," of undermining ethics altogether, but I think that Nietzsche believed in an elitist morality in which the "superior" egoists cooperated with one another in their struggle against the herd, the mediocre masses of mankind.

4. Thomas Hobbes, *Leviathan,* Ch. 13.

5. Joel Feinberg, "Psychological Egoism," in his *Reason and Responsibility* (Wadsworth, 1985).

6. Ayn Rand, *The Virtue of Selfishness* (New American Library, 1964), pp. vii and 27–32; 80 ff.

7. See Gregory S. Kavka, *Hobbesian Moral and Political Theory* (Princeton University Press, 1986), pp. 64–82, where the "predominant" interpretation is set forth. I think Hobbes is unclear regarding the matter, but I am willing to call Kavka's position "revised Hobbesianism." It is a more charitable position.

8. See Jesse Kalin, "In Defense of Egoism," in *Ethical Theory*, ed. Louis Pojman (Wadsworth, 1989), p. 93 f.

9. Brian Medlin, "Ultimate Principles and Ethical Egoism," *Australasian Journal of Philosophy* (1957), pp. 111–118; reprinted in Louis Pojman, *Ethical Theory*, pp. 81–85.

10. Kalin, "In Defense of Egoism."

11. Richard Dawkins, *The Selfish Gene* (Oxford University Press, 1976), Ch. 10.

12. J. L. Mackie, "The Law of the Jungle: Moral Alternatives and Principles of Evolution," *Philosophy* 53 (1978).

FOR FURTHER REFLECTION

1. Evaluate whether this statement, which I first encountered in a student paper, is true or false:

   "Everyone is an egoist, for everyone always tries to do what will bring them satisfaction."

2. Distinguish between individual and universal ethical egoism. Which theory appeals to you more? Does either constitute an adequate ethical theory? Explain your answer.

3. Chapter 1 began with the story of the killing of Kitty Genovese. Review that story, and discuss how an ethical egoist would respond to the plight of Kitty Genovese. Would egoists admit that they have a duty to come to the aid of Ms. Genovese?

4. Discuss the three arguments in favor of ethical egoism and the four against it. Which side has the best arguments? Why?

5. Does the egoist have a point in believing that most moral systems fail to recognize adequately that morality should be in our best interest? In this light, ethical egoism could be seen as an attempt to compensate for the inadequacies of other ethical views that emphasize doing duty for duty's sake or for the sake of others. We will discuss this point at length in Chapter

9, but you may want to work out your initial response now.

6. Some philosophers, beginning with Plato, have argued that ethical egoism is irrational, since it precludes psychological health. In an article entitled "Ethical Egoism and Psychological Dispositions" (*American Philosophical Quarterly* 17(1), 1980), Laurence Thomas sets forth the following argument:

P1. A true friend could never, as a matter of course, be disposed to harm or to exploit anyone with whom he is a friend [definition of a friend].

P2. An egoist could never be a true friend to anyone [for the egoist must be ready to exploit others whenever it is in his or her interest].

P3. Only someone with an unhealthy personality could never be a true friend to anyone [definition of a healthy personality; that is, friendship is a necessary condition for a healthy personality].

P4. Ethical egoism requires that we have a kind of disposition which is incompatible with our having a healthy personality [from P1–P3].

Conclusion: Therefore, from the standpoint of our psychological

makeup, ethical egoism is unacceptable as a moral theory.

Do you agree with Thomas? How
might the ethical egoist respond?

7. What is the relationship between
ethics and evolution? How does this
relationship throw light on egoism?
What is the significance of reciprocity
for ethics?

FOR FURTHER READING

Baier, Kurt. *The Moral Point of View.* Cornell University Press, 1958.

Brandt, Richard. "Rationality, Egoism, and Morality," *The Journal of Philosophy,* 69 (1972).

Falk, W. D. "Morality, Self, and Others," in *Ethics,* ed. J. J. Thomson and G. Dworkin. Harper & Row, 1968.

Gauthier, David, ed. *Morality and Rational Self-Interest.* Prentice-Hall, 1970.

Gauthier, David. *Morality by Agreement.* Clarendon Press, 1986.

MacIntyre, Alasdair. "Egoism and Altruism," in *The Encyclopedia of Philosophy,* ed. Paul Edwards. Macmillan, 1967.

Nagel, Thomas. *The Possibility of Altruism.* Clarendon Press, 1970.

Pojman, Louis, ed. *Ethical Theory: Classical and Contemporary Readings,* 2nd ed. Wadsworth, 1995. Contains essays by

Feinberg, Medlin, Kalin, Ruse, and Sober.

Rachels, James. *The Elements of Moral Philosophy.* Random House, 1986, Chs. 5 and 6.

Ruse, Michael. *Sociobiology: Sense or Nonsense?* D. Reidel, 1984.

Sidgwick, Henry. *The Methods of Ethics,* 7th ed. Hackett, 1981.

Singer, Peter. *The Expanding Circle: Ethics and Sociobiology.* Oxford University Press, 1983. A good discussion of egoism in the light of sociobiology.

Slote, Michael. "An Empirical Basis for Psychological Egoism," *Journal of Philosophy,* 61, (1964).

Thomas, Laurence. "Ethical Egoism and Psychological Dispositions," *American Philosophical Quarterly,* 17(1) (January 1980).

5

Value:
The Quest
for the Good

There is beauty in sky and cloud and sea, in lilies and in sunsets, in the glow of bracken in autumn and in the enticing greenness of a leafy spring. Nature, indeed, is infinitely beautiful, and she seems to wear her beauty as she wears color or sound. Why then should her beauty belong to us rather than to her? Human character and human dispositions have value or worth, which belongs to them in the same sense as redness belongs to the cherry.

JOHN LAIRD, *A STUDY IN REALISM*

We never strive for, wish for, long for, or desire anything, because we deem it to be good, but, rather, we deem a thing good, because we strive for it, wish for it, long for it, or desire it.

BENEDICT DE SPINOZA, *ETHICS*

What sorts of things are valuable? Do you have a clear idea of what your values are? For example, do you believe in the sanctity of life? Do you place an absolute value on life? What would you say if I told you that I had invented a marvelous Convenience Machine that would save us a lot of time and energy but result in the deaths of over 80,000

Americans per year? Would you use this machine? Would you refuse to use it on the grounds that the value of life exceeds any amount of convenience? What if our economy were centered around the use of this machine? Would you say that we ought to change our economy in order to save more lives?

Well, we have this Convenience Machine, in several brands: Chevrolet, Ford, Chrysler, Nissan, Honda, Mercedes, and so on. Motor vehicle accidents in the United States result in about 50,000 deaths a year; another 30,000 deaths are caused by diseases brought on by automobile pollution. Half the air pollution produced in the United States is from motor vehicle exhaust. How much do you really value life?

Perhaps we really do not value life as an absolute. Some people say that it is the quality of life rather than life itself that is valuable. The ancient Greeks and Romans believed that when life became burdensome, one had the obligation to commit suicide, for it was not the quantity of life that counted, but the quality. As the Roman Stoic philosopher Seneca (4 B.C.?–65 A.D.) said, "Mere living is not a good, but living well." Although the Christian tradition has generally condemned suicide, Jesus seems to agree that it is not mere living that is important, but a certain type of living. Speaking of the man who betrayed him, Jesus said, "It were better for that man that he were never born" (Matt. 26).

What makes life worth living? What things are good or bad in themselves? Are values subjective or objective? What is the relation of values to morality? What is the valuable life, the good or happy life? Before reading any further, make a list of your values. What things do you consider good or desirable? Reflect a moment on why you chose the things you did and how they relate to each other.[1]

The term *value* (from the Latin *valere,* meaning "to be of worth") is highly elastic. Sometimes it is used narrowly as a synonym for *good* or *valuable,* and sometimes it is used broadly for the whole scope of evaluative terms, ranging from the highest good through the indifferent to the worst evil, comprising positive, neutral, as well as negative "values." In the narrow sense the opposite of *value* is *evil* or *disvalue,* but in the broader sense its opposite is *fact,* that which suggests that values are not recognized in the same way as empirical facts are. In a comprehensive value theory (sometimes referred to as an "axiology"), the broader meaning of the word is used. In this chapter we shall generally refer to negative value as *disvalue,* use *value* to signify what is good or valuable, and use *axiology* to refer to the whole range of positive and negative values. The range may be illustrated by the following chart.

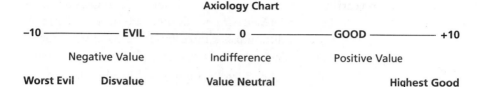

Axiology Chart

The central questions in value theory are these:

1. What are the different types of values, and how are they related to each other?
2. What things or activities are valuable or good?
3. Are values objective or subjective? That is, do we desire the Good because it is good, or is the Good good because we desire it?
4. What is the relation of value to morality?
5. What is the good life?

Let us briefly examine each of these questions.

WHAT TYPES OF VALUE ARE THERE?

Let me begin with an excerpt from Plato's *Republic* that features a dialogue between Socrates and Plato's brother Glaucon.

SOCRATES (S): Tell me, do you think there is a kind of good which we welcome not because we desire its consequences but for its own sake: joy, for example, and all the harmless pleasures which have no further consequences beyond the joy which one finds in them?

GLAUCON (G): Certainly, I think there is such a good.

S: Further, there is the good which we welcome for its own sake and also for its consequences, knowledge, for example, and sight and health. Such things we somehow welcome on both accounts.

G: Yes.

S: Are you also aware of a third kind, such as physical training, being treated when ill, the practice of medicine, and other ways of making money? We should say that these are wearisome but beneficial to us; we should not want them for their own sake, but because of the rewards and other benefits which result from them.[2]

The question "What things are good or valuable?" is ambiguous. We need first to separate the kinds of values or goods there are. In the quotation from Plato's *Republic* Socrates distinguishes three kinds of goods: (1) purely intrinsic goods (of which simple joys are an example); (2) purely instrumental goods (of which medicine and making money are examples); and (3) combination goods (such as knowledge, sight, and health), which are good in themselves *and* good as a means to further goods.

Examine the list you made of things you value, and see if you can distinguish the three kinds of goods mentioned by Socrates. The essential difference is between *intrinsic* and *instrumental* goods. We consider some things good or worthy of desire (desirable) in themselves and other things good or desirable only because of their consequences. Intrinsic goods are good because of their nature. They are not derived from other goods, whereas instrumental goods are worthy of desire because they are effective means of attaining our intrinsic goods.

We may further distinguish an *instrumental good* from a *good instrument*. If something is an instrumental good, it is a means to attaining something that is intrinsically good; but merely to be a good instrument is to be an effective means to any goal, good or bad. For example, poison is a good instrument for murdering someone, but murder is not an intrinsically good thing; thus poison, in this use at least, is not an instrumental good.

Look at your list of values. It probably contains many things that are instrumental values. Socrates in our selection from the *Republic* mentions two instrumental values: medicine and money. Medicine is an instrumental good in that it can hardly be valued for its own sake. We can ask, "What is medicine for?" The answer is, "It is to promote health." But is health an intrinsic value or an instrumental one? Can we ask, "What is health for?" Some will agree with Socrates that health is good for itself and for other things as well, such as happiness and creative activity. Others will dispute Socrates' contention and judge health to be wholly an instrumental good. We will look at this more closely in the next section.

Money is Socrates' other example of an instrumental value. Few, if any, of us really value money for its own sake, but almost all of us value it for what it can buy. When we ask, "What is money for?" we arrive at such goods as food and clothing, shelter and automobiles, entertainment and education. But are any of these really intrinsic goods, or are they all instrumental goods? When we ask, for example, "What is entertainment for?" what answer do we come up with? Most of us would mention enjoyment or pleasure, Socrates' example of an intrinsic good. Can we further ask, "What is enjoyment or pleasure for?" We will examine this question in the next section. But before we do we need to ask whether the notion of intrinsic values makes any sense.

Are there any intrinsic values? Are there any entities whose values are not derived from something else, that is, that are sought for their own sake, that are just good in themselves? Or are all values relative to desirers, that is, instrumental to goals that are the creation of choosers? Those who espouse the notion of intrinsic value usually argue that pleasure is an example of an intrinsic value and pain an example of an intrinsic disvalue: It is good to experience pleasure and bad to experience pain. Naturally, these philosophers admit that individual experiences of pleasure can be bad (because they result in some other disvalue, such as a hangover after a drinking spree) and individual painful experiences can be valuable (for example, having a painful operation to save one's life). The intrinsicalist affirms that pleasure is just better than pain. We can see this straight off. We do not need any arguments to convince us that pleasure is good or that gratuitous pain is intrinsically bad. Suppose we see a man torturing a child and order him to stop at once. If he replies, "I agree that the child is experiencing great pain, but why should I stop torturing her?" we would suspect some mental aberration on his part.

The nonintrinsicalist denies that the preceding arguments have any force. The notion that the experience itself could have any value is unclear. It is only by our choosing pleasure over pain that the notion of value begins to have meaning. In a sense, all value is extrinsic, or a product of choosing. Many existentialists, most notably Jean-Paul Sartre, believe that we invent our values by arbitrary choice. The freedom to create our values and thus to define ourselves is godlike and, at the same time, deeply frightening, for we have no one to blame for our failures but ourselves. "We are condemned to freedom . . . Value is nothing else but the meaning that you choose. One may choose anything so long as it is done from the ground of freedom."[3]

But this seems false. We do not choose most of our values in the same way we choose to have soup or salad with our meal. We cannot help valuing pleasure, health, happiness, and love and disvaluing pain and suffering. With regard to the fundamental values, they choose us, not we them. It is as though God or evolution preprogrammed us to desire them. And when we find someone who does not value (or claims not to value) happiness or love, we tend to explain this anomaly as a product of unfortunate circumstances.

WHAT THINGS ARE GOOD?

Philosophers divide into two broad camps: hedonists and nonhedonists. The hedonist (from *hedon,* Greek for "pleasure") asserts that all pleasure is good, that pleasure is the only thing good in itself, and that all other goodness is derived from this value. An experience is good in itself if and only if it provides some pleasure and to the extent that it provides pleasure. Sometimes this definition is widened to include the amelioration of pain, pain being seen as the only thing bad in itself. For simplicity's sake we will use the former definition, realizing that it may need to be supplemented by reference to pain.

Hedonists subdivide into (a) *sensualists,* who equate all pleasure with sensual titillation, and (b) *satisfactionists,* who equate all pleasure with satisfaction or enjoyment, which may not involve sensuality. Satisfaction is a pleasurable state of consciousness, such as we might experience after accomplishing a successful venture or receiving a gift. The opposite of sensual enjoyment is physical pain; the opposite of satisfaction is displeasure or dissatisfaction.

The Greek philosopher Aristippus (ca. 435–366 B.C.) and his school, the Cyrenaics, espoused the sensualist position; that the only (or primary) good was sensual pleasure and that this goodness was defined in terms of its intensity. This was also Mustapha Mond's philosophy in Aldous Huxley's *Brave New World.* The following dialogue is between Mustapha Mond, the genius technocrat who governs the brave new world and the malcontent, "Savage," who believes that this hedonic paradise lacks something.

SAVAGE: Yes, that's just like you. Getting rid of everything unpleasant instead of learning to put up with it. Whether 'tis better in the mind to suffer the slings and arrows of outrageous fortune, or to take arms against a sea of troubles and by opposing end them . . . But you don't do either. Neither suffer nor oppose. You just abolish the slings and arrows. It's too easy . . . Isn't there something in living dangerously?

MUSTAPHA MOND: There's a great deal in it . . . Men and women must have their adrenals stimulated from time to time . . . It's one of the conditions of perfect health. That's why we've made the VPS treatment compulsory.

SAVAGE: VPS?

MOND: Violent Passion Surrogate. Regularly once a month. We flood the whole system with adrenin. It's the complete physiological equivalent of fear and rage . . . without any of the inconveniences.

SAVAGE: But I like the inconvenience.

MOND: In fact you're claiming the right to be unhappy . . . Not to mention the right to grow old and ugly and impotent; the right to have syphilis and cancer; the right to have too little to eat; the right to live in constant apprehension of what may happen tomorrow; the right to be tortured by unspeakable pains of every kind.

SAVAGE (after a long silence): I claim them all.

MOND (shrugging his shoulders): You're welcome.[4]

The brave new world is a society of the future where people have been liberated from disease, violence, and crime through immunization, genetic engineering, and behavior modification. They are protected from depression and unhappiness through a drug, *soma,* that offers them euphoric sensations. Mustapha Mond, the brilliant manager of the society, defends this hedonistic utopia against one of the few remaining malcontents, the "Savage," who complains that something of value is missing in this "utopia."

All but sensuously deprived adolescents (or those in a similar psychological state) would probably agree that the brave new world is lacking something. The sensuous version of pleasure is too simple.

Most hedonists since the third century B.C. follow Epicurus (342–270 B.C.), who had a broader view of pleasure:

It is not continuous drinkings and revellings, nor the satisfaction of lusts, nor the enjoyment of fish and other luxuries of the wealthy table, which produce a happy life, but sober reasoning, searching out the motives for all choice and avoidance, and banishing mere opinions, to which are due the greatest disturbance of the spirit.[5]

The distinction between pleasure as satisfaction and as sensation is important, and failure to recognize it results in confusion and paradox. One example of this is the paradox of masochism. How can it be that the masochist enjoys (i.e., takes pleasure in) pain, which is the opposite of pleasure? "Well," the hedonist responds, "because of certain psychological aberrations, the masochist enjoys (qua satisfaction) what is painful (qua sensation)." He or she does not enjoy (qua sensation) what is painful (qua sensation). There is also a two-level analysis to explain the masochist's behavior: On a lower, or basic, level he is experiencing either pain or dissatisfaction, but on a higher level he approves and finds satisfaction from that pain or dissatisfaction.

Nonhedonists divide into two camps: Monists and Pluralists. *Monists* believe there is a single intrinsic value but that it is not pleasure. Perhaps it is a transcendent value, "the Good," which we do not fully comprehend but which is the basis of all our other values. This seems to be Plato's view. *Pluralist nonhedonists* generally admit that pleasure or enjoyment is an intrinsic good, but add that there are other intrinsic goods as well, such as knowledge, friendship, freedom, love, conscientiousness, and life itself.

Hedonists such as Jeremy Bentham (1748–1832) argue that though these qualities are good, their goodness is *derived* from the fact that they bring pleasure or satisfaction. Such hedonists ask of each of the previously mentioned values, what is it for? What is knowledge for? If it gave no one any satisfaction or enjoyment, would it really be good? Why do we feel there is a significant difference between knowing how many stairs there are in New York City and whether or not there is life after death? We normally do not value knowledge of the first kind, but knowledge of the second kind is relevant for our enjoyment.

The hedonist asks; "What are friendship and love for?" If we were made differently and got no satisfaction out of love and friendship, would they still be valuable? Are they not highly valuable, significant instrumental goods, because they bring enormous satisfaction?

Even moral commitment or conscientiousness is not good in itself, avers the hedonist. Morality is not intrinsically valuable, but is meant to serve human need, which in turn has to do with bringing about satisfaction.

And life certainly is not intrinsically good. It is quality that counts. An amoeba or a permanently comatose patient has life but no intrinsic value. Only when consciousness appears does the possibility for value arrive. Consciousness is a necessary but not a sufficient condition for satisfaction.

The nonhedonist responds that this is counterintuitive. Consider, for example, the possibility of living in a Pleasure Machine. We have invented a complex machine into which people may enter in order to find pure and constant pleasure. Attached to their brains will be electrodes that send currents to the limbic area of the cerebral cortex and other parts of the brain, producing very powerful sensations of pleasure. When people get into the machine, they experience these wonderful feelings. Would you enter such a machine?

If all you want is pleasure or satisfaction, then the Pleasure Machine seems the right choice. You're guaranteed all the pleasure you've ever dreamt of—without frustration or competition from other people. But if you want to *do* something and *be* something (e.g., have good character or a certain quality of personality) or experience reality (e.g., friendship and competition), then you might think twice about this choice. Is the Pleasure Machine not just another addiction—like alcohol, cocaine, or "crack"? Once in the machine, would we become forever addicted to it?

Or suppose there were two worlds with the same number of people and the same amount of total pleasure, but in World I the people were selfish and even evil, whereas in World II the people were deeply moral. Wouldn't it seem that World II was intrinsically better than World I?

Or imagine two lives, those of Suzy and Izzy. Suzy possesses 100 hedons (units of pleasure), even though she is severely retarded and physically handicapped, whereas Izzy enjoys great mental acumen and physical prowess but has only 99 hedons. Isn't it obvious that Izzy has the better life? But hedonists are committed to saying that Suzy's life is better, which seems implausible.

It was these sorts of cases that led John Stuart Mill (1806–1873)—in his classic work, *Utilitarianism*—to modify the hedonic doctrine, admitting that "it is better to be a human dissatisfied than a pig satisfied; better to be Socrates dissatisfied than a fool satisfied."[6] He suggested that there were different qualities of pleasure and that those who had experienced the different kinds could distinguish among them. Whether the notion of *quality of pleasure* can save hedonism is a controversial matter, but many of us feel uneasy with the idea that pleasure alone is good. Some broader notion, such as *happiness* or *object of desire* seems a more adequate candidate for what we mean by value. We will discuss these criteria in upcoming sections.

ARE VALUES OBJECTIVE OR SUBJECTIVE?

Do we desire the Good because it is good, or is the Good good because we desire it? The objectivist holds that values are worthy of desire whether or not anyone actually desires them; they are somehow independent of us. The subjectivist holds, to the contrary, that values are dependent on desirers, are relative to desirers.

The classic objectivist view on values (the absolutist version) was given by Plato (428–348 B.C.), who taught that the Good was the highest form, was ineffable, godlike, independent, and knowable only after a protracted education in philosophy. We desire the Good because it is good. Philosophers in the Platonic tradition, such as John Laird (see the first quote at the beginning of this chapter) and G. E. Moore, hold to the independent existence of values apart from human or rational interest. Moore claims that the Good is a simple, unanalyzable quality, such as the color yellow, but one that must be known through intuition. Moore believes that a world with beauty is more valuable than one that is a garbage dump, regardless of whether there are conscious beings in those worlds:

Let us imagine one world exceedingly beautiful. Imagine it as beautiful as you can...and then imagine the ugliest world you can possibly conceive. Imagine it simply one heap of filth."[7]

Moore asks us whether, even if there were no conscious being who might derive pleasure or pain in either world, we would prefer the first world to exist rather than the second.

Other, weaker objectivist versions treat values as *emergent* properties or qualities in the nature of things. That is, just as the wetness of water is not in the H_2O molecules but in the interaction of our nervous system with millions of those molecules, and just as smoothness is not in the table I am touching but in the relationship between the electrical charges of the subatomic particles of which the table is made up and my nervous system, so values (or good qualities) emerge in the relationship between conscious beings and physical and social existence.

For example, if we were not beings with desires, we would not be in a position to appreciate values; but once there are such beings, certain things (such as pleasure, knowledge, health) will be valuable and others not valuable, depending on objective factors. Perhaps this should be called a mixed view, for it recognizes both a subjective and an objective aspect to value.

Subjectivism treats values as merely products of conscious desire. The quote from Spinoza's *Ethics* at the beginning of this chapter represents this position. R. B. Perry (1876–1957), in his interest theory of values, states that a value is simply the object of interest.[8] Values are created by desires, and they are valuable just to that degree to which they are desired: The stronger the desire, the greater the value. The difference between the subjectivist and the weak objectivist position (or mixed view) is simply that the subjectivist makes no normative claims about "proper desiring," instead judging all desires as equal. Anything one happens to desire is, by definition, a value, a good.

The objectivist responds that we can separate the Good from what one desires. We can say, for example, that Joan desires more than anything else to get into the Pleasure Machine, but it is not good; or that John desires more than anything else to join the Ku Klux Klan, but it is not good (not even for John). There is something just plain bad about the Pleasure Machine and the Klan, even if Joan and John never experience any dissatisfaction on account of them.

On the other hand, suppose Joan does not want to have any friends and John does not want to know any history or science (beyond whatever is necessary for his needs as a mudwrestler). The objectivist would reply that it really would be an objectively good thing if Joan did have friends and if John knew something about history and science.

Perhaps a way to adjudicate the disagreement between the subjectivist and the objectivist is to imagine an Ideal Desirer, a person who is impartial and has maximal knowledge of the consequences of all actions. What the Ideal Desirer chose would be by definition the "good," and what he or she disdained would be the "bad."

WHAT IS THE RELATION
OF VALUE TO MORALITY?

Typically, value theory is at the heart of moral theory. The question, however, is whether moral right and wrong are themselves intrinsic values (as Kant states, the moral law is "a jewel that shines in its own light") or whether rightness and wrongness are defined by their ability to further nonmoral values, such as pleasure, happiness, health, and political harmony. In order to begin to understand this question and to get a panoramic view of the workings of morality (at the cost of oversimplifying and biasing the discussion), let me offer a Schema of the Moral Process (see Figure 1) that may help in locating the role of values in moral theory and may thereby provide a bridge to the discussion of various moral theories that follows in the next two chapters.

The location of values in the schema of the moral process (box 3) indicates that values are central to the domain of morality. Examples of values are life, loving relationships, freedom, privacy, happiness, creative activity, knowledge, health, integrity, and rationality. From our values we derive principles (box 4), which we may call action-guiding value "instantiators" or "exemplifiers" (because they make clear the action-guiding or prescriptive force latent in values). From the value "life" we derive the principles "Promote and protect life" and/or "Thou shalt not kill." From the value "freedom" we derive the principle "Thou shalt not deprive another of his or her freedom." From the value "privacy" we derive the principle "Respect every person's privacy." From the value "happiness" we derive the principle "Promote human happiness," and so forth with all the other values.

This schema makes no judgment as to whether values are objective or subjective, intrinsic or instrumental. Neither does it take a stand on whether values or principles are absolute; they need not be absolute. Most systems allow that all or most values and principles are prima facie or overridable. That is, they are considerations that direct our actions, and whenever they clash, an adjudication must take place in order to decide which principle overrides the other in the present circumstances.

We often find ourselves in moral situations in which one or more principles apply. We speak of making a judgment as to which principle applies to our situation or which principle wins out in the competition when two or more principles apply (see box 5). The correct principle defines our duty. For example, we have the opportunity to cheat on a test and immediately judge that the principle of honesty (derived from the value integrity) applies to our situation. Or there might be an interpersonal disagreement in which two or more people differ on which of two values outweighs the other in importance, as when Mary argues that Jill should not have an abortion because the value of life outweighs Jill's freedom and bodily integrity, but John argues that Jill's freedom and bodily integrity outweigh the value of life.

After we judge which principle applies, we are not yet finished with the moral process. We must still *decide* to do the morally right act. Then finally, we must actually *do* the right act.

Note the possibilities for failure all along the way. We may fail to apply the right principle to the situation (the arrow between boxes 4 and 5). For example, we may simply neglect to bring to mind the principle against cheating. This is a failure of application. But even after we make the correct judgment, we may fail to make the right choice, deciding to cheat anyway. In this case we have a perverse will (the arrow between boxes 5 and 6). Finally, we may make the correct choice, but fail to carry out our decision (the arrow between boxes 6 and 7). We call this *weakness of will:* We mean to do the right act but simply are too morally weak to accomplish it. In our example we meant to refrain from cheating but couldn't control ourselves. "The good that I would, I do not, but the evil that I would not, that I do."[9]

A more controversial matter concerns the deep structure in which values are rooted. Some theories deny that there is any deep structure, but assert instead that values simply exist in their own right—independently, as it were. More often, however, values are seen as rooted in whole forms of life (box 2) that can be actual or ideal, such as Plato's hierarchical society or Aristotle's aristocracy or the Judeo-Christian notion of the kingdom of God (the ideal synagogue or church). Ways of life or cultures are holistic and hierarchical combinations of beliefs, values, and practices.

The deepest question about morality is whether and how these forms of life are justified (box 1). Are some forms of life better or more justified than others? If so, how does one justify a form of life? Candidates for justification are ideas such as God's will, human happiness, the flourishing of all creation, the canons of impartiality and knowledge, a deeply rational social contract (Hobbes and Rawls), and the like. For example, a theist

FIGURE 1 Schema of the Moral Process

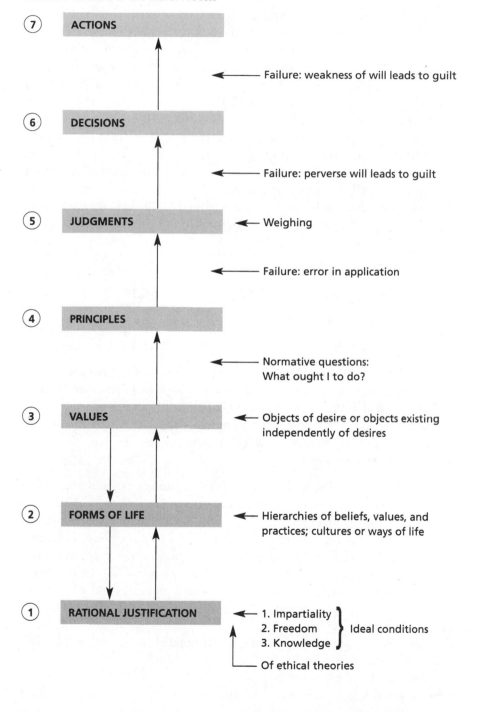

might argue that the ideal system of morality (that is, the ideal form of life) is justified by being commanded by God. A naturalist or humanist might argue that the ideal system is justified by the fact that it best meets human need or that it would be the one chosen by ideally rational persons. Some ethicists would deny that there is any ideal justification at all and would contend that each moral system is correct simply by being chosen by the culture or individual. In Chapter 2 we called the latter type of ethicists "ethical relativists."

The main point of the schema, however, is not to decide on the exact deep structure of morality but to indicate that values are rooted in cultural constructs and are the foundation for moral principles upon which moral reasoning is based. We could also devise a similar schema for the relationship between values and virtues (to be discussed in Chapter 8). Each virtue is based on a value and each vice on a disvalue.

WHAT IS THE GOOD LIFE?

Finally, we want to ask what kind of life is most worth living. Aristotle (384–322 B.C.) wrote long ago that what all people seek is happiness.

> There is very general agreement; for both the common person and people of superior refinement say that it is happiness, and identify living well and doing well with being happy; but with regard to what happiness is they differ, and the many do not give the same account as the wise. For the former think it is some plain and obvious thing, like pleasure, wealth or honor.[10]

What is happiness? Again, the field divides up among objectivists, subjectivists, and combination theorists. The objectivists, following Plato and Aristotle, distinguish happiness from pleasure and speak of a single ideal for human nature; if we do not reach that ideal, then we have failed. Happiness (Greek, *eudaimonia;* literally "good demon") is not merely a subjective state of pleasure or contentment but the kind of life we would all want to live if we understood our essential nature. Just as knives and forks and wheels have functions, so do species, including the human species. Our function (sometimes called our "essence") is to live according to reason and thereby to become a certain sort of highly rational, disciplined being. When we fulfill the ideal of living the virtuous life, we are truly happy.

Plato speaks of happiness as "harmony of the soul." Just as the body is healthy when it is in harmony with itself, and the political state is a good state when it is functioning harmoniously, so the soul is happy when all its features are functioning in harmonious accord, with the rational faculty ruling over the spirited and emotional elements. Though we no doubt know when we are happy and feel good about ourselves, the subjective feeling does not itself define happiness, for people who fail to attain human excellence can also feel happy, via self-deception or ignorance.

The objectivist view fell out of favor with the rise of the evolutionary account of human nature, which undermined the sense of a preordained essence or function. Science cannot discover any innate *telos,* or goal, to which all people must strive. The contemporary bias is in favor of value pluralism, that is, the view that there are many ways of finding happiness: "Let a thousand flowers bloom." This leads to subjectivism.

The subjectivist version of happiness states that happiness is in the eyes of the beholder. You are just as happy as you think you are—no more, no less. The concept is not a descriptive one, but a first-person evaluation. I am the only one who decides or knows whether I am happy. If I feel happy, I am happy, even though everyone else despises my lifestyle. Logically, happiness has nothing to do with virtue, though—due to our social nature—it usually turns out that we will feel better about ourselves if we are virtuous.

The combinational view tries to incorporate aspects of both the objectivist and the subjectivist views. One version is John Rawls's "plan-of-life" conception of happiness: There is a plurality of life plans open to each person, and what is important is that the plan be an integrated whole, freely chosen by the person, and that the person be successful in realizing his or her goals. This view is predominantly subjective in that it recognizes the person as the autonomous chooser of goals and a plan. Even if a person should choose a life plan

> whose only pleasure is to count blades of grass in various geometrically shaped areas such as park squares and well-trimmed lawns, . . . our definition of the good forces us to admit that the good for this man is indeed counting blades of grass.[11]

However, Rawls recognizes an objective element in an otherwise subjective schema. There are primary goods that are necessary to any worthwhile life plan: "rights and liberties, powers and opportunities, income and wealth, . . . self-respect, . . . health and vigor, intelligence and imagination."[12] The primary goods function as the core (or the hub of the wheel) from which may be derived any number of possible life plans (the spokes). But unless these primary goods (or most of them) are present, the life plan is not an authentic manifestation of an individual's autonomous choice of his or her own selfhood. So it is perfectly possible that people believe themselves to be happy when they really are not.

Although subjectivist and plan-of-life views dominate the literature today, there is some movement back to an essentialist, or Aristotelian, view of happiness as a life directed toward worthwhile goals. Some lifestyles are more worthy than others, and some may be worthless. Philosopher Richard Kraut asks us to imagine a man who has as his idea of happiness the state of affairs of being loved, admired, or respected by his friends and who would hate to have his "friends" only pretend to care for him. Suppose his "friends" really do hate him but "orchestrate an elaborate deception, giving him every reason to believe that they love and admire him, though in fact they don't. And he is taken in by the illusion."[13] Can we really call this man happy?

Or suppose that a woman centers her entire life around an imaginary Prince Charming. She refuses to date—let alone marry—perfectly eligible young men; she turns down educational travel opportunities lest they distract her from this wonderful future event; for 95 years she bores all her patient friends with tales of the prince's imminent appearance. As death approaches at 96, after a lifetime of disappointment, she discovers that she's been duped; she suddenly realizes that what appeared to be a happy life was a stupid, self-deceived, miserable existence. Would we say that our heroine was happy up until her death-bed revelation? Do these thought experiments not indicate that our happiness depends, at least to some extent, on reality and not simply on our own evaluation?

Or suppose that we improve on our Pleasure Machine, turning it into a Happiness Machine.[14] This machine is a large tub that is filled with a chemical solution. Electrodes are attached to many more parts of your brain. You work with the technician to program all the "happy experiences" that you have ever wanted. Suppose that includes wanting to be a football star, a halfback who breaks tackles like a dog shakes off fleas and who has a penchant for scoring last-minute game-winning touchdowns. Or perhaps you've always wanted to be a movie star and to bask in the public's love and admiration. Or maybe you've wanted to be the world's richest person, living in the splendor of a magnificent castle, with servants faithfully at your beck and call. In fact, with the Happiness Machine you can have all of these plus passionate romance and the love of the most beautiful (or handsome) persons in the world. All of these marvelous adventures would be simulated, and you would truly believe you were experiencing them. Would you enter the Happiness Machine?

What if I told you that once you were unplugged, you could either stay out or go in for another round, but that no one who entered the machine ever chose to leave of his or her own accord, having become addicted to its pleasures and believing that reality could never match its ecstasy. Now you have an opportunity to enter the Happiness Machine for the first time. Will you enter? If so, why? If not, are you not voting against making the subjectivist view (or even the plan-of-life view) the sole interpretation of happiness?

When I ask this question in class, I get mixed responses. Many students say they would enter the Happiness Machine; most say they would not. I myself would not, for the same reason that I do not use drugs and rarely watch television or spectator sports—because some very important things are missing that are necessary for the happy life. What are these vital missing ingredients?

1. **Action.** You are entirely passive in the machine, a mere spectator. But the good life requires participation in our own destiny. We don't just want things to happen to us; we want to accomplish things, even at the risk of failure.

2. **Freedom.** Not only do we want to do things, but we want to make choices. In the Happiness Machine we are entirely determined by a preordained plan—we cannot do otherwise. In fact, we cannot do anything but react to what has been programmed into the machine.

3. **Character.** Not only do we want to do things and act freely, but we want to *be* something and someone. In the machine we lose our identity. We are defined only by our experience, but have no character. We are not persons who act out of set dispositions, for we never act at all. We are mere floating blobs in a glorified bathtub.

4. **Relationships.** There are no real people in our Happiness Machine life. We subsist in splendid solipsism. All the world is a figment of our imagination as dictated by the machine; our friends and loved one are mere products of our fancy. But we want to love and be loved by real people, not by phantasms.

In sum, the Happiness Machine is a myth, all *appearance* and no *reality*—a bliss bought at too high a price, a deception! If this is so and if reality is a necessary condition for the truly worthwhile life, then we cannot be happy in the Happiness Machine. But neither can we be happy outside of the Happiness Machine when the same necessary ingredients are missing: activity, freedom, moral character, loving relationships, and a strong sense of reality.

The objective and subjective views of happiness assess life from different perspectives, with the objectivist assuming that there is some kind of independent standard of assessment and the subjectivist denying it. Even though there seems to be an immense variety of lifestyles that could be considered intrinsically worthwhile or happy, and even though some subjective approval or satisfaction seems necessary before we are willing to attribute the adjective "happy" to a life, there do seem to be limiting conditions on what may count as happy. We have a notion of *fittingness* for the good life, which would normally *exclude* being severely retarded, being a slave, or being a drug addict (no matter how satisfied) and which would *include* being a deeply fulfilled, autonomous, healthy person. It is better to be Socrates dissatisfied than to be the pig satisfied, but only the satisfied Socrates is happy.

This moderate objectivism is set forth by John Stuart Mill. Happiness, according to Mill, is

> not a life of rapture; but moments of such, in an existence made up of few and transitory pains, many and various pleasures, with a decided predominance of the active over the passive, and having as the foundation of the whole, not to expect more from life than it is capable of bestowing.[15]

This conception of happiness is worth pondering. It includes "activity," "freedom," and "reality" components, which exclude being satisfied by the passive experience in the Happiness Machine, and it supposes (the context tells us this) that some pleasing experiences are better than others. I would add to Mill's definition the ingredients of moral character and loving relations. A closer approximation might go like this:

> Happiness is a life in which exist free action (including meaningful work), loving relations, and moral character, and in which the individual is not plagued by guilt and anxiety but is blessed with peace and satisfaction.

The *satisfaction* should not be confused with complacency; rather it means contentment with one's lot—even as one strives to improve it. Whether this neo-objectivist, Millian view of happiness is adequate, you must decide.

While Mill's view of happiness can be judged independently from his view of ethics, Mill himself saw his conception of happiness as playing a substantial role in his view of utilitarianism. If he is right about utilitarianism, we will have significant support for his view of happiness. So let's turn next to utilitarianism.

NOTES

1. Here is an outline of types of value, based on a classification scheme by Nicholas Rescher, *Introduction to Value Theory* (Prentice-Hall, 1969), p. 16:

Category of Value	Sample Values
1. Material and physical	Health, comfort, physical security
2. Economic	Economic security, productiveness
3. Moral	Honesty, fairness, kindness
4. Social	Generosity, politeness, graciousness
5. Political	Freedom, justice
6. Aesthetic	Beauty, symmetry, grace
7. Religious	Piety, obedience, faith
8. Intellectual	Intelligence, clarity, knowledge

2. Plato's *Republic,* Book II, trans. by G. M. A. Grube.

3. Jean-Paul Sartre, *Existentialism and Human Emotions,* trans. Bernard Frechtman (Philosophical Library, 1957), pp. 23, 48 f.

4. Adapted from Aldous Huxley, *Brave New World* (Harper & Row, 1932), pp. 286 f.

5. Epicurus, "Letter to Manoeceus," trans. C. Bailey, in W. J. Oates, ed., *The Stoics and Epicurean Philosophers* (Random House, 1940), p. 32.

6. From John Stuart Mill, *Utilitarianism* (1863); reprinted in Louis Pojman,

ed., *Ethical Theory.* (Wadsworth, 1989), p. 165.

7. G E. Moore, *Principia Ethica* (Cambridge University Press, 1903), pp. 83 ff.

8. R. B. Perry, *Realms of Value* (Harvard University Press, 1954): "A thing— any thing—has value, or is valuable, in the original and generic sense when it is the object of an interest— any interest. Or, whatever is an object of interest is ipso facto valuable." Similarly, Roger Beehler states that "value is the shadow cast by human affection or desire" [*The Moral Life,* (Oxford University Press, 1978), p. 143].

9. St. Paul, in Rom. 7.

10. Aristotle, *Nicomachean Ethics,* trans. W. D. Ross (Oxford University Press, 1925) Book I:4, p. 1095.

11. John Rawls, *A Theory of Justice* (Harvard University Press, 1971), p. 432. See Paul Taylor's discussion in his *Principles of Ethics* (Wadsworth, 1989) Ch. VI.

12. Rawls, *A Theory of Justice,* p. 62.

13. Richard Kraut, "Two Concepts of Happiness," *Philosophical Review* (1979); reprinted in Pojman, *Ethical Theory.*

14. My discussion here has profited from Robert Nozick's original discussion of the experience machine in his *Anarchy, State and Utopia* (Blackwell's, 1974), pp. 42–45.

15. John Stuart Mill, *Utilitarianism* (1863), Ch. II; reprinted in Pojman, *Ethical Theory.*

FOR FURTHER REFLECTION

1. Reflect on the five questions mentioned at the beginning of this chapter, and try to give your own considered response to each one:

a. What are the different types of values, and how are they related to each other?

b. What things or activities are valuable or good?

c. Are values objective or subjective? That is, do we desire the Good because it is good, or is the Good good because we desire it?

d. What is the relation of value to morality?

e. What is the good life?

2. Review Figure 1 (Schema of the Moral Process); then take a moral dispute and illustrate how opponents would form a chain of reason-action with regard to that issue. You might choose the issue of abortion. Certain pro-choice people might make their overriding value the mother's right to privacy or autonomy (as in the 1973 *Rowe v. Wade* decision), whereas the right-to-life advocate would likely insist that the basic value is the sanctity of human life. Work out the process each person would go through in reaching action.

3. Is life itself an intrinsic value? Or is the value in the quality of life? If life itself is intrinsically good, how good is it in itself? Remember that the definition of life includes more than humans and animals (*life* is "an organismic state characterized by capacity for metabolism, growth, reaction to stimuli, and reproduction," according to *Merriam Webster's Collegiate Dictionary*, 10th ed.).

4. In *Brave New World* Aldous Huxley portrays a society living according to a hedonistic worldview. People have been liberated from disease, violence, and crime through immunization, genetic engineering, and behavior modification. They are protected from depression and unhappiness through a drug, *soma*, that offers them euphoric sensations. Go over the dialogue presented earlier in this chapter in which Mustapha Mond, the brilliant manager of the society, defends this hedonistic utopia against one of the few remaining malcontents, the "Savage."

In your opinion, what, if anything, is missing in the brave new world? Would you exchange our world of disease, violence, and crime for this benign hedonistic utopia? Why or why not?

5. Go over the different theories of happiness discussed at the end of this chapter. Which one seems closest to the truth?

6. Would you enter the Happiness Machine? Why or why not? Compare the experience of being in the Happiness Machine with that of watching television or spectator sports or playing computer games such as Nintendo. How are they similar or different?

FOR FURTHER READING

Alston, William. "Pleasure," in *Encyclopedia of Philosophy*, ed. Paul Edwards. Macmillan, 1969. An excellent discussion of various theories of pleasure.

Aristotle. *Nicomachean Ethics*, Books I, X. There are several good translations, including those of T. E. Irwin, Martin Ostwald, W. D. Ross, and J. A. K. Thomson.

Bond, E. J. *Reason and Value*. Cambridge University Press, 1983. A thoughtful defense of objectivism in values.

Brandt, Richard B. "Happiness," in *Encyclopedia of Philosophy*, ed. Paul Edwards. Macmillan, 1969.

Brandt, Richard B. *A Theory of the Good and the Right*. Oxford University Press, 1979. Advanced, but important for anyone who wishes to go deeply into the subject.

Hospers, John. *Human Conduct: Problem of Ethics.* Harcourt Brace Jovanovich, 1972, Ch. 2–8. An accessible introduction.

Nagel, Thomas. *The View from Nowhere.* Oxford University Press, 1986.

Nietzsche, Friedrich. *Beyond Good and Evil,* trans. Walter Kaufmann. Random House, 1966.

Perry, Ralph B. *Realms of Value.* Harvard University Press, 1954.

Pojman, Louis, ed. *Ethical Theory: Classical and Contemporary Readings,* 2nd ed. Wadsworth, 1995. Part IV, especially, contains several important selections on the nature of value and happiness.

Rescher, Nicholas. *Introduction to Value Theory.* Prentice-Hall, 1982.

Rorty, Amelie Oksenberg, ed. *Essays on Aristotle's Ethics.* University of California Press, 1980. Contains important articles on *eudaimonia* and other subjects.

Ross, W. D. *The Right and the Good.* Oxford University Press, 1930. Chapters III–VII contain a seminal discussion of the nature of Good.

Taylor, Paul. *Principles of Ethics.* Wadsworth, 1975, Ch. 6.

Taylor, Richard. *Good and Evil.* Macmillan, 1970. One of the liveliest introductions to ethics from the perspective of value theory.

Von Wright, G. H. *The Varieties of Goodness.* Routledge & Kegan Paul, 1963. A rich analysis of values.

6

Utilitarianism

The Greatest Happiness for the Greatest Number.

FRANCIS HUTCHESON, *AN INQUIRY CONCERNING MORAL GOOD AND EVIL*

S uppose you are on an island with a dying millionaire. As he lies dying,
he entreats you for one final favor:

> I've dedicated my whole life to baseball and for 50 years have gotten
> endless pleasure, and some pain, rooting for the New York Yankees.
> Now that I am dying, I want to give all my assets, $2 million, to the
> Yankees. Would you take this money [he indicates a box containing
> the money in large bills] back to New York and give it to the Yankees'
> owner, George Steinbrenner, so that he can buy better players?

You agree to carry out his wish, at which point a huge smile of relief and
gratitude breaks out on his face as he expires in your arms. After traveling
to New York, you see a newspaper advertisement placed by your favorite
charity, World Hunger Relief Organization (whose integrity you do not
doubt), pleading for $2 million to be used to save 100,000 people dying
of starvation in East Africa. Not only will the $2 million save their lives,
but it will also purchase equipment and the kinds of fertilizers necessary to

build a sustainable economy. You decide to reconsider your promise to the dying Yankee fan, in light of this advertisement. What should you do with the money?

Or suppose there are two men starving to death on a raft afloat in the Pacific Ocean. One day they discover some food in an inner compartment of a box on the raft. They have reason to believe that the food will be sufficient to keep one of them alive until the raft reaches a certain island where help is available but that if they share the food both of them will most likely die. Now, one man is a brilliant scientist who has in his mind a cure for cancer. The other man is undistinguished. Otherwise there is no relevant difference between the two. What is the morally right thing to do? Share the food and hope against the odds for a miracle? Flip a coin in order to see which man gets the food? Give the food to the scientist?

What is the right thing to do in these kinds of situations? Consider some traditional moral principles and see if they help us come to a decision. One principle often given to guide action is "Let your conscience be your guide." I recall this principle with fondness, for it was the one my father taught me at an early age, and it still echoes in my mind. But does it help here? No, since conscience is primarily a function of upbringing. People's consciences speak to them in different ways according to how they were brought up. Depending on upbringing, some people feel no qualms about committing terrorist acts, whereas others feel the torments of conscience over stepping on a gnat. Suppose your conscience tells you to give the money to the Yankees and my conscience tells me to give the money to the World Hunger Relief Organization. How can we even discuss the matter? If conscience is the end of it, we're left mute.

Another principle urged on us is "Do whatever is most loving." St. Augustine (354–430) said, "Love God and do whatever you want." Love is surely a wonderful value. But is it enough to guide our actions when there is a conflict of interest? "Love is blind," it has been said, "but reason, like marriage, is an eye-opener." Whom should I love in the case of the disbursement of the millionaire's money—the millionaire, or the starving people? How do I apply the principle of love in the case of the two starving men on the raft? Should I take into consideration the needs of the two men, their families, those in need of a cure for cancer, everyone? It's not clear how love alone will settle anything. In fact, it is not obvious that we must always do what is most loving. Should we always treat our enemies in loving ways? Or is it morally acceptable to hate those who have purposely and unjustly harmed us, our loved ones, or other innocent people? Should the survivors of Auschwitz love Adolph Hitler?

We will deal with these questions later. Here we must be content to notice that love alone does not solve difficult moral issues.

A third principle often given to guide our moral actions is the Golden Rule: "Do unto others as you would have them do unto you." This, too, is a noble rule of thumb, one that works in simple, commonsense situations. But it has problems. First of all, it cannot be taken literally. Suppose I love to hear loud rock 'n' roll music. Since I would want you to play it loudly for me, I reason that I should play it loudly for you—even though I know that you hate the stuff. So the rule must be modified: "Do unto others as you would have them do unto you if you were in their shoes." However, this still has problems. If I were in Sirhan Sirhan's (the assassin of Robert Kennedy), I'd want to be released from the penitentiary; but it's not clear that he should be released. If I put myself in the place of a sex-starved individual, I might want to have sex with the next available person; but it's not obvious that I must comply with that wish. Likewise, the Golden Rule doesn't tell me to whom to give the millionaire's money or the food on the life raft.

Conscience, love, and the Golden Rule are all worthy rules of thumb to help us through life. They work for most of us, most of the time, in ordinary moral situations. But in more complicated cases, especially when there are legitimate conflicts of interests, they are limited.

A more promising strategy for solving dilemmas is that of following definite moral rules. Suppose you decided to give the millionaire's money to the Yankees in order to keep your promise or because to do otherwise would be stealing. The principle you followed would be "Always keep your promise" and/or "Thou shalt not steal" (the Eighth Commandment). Principles are important in life. All learning involves understanding a set of rules. As Oxford University philosopher R. M. Hare says:

> To learn to do anything is never to learn to do an individual act; it is always to learn to do acts of a certain kind in a certain kind of situation; and this is to learn a principle. . . . Without principles we could not learn anything whatever from our elders. . . . Every generation would have to start from scratch and teach itself. But . . . self-teaching, like all other teaching, is the teaching of principles.[1]

If you decided to act on the principle of keeping promises or of not stealing in the case of the millionaire's money, or if you decided to share the food in the case of the two men on the life raft on the basis of the principle of fairness or equal justice, then you adhered to a type of moral theory called *deontology*. If, on the other hand, you decided to give the money to the World Hunger Relief Organization in order to save an enormous number of lives and restore economic solvency to the region, you sided with a type of theory called *teleological* ethics. Sometimes it is referred to as *consequentialist ethics.* You also sided with the teleologist if you decided to give the food to the scientist because he would probably do more good with his life.

Traditionally, two major types of ethical systems have dominated the field: *deontological* (from the Greed *deon,* meaning "duty," and *logos,* meaning "logic"), in which the locus of value is the act or kind of act; and *teleological* (from the Greek *teleos,* meaning "having reached one's end" or "goal-directed"), in which the locus of value is the outcome or consequences of the act. Whereas teleological systems see the ultimate criterion of morality in some nonmoral value that results from acts, deontological systems see certain features in the act itself as having intrinsic value. For example, a teleologist would judge whether lying was morally right or wrong by the consequences it produced, but a deontologist would see something intrinsically wrong in the very act of lying. In this chapter we will consider the dominant version of teleological ethics—*utilitarianism.* In Chapter 7 we'll examine Immanuel Kant's ethics as the major form of deontological ethics. Then in Chapter 8 we shall look at a third type of theory, virtue-based ethics. Let us turn to teleological ethics.

As we mentioned earlier, a teleologist is a person whose ethical decision-making aims solely at maximizing nonmoral goods, such as pleasure, happiness, welfare, and the amelioration of suffering. That is, the standard of right or wrong action for the teleologist is the comparative consequences of the available actions: That act is right that produces the best consequences. Whereas the deontologist is concerned only with the rightness of the act itself, the teleologist asserts that there is no such thing as an act having intrinsic worth. While there is something intrinsically bad about lying for the deontologist, the only thing wrong with lying for the teleologist is the bad consequences it produces. If you can reasonably calculate that a lie will do even slightly more good than telling the truth, then you have an obligation to lie.

We have already noticed one type of teleological ethics: ethical egoism, the view that the act that produces the most amount of good for the agent is the right act. Egoism is teleological ethics narrowed to the agent him- or herself. Utilitarianism, on the other hand, is a universal teleological system. It calls for the maximization of goodness in society, that is, the greatest goodness for the greatest number. We turn now to an examination of utilitarianism.

WHAT IS UTILITARIANISM?

One of the earliest examples of utilitarian reasoning is found in Sophocles' *Antigone* (ca. 440 B.C.), in which we find King Creon faced with the tragic task of sacrificing his beloved niece, Antigone, who had violated the law by performing funeral rites over her brother, Polynices. Creon judges that it is necessary to sacrifice one person rather than expose his society to the dangers of rebelliousness—regardless of that person's innocence.

> And whoever places a friend above the good of his own country,
> I have no use for him. . . . I could never stand by silent, watching
> destruction march against our city, putting safety to rout, nor could
> I ever make that man a friend of mine who menaces our country.
> Remember this: our country is our safety.[2]

In the New Testament, Caiphas, the High Priest, advises the Council to deliver Jesus to the Romans for execution: "You know nothing at all; you do not understand that it is expedient that one man should die for the people, and that the whole nation should not perish" (John 11:50). Sometimes Jesus himself is interpreted as adhering to utilitarianism, as when he breaks the Sabbath laws in order to do good, saying that "The Sabbath was made for man, not man for the Sabbath" (Mark 2:27).

However, as a moral philosophy, utilitarianism begins with the work of Scottish philosophers Frances Hutcheson (1694–1746), David Hume (1711–1776), and Adam Smith (1723–1790); and comes into its classical stage in the writings of English social reformers Jeremy Bentham (1748–1832) and John Stuart Mill (1806–1873). They were the nonreligious ancestors of the 20th-century secular humanists, optimistic about human nature and our ability to solve our problems without recourse to providential grace. Engaged in a struggle for legal as well as moral reform, they were impatient with the rule-bound character of law and morality in 18th- and 19th-century Great Britain and tried to make the law serve human needs and interests.

Bentham's concerns were mostly practical rather than theoretical. He worked for a thorough reform of what he regarded as an irrational and outmoded legal system. He might well have paraphrased Jesus, making his motto "Morality and Law were made for man, not man for Morality and Law." What good was adherence to outworn deontological rules that served no useful purpose, that only kept the poor from enjoying a better life, and that supported punitive codes that served only to satisfy sadistic lust for vengeance?

The changes the utilitarians proposed were not done in the name of justice, for—they believed—even justice must serve the human good. The poor were to be helped, women were to be liberated, and criminals were to be rehabilitated if possible, not in the name of justice, but because doing so could bring about more utility: ameliorate suffering and promote more pleasure or happiness.

The utilitarian view of punishment is a case in point. Whereas deontologists believe in retribution—that all the guilty should be punished in proportion to the gravity of their crime—the utilitarians' motto is "Don't cry over spilt milk!" They believe that the guilty should be punished only if the punishment would serve some deterrent (or preventive) purpose. Rather than punish John in exact proportion to the heinousness of his deed, we ought to find the right punishment that will serve as the optimum deterrent.

The proper amount of punishment to be inflicted upon the offender is the amount that will do the most good (or the least harm) to all those who will be affected by it. The measure of harm inflicted on the criminal, John, should be preferable to the harm avoided by setting that particular penalty rather than one slightly lower. If punishing John will do no good (because John is not likely to commit the crime again and no one will be deterred by the punishment), then John should go free.

It is the *threat* of punishment that is the important thing. Every *act* of punishment is an admission of the failure of the threat; if the threat were successful, there would be no punishment to justify. Of course, utilitarians believe that, given human failing, punishment is vitally necessary as a deterrent, so that the guilty will seldom if ever be allowed to go free.

There are two main features of utilitarianism: the *consequentialist principle* (or its teleological aspect) and the *utility principle* (or its hedonic aspect). The consequentialist principle states that the rightness or wrongness of an act is determined by the goodness or badness of the results that flow from it. It is the end, not the means, that counts; the end justifies the means. The utility principle states that the only thing that is good in itself is some specific type of state (e.g., pleasure, happiness, welfare). Hedonistic utilitarianism views pleasure as the sole good and pain as the only evil. To quote Bentham, the first one to systematize classical utilitarianism, "Nature has placed mankind under the governance of two sovereign masters, pain and pleasure. It is for them alone to point out what we ought to do, as well as what we shall do."[3] An act is right if it either brings about more pleasure than pain or prevents pain, and an act is wrong if it either brings about more pain than pleasure or prevents pleasure from occurring.

Bentham invented a scheme for measuring pleasure and pain that he called the *hedonic calculus:* The quantitative score for any pleasure or pain experience is obtained by summing the seven aspects of a pleasurable or painful experience: its intensity, duration, certainty, nearness, fruitfulness, purity, and extent. Adding up the amounts of pleasure and pain for each possible act and then comparing the scores would enable us to decide which act to perform. With regard to our example of deciding between giving the dying man's money to the Yankees or to the East African famine victims, we would add up the likely pleasures to all involved, for all seven qualities. If we find that giving the money to the famine victims will cause at least 3 million *hedons* (units of happiness) but that giving the money to the Yankees will cause less than 1,000 hedons, we would have an obligation to give the money to the famine victims.

There is something appealing about Bentham's utilitarianism. It is simple in that there is only one principle to apply: Maximize pleasure and minimize suffering. It is commonsensical in that we think that morality really is about ameliorating suffering and promoting benevolence. It is scientific: Simply make quantitative measurements and apply the principle impartially, giving no special treatment to ourselves or to anyone else because of race, gender, or religion.

However, Bentham's philosophy may be too simplistic in one way and too complicated in another. It may be too simplistic in that there are other values than pleasure (as we saw in the previous chapter), and it seems too complicated in its artificial hedonic calculus. The calculus is encumbered with too many variables and has problems assigning scores to the variables. For instance, what score do we give a cool drink on a hot day or a warm shower on a cool day? How do we compare a 5-year-old's delight over a new toy with a 50-year-old's delight with a new lover? Can we take your second car from you and give it to Beggar Bob, who does not own a car and would enjoy it more than you? And if it's simply the overall benefits of pleasure that we are measuring, then if Jack or Jill would be "happier" in the Pleasure Machine or the Happiness Machine or on drugs than in the "real world," would we not have an obligation to ensure that these conditions obtain? Because of such considerations, Bentham's version of utilitarianism was, even in his own day, referred to as the "pig-philosophy," since a pig enjoying his life would constitute a higher moral state than a slightly dissatisfied Socrates.

It was to meet these sorts of objections and save utilitarianism from the charge of being a pig-philosophy that Bentham's brilliant successor, John Stuart Mill, sought to distinguish happiness from mere sensual pleasure. His version of utilitarianism—*eudaimonistic* (from the Greek *eudaimonia,* meaning "happiness") utilitarianism—defines happiness in terms of certain types of higher-order pleasures or satisfactions, such as intellectual, aesthetic, and social enjoyments, as well as in terms of minimal suffering. That is, there are two types of pleasures: the lower, or elementary (e.g., eating, drinking, sexuality, resting, and sensuous titillation), and the higher (e.g., intellectuality, creativity, and spirituality). Though the lower pleasures are more intensely gratifying, they also lead to pain when overindulged in. The spiritual, or achieved, pleasures tend to be more protracted, continuous, and gradual.

Mill argues that the higher, or more refined, pleasures are superior to the lower ones: "A being of higher faculties requires more to make him happy, is capable probably of more acute suffering, and certainly accessible to it at more points, than one of an inferior type," but still he is qualitatively better off than the person without these higher faculties. "It is better to be a human being dissatisfied than a pig satisfied; better to be Socrates dissatisfied than a fool satisfied."[4] Humans are the kind of creatures who require more to be truly happy. They want the lower pleasures, but they also want deep friendship, intellectual ability, culture, ability to create and appreciate art, knowledge, and wisdom.

But, one may object, how do we know that it really is better to have these higher pleasures? Here Mill imagines a panel of experts, and says that of those who have had wide experience of pleasures of both kinds almost all give a decided preference to the higher type. Since Mill was an *empiricist*—one who believed that all knowledge and justified belief was based in experience—he had no recourse but to rely on the composite consensus of human history. By this view, people who experience both rock music and classical music will, if they appreciate both, prefer Bach and Beethoven to the Rolling Stones or the Dancing Demons. That is, we generally move up from appreciating simple things (e.g., nursery rhymes) to more complex and intricate things (e.g., poetry that requires great talent) rather than the other way around.

Mill has been criticized for not giving a better reply—for being an elitist and for unduly favoring the intellectual over the sensual. But he has a point. Don't we generally agree, if we have experienced both the lower and the higher types of pleasure, that even though a full life would include both, a life with only the former is inadequate for human beings? Isn't it better to be Socrates dissatisfied than the pig satisfied—and better still to be Socrates satisfied?

The point is not merely that humans would not be satisfied with what satisfies a pig, but that somehow the quality of these pleasures is *better*. But what does it mean to speak of better pleasure? Is Mill assuming some nonhedonic notion of intrinsic value to make this distinction—that is, that knowledge, intelligence, freedom, friendship, love, health, and so forth are good things in their own right? Or is Mill simply saying that the lives of humans are generally such that they will be happier with more developed, refined, spiritual values? Which thesis would you be inclined to defend?

The formula he comes up with, finally, is the following:

> Happiness . . . [is] not a life of rapture; but moments of such, in an existence made up of few and transitory pains, many and various pleasures, with a decided predominance of the active over the passive, and having as the foundation of the whole, not to expect more from life than it is capable of bestowing.[5]

It does seem that intellectual activity, autonomous choice, and other non-hedonic qualities supplement the notion of pleasure.

TWO TYPES OF UTILITARIANISM

There are two classical types of utilitarianism: *act-* and *rule-utilitarianism*. In applying the principle of utility, act-utilitarians, such as Bentham, say that ideally we ought to apply the principle to all of the alternatives open to us at any given moment. We may define act-utilitarianism in this way:

> *Act-utilitarianism:* An act is right if and only if it results in as much good as any available alternative.

Of course, we cannot do the necessary calculations to determine which act is the correct one in each case, for often we must act spontaneously and quickly. So rules of thumb (e.g., "In general don't lie," and "Generally keep your promises") are of practical importance. However, the right act is still that alternative that results in the most utility.

The obvious criticism of act-utility is that it seems to fly in the face of fundamental intuitions about minimally correct behavior. Consider Richard Brandt's criticism of act-utilitarianism:

> It implies that if you have employed a boy to mow your lawn and he has finished the job and asks for his pay, you should pay him what you promised only if you cannot find a better use for your money. It implies that when you bring home your monthly paycheck you should use it to support your family and yourself only if it cannot be used more effectively to supply the needs of others. It implies that if your father is ill and has no prospect of good in his life, and maintaining him is a drain on the energy and enjoyments of others, then, if you can end his life without provoking any public scandal or setting a bad example, it is your positive duty to take matters into your own hands and bring his life to a close.[6]

Rule-utilitarians like Brandt attempt to offer a more credible version of the theory. They state that an act is right if it conforms to a valid rule within a system of rules that, if followed, will result in the best possible state of affairs (or the least bad state of affairs, if it is a question of all the alternatives being bad). We may define rule-utilitarianism this way:

> *Rule-utilitarianism:* An act is right if and only if it is required by a rule that is itself a member of a set of rules whose acceptance would lead to greater utility for society than any available alternative.

An oft-debated question in ethics is whether rule-utilitarianism is a consistent version of utilitarianism. Briefly, the argument that rule-utilitarianism is an inconsistent version that must either become a deontological system or transform itself into act-utilitarianism goes like this: Imagine that following the set of general rules of a rule-utilitarian system yields 100 hedons (positive utility units). We could always find a case where breaking the general rule would result in additional hedons without decreasing the sum of the whole. So, for example, we could imagine a situation in which breaking the general rule "Never lie" in order to spare someone's feelings would create more utility (e.g., 102 hedons) than keeping the rule would. It would seem that we could always improve on any version of rule-utilitarianism by breaking the set of rules whenever we judge that by so doing we could produce even more utility than by following the set.

One way of resolving the difference between act- and rule-utilitarians is to appeal to the notion of *levels of rules.* For the sophisticated utilitarian there will be three levels of rules to guide actions. On the lowest level is a set of utility-maximizing rules of thumb that should always be followed unless there is a conflict between them, in which case a second-order set of conflict-resolving rules should be consulted. At the top of the hierarchy is the *remainder rule* of act utilitarianism: When no other rule applies, simply do what your best judgment deems to be the act that will maximize utility.

An illustration of this might be the following: Two of our lower-order rules might be "Keep your promises" and "Help those in need when you are not seriously inconvenienced in doing so." Suppose you promised to meet your teacher at 3 P.M. in his office. On your way there you come upon an accident victim stranded by the wayside who desperately needs help. It doesn't take you long to decide to break the appointment with your teacher, for it seems obvious in this case that the rule to help others overrides the rule to keep promises. We might say that there is a second-order rule prescribing that the first-order rule of helping people in need when you are not seriously inconvenienced in doing so overrides the rule to keep promises. However, there may be some situation where no obvious rule of thumb applies. Say you have $50 you don't really need now. How should you use this money? Put it into your savings account? Give it to your favorite charity? Use it to throw a party? Here and only here, on the third level, the general act-utility principle applies without any other primary rule; that is, do what in your best judgment will do the most good.

It is a subject of keen debate whether John Stuart Mill was a rule- or an act-utilitarian. He doesn't seem to have noticed the difference, and there seem to be aspects of both theories in his work. Philosophers like J. J. C. Smart and Kai Nielsen hold views that are clearer examples of act-utilitarianism. Nielsen attacks what he calls *moral conservatism,* which is any

> normative ethical theory which maintains that there is a privileged
> moral principle or cluster of moral principles, prescribing determinate
> actions, with which it would always be wrong not to act in accordance
> no matter what the consequences.

For Nielsen, no rules are sacrosanct; but differing situations call forth different actions, and potentially any rule could be overridden (though in fact we may need to treat some as absolutes for the good of society).

Nielsen's argument in favor of utilitarianism makes strong use of the notion of *negative responsibility:* We are responsible not only for the consequences of our actions, but also for the consequences of our non-actions. Suppose that you are the driver of a trolley car and suddenly discover that your brakes have failed. You are just about to run over five workmen on the track ahead of you. However, if you act quickly, you can turn the trolley onto a side track where only one man is working. What should you do? One who makes a strong distinction between active and passive evil (*allowing* versus *doing* evil) would argue that you should do nothing and merely allow the trolley to kill the five men, but one who denies that this is an absolute distinction would prescribe that you do something positive in order to minimize evil. Negative responsibility means that you are going to be responsible for someone's death in either case. Doing the right thing, the utilitarian urges, means minimizing the amount of evil. So you should actively cause the one death in order to save the other five lives.[7]

Critics of utilitarianism contend either that negative responsibility is not a strict duty or that it can be worked into other systems besides utilitarianism.

THE STRENGTHS AND WEAKNESSES OF UTILITARIANISM

Whatever the answers to these questions, utilitarianism does have two very positive features. It also has several problems. The first attraction or strength is that it is a single principle, an absolute system with a potential answer for every situation. Do what will promote the most utility! It's good to have a simple, action-guiding principle that is applicable to every occasion—even if it may be difficult to apply (life's not simple). Its second strength is that utilitarianism seems to get to the substance of morality. It is not merely a formal system (i.e., a system that sets forth broad guidelines for choosing principles but offers no principles; such a guideline would be "Do whatever you can universalize"), but rather has a material core: promoting human (and possibly animal) flourishing and ameliorating suffering. The first virtue gives us a clear decision procedure in arriving at our answer about what to do. The second virtue appeals to our sense that morality is made for humans (and other animals?) and that morality is not so much about rules as about helping people and alleviating the suffering in the world.

Utilitarianism seems commonsensical. For instance, it gives us clear and reasonable guidance in dealing with the Kitty Genovese case (Chapter 1): We should call the police or do what is necessary to help her (so long as helping her does not create more disutility than leaving her alone). And in the case of deciding what to do with the $2 million of the dead millionaire, something in us says that it is absurd to keep a promise to a dead person when it means allowing hundreds of thousands of famine victims to die (how would we like it if we were in their shoes?). Far more good can be accomplished by helping the needy than by giving the money to the Yankees!

Problems in Formulating Utilitarianism

But there are problems with utilitarianism that need to be addressed before we can give it a "philosophically clean bill of health." The first set of problems occurs in the very formulation of utilitarianism: "The greatest happiness for the greatest number." Notice that we have two superlatives in this formula, two "greatest" things: "happiness" and "number." Whenever we have two variables, we invite problems of incommensurability, that is, of not being able to decide which of the variables to rank first when they seem to conflict. In order to see this point, consider the following example: I am offering a $1,000 prize to the person who runs the longest distance in the shortest amount of time. Three people participate: Joe runs 5 miles in 31 minutes, John runs 7 miles in 50 minutes, and Jack runs 1 mile in 6 minutes. Who should get the prize? John has fulfilled one part of the requirement (run the longest distance), but Jack has fulfilled the other requirement (run the shortest amount of time).

This is precisely the problem with utilitarianism. Should we concern ourselves with spreading happiness around so that the greatest number obtain it (in which case we should get busy and procreate a larger population)? Or should we be concerned that the greatest possible amount of happiness obtains in society (in which case we might be tempted to allow some people to become far happier than others, so long as their increase offsets the losers' diminished happiness)? Should we worry about total happiness or about highest average? What is the place of distribution requirements? And just whose happiness are we talking about anyway—all sentient beings, or all human beings, or all rational beings (which might exclude some human beings and include some higher animals)? Finally, how do we measure happiness and make interpersonal comparisons between the happiness of different people?

Utilitarians struggle to resolve these problems. Since some of these questions take us into metaphysics (e.g., what is a person, and to what degree is a person continuous with him- or herself over time?) and into economics (what is the best way to distribute goods over a society?), we cannot answer them here.

The Problem of Knowing the Comparative Consequences of Actions

Sometimes utilitarians are accused of playing God. They seem to hold to an ethical theory that demands godlike powers, particularly knowledge of the future. Of course, we normally do not know the long-term consequences of our actions, for life is too complex and the consequences go on into the indefinite future. One action causes one state of affairs, which in turn causes another state of affairs, indefinitely, so that calculation becomes impossible. Recall the nursery rhyme:

> For want of a nail
> The shoe was lost;
> For want of a shoe
> The horse was lost;
> For want of a horse

The rider was lost;
For want of a rider
The battle was lost;
For want of a battle
The kingdom was lost;
And all for the want
Of a horseshoe nail.

Poor, unfortunate blacksmith! What utilitarian guilt he must bear all the rest of his days!

But it is ridiculous to blame the loss of one's kingdom on the poor, unsuccessful blacksmith, and utilitarians are not so foolish as to hold him responsible for the bad situation. Instead, following C. I. Lewis, they distinguish three kinds of consequences: (1) actual consequences of an act, (2) consequences that could reasonably have been expected to occur, and (3) intended consequences.[8] An act is *absolutely* right if it has the best actual consequences. An act is *objectively* right if it is reasonable to expect that it will have the best consequences. An act is *subjectively* right if its agent intends or actually expects it to have the best consequences. It is the second kind of rightness, that based on reasonable expectations, that is central here, for only the subsequent observer of the consequences is in a position to determine the actual results. The most that the agent can do is to use the best information available and do what a reasonable person would expect to produce the best overall results. Suppose, for example, that while Hitler's grandmother was carrying little Adolph up the stairs to her home, she slipped and had to choose between dropping infant Adolph and allowing him to be fatally injured, and breaking her arm. According to the formula just given, it would have been *absolutely* right for her to let him be killed because history would have turned out better. But it would not have been within her power to know that. She did what any reasonable person would do—she saved the baby's life at the risk of injury to herself. She did what was *objectively* right. The utilitarian theory holds that by generally doing what reason judges to be the best act based on likely consequences, we will in general actually promote the best consequences.

EXTERNAL CRITICISMS OF UTILITARIANISM

There are several other objections opponents raise against utilitarianism. We shall discuss five of them: (1) the no-rest objection, (2) the absurd-implications objection, (3) the integrity objection, (4) the justice objection, and (5) the publicity objection. We will first go through all of the objections and then offer a utilitarian response to each of them.

Problem 1: The No-Rest Objection

According to utilitarianism one should always do that act that promises to promote the most utility. But there is usually an infinite set of possible acts to choose from, and even if I can be excused from considering all of them, I can be fairly sure that there is often a preferable act that I could be doing. For example, when I am about to go to the cinema with a friend, I should ask myself if helping the homeless in my community wouldn't promote more utility. When I am about to go to sleep, I should ask myself whether I could at that moment be doing something to help save the ozone layer. And why not simply give all my assets (beyond what is absolutely necessary to keep me alive) to the poor in order to promote utility? Following utilitarianism, I should get little or no rest, and, certainly, I have no right to enjoy life when, by sacrificing, I can make others happier.

Problem 2: The Absurd-Implications Objection

W. D. Ross has argued that utilitarianism is to be rejected because it is counterintuitive. If we accept it, we would have to accept an absurd implication. Consider two acts, A and B, that will both result in 100 hedons (units of pleasure of utility). The only difference is that A involves telling a lie and B involves telling the truth. The utilitarian must maintain that the two acts are of equal value. But this seems implausible; truth seems to be an intrinsically good thing.

Similarly, in Arthur Koestler's *Darkness at Noon,* Rubashov writes of the communist philosophy in the former Soviet Union:

> History has taught us that often lies serve her better than the truth; for man is sluggish and has to be led through the desert for forty years before each step in his development. And he has to be driven through the desert with threats and promises, by imaginary terrors and imaginary consolations, so that he should not sit down prematurely to rest and divert himself by worshipping golden calves.[9]

According to this interpretation, orthodox Soviet communism justified its lies and atrocities via utilitarian ideas. Something in us revolts at this kind of value system. Truth is sacred and must not be sacrificed on the altar of expediency.

Problem 3: The Integrity Objection

Bernard Williams argues that utilitarianism violates personal integrity by commanding that we violate our most central and deeply held principles. He illustrates this with the following example:

> Jim finds himself in the central square of a small South American town. Tied up against the wall are a row of twenty Indians, most terrified, a few defiant, in front of them several armed men in uniform. A heavy man in a sweat-stained khaki shirt turns out to be the captain in charge and, after a good deal of questioning of Jim which establishes that he got there by accident while on a botanical expedition, explains that the Indians are a random group of inhabitants who, after recent acts of protest against the government, are just about to be killed to remind other possible protesters of the advantages of not protesting. However, since Jim is an honored visitor from another land, the captain is happy to offer him a guest's privilege of killing one of the Indians himself. If Jim accepts, then as a special mark of the occasion, the other Indians will be let off. Of course, if Jim refuses, then there is no special occasion, and Pedro here will do what he was about to do when Jim arrived, and kill them all. Jim, with some desperate recollection of schoolboy fiction, wonders whether if he got hold of a gun, he could hold the captain, Pedro and the rest of the soldiers to threat, but it is quite clear from the set-up that nothing of that kind is going to work: any attempt of that sort of thing will mean that all the Indians will be killed, and himself. The men against the wall, the other villagers, understand the situation, and are obviously begging him to accept. What should he do?[10]

Williams asks rhetorically,

> How can a man, as a utilitarian agent, come to regard as one satisfaction among others, and a dispensable one, a project or attitude round which he has built his life, just because someone else's projects have so structured the causal scene that *that* is how the utilitarian sum comes out?

Williams' conclusion is that utilitarianism leads to personal alienation, and so is deeply flawed.

Problem 4: The Justice Objection

Suppose that a rape and murder is committed in a racially volatile community. As the sheriff of the town, you have spent a lifetime working for racial harmony. Now, just when your goal is being realized, this incident occurs. The crime is thought to be racially motivated, and a riot is about to break out that will very likely result in the death of several people and create long-lasting racial antagonism. You see that you could frame a tramp for the crime so that a trial will find him guilty and he will be executed. There is every reason to believe that a speedy trial and execution will head off the riot and save community harmony. Only you (and the real criminal, who will keep quiet about it) will know that an innocent man has been tried and executed. What is the morally right thing to do? The utilitarian seems committed to framing the tramp, but many would find this appalling.

Or take this hypothetical situation: You are a utilitarian physician who has five patients under your care. One needs a heart transplant, one needs two lungs, one needs a liver, and the last two each need a kidney. Now into your office comes a healthy bachelor needing an immunization. You judge that he would make a perfect sacrifice for your five patients. Via a utility-calculus, you determine that, without doubt, you could do the most good by injecting the healthy man with a fatal drug, and then using his organs to save your five other patients.[11]

This cavalier view of justice offends us. The very fact that utilitarians even countenance such actions—that they would misuse the legal system or the medical system to carry out their schemes—seems frightening. It reminds us of the medieval Roman Catholic bishop's justification for heresy hunts and inquisitions and religious wars:

> When the existence of the Church is threatened, she is released from the commandments of morality. With unity as the end, the use of every means is sanctified, even cunning, treachery, violence, simony, prison, death. For all order is for the sake of the community, and the individual must be sacrificed to the common good.[12]

Problem 5: The Publicity Objection

It is usually thought that moral principles must be known to all, so that all may freely obey the principles. But utilitarians usually hesitate to recommend that everyone act as a utilitarian, especially an act-utilitarian, for it takes a great deal of deliberation to work out the likely consequences of alternative courses of action. It would be better if most people acted simply as deontologists.[13] So utilitarianism seems to contradict our notion of publicity.

UTILITARIAN RESPONSES
TO STANDARD OBJECTIONS

The objections just discussed are weighty and complicated, but let's allow the utilitarians to make an initial defense. What sorts of responses are open to utilitarians?

A General Defense

A sophisticated version of utilitarianism can offset at least some of the force of these criticisms. There is the *multilevel strategy,* which goes like this:[14] We must split considerations of utility into two levels, with the lower level dealing with a set of rules that we judge to be most likely to bring about the best consequences most of the time. We'll call this the *rule-utility* feature of utilitarianism. Normally, we have to live by the best rules our system can devise; rules of honesty, promise-keeping, obedience to the law, and justice will be among them.

But sometimes the rules conflict or clearly will not yield the best consequences. In these infrequent cases we will need to suspend or override the rule in favor of the better consequences. We call this the *act-utility* feature of utilitarianism. This second level of consideration is referred to only when there is dissatisfaction with the rule–utility feature. An example might be the rule against breaking a promise. Normally, the most utility will come via keeping one's promises. But what if I promise to meet you at the movies tonight at 7 o'clock, and, unbeknownest to you, on the way to our rendezvous I come across an accident and am able to render great service to the injured parties? Unfortunately, I cannot contact you, and you are inconvenienced as you wait in front of the theater for an hour. I have broken a utility rule in order to maximize utility, and I am justified in doing so.

As another example, let us repeat the trolley car story: You are a trolley car driver who sees five workers on the track before you when you suddenly realize that the brakes have failed. Fortunately, the track has a spur leading off to the right onto which you can turn the trolley. Unfortunately, there is one person on this spur of track. You can turn the trolley to the right, killing that one person, or you can continue on the main trolley, in which case the five workers will die.[15] Under traditional views, there is a distinction between killing and letting die, that is, between actively killing and passively allowing death. But the utilitarian rejects this distinction, maintaining instead that you should turn onto the spur, thereby causing the lesser evil, for the only relevant issue is expected utility. So the normal rule against actively causing an innocent to die is suspended in favor of the utility principle. This is the kind of defense the sophisticated utilitarian is likely to lodge against *all* five of the criticisms.

Response to Problem 1

The utilitarian responds to Problem 1, the no-rest objection, by insisting that a rule prescribing rest and entertainment is actually the kind of rule that would have a place in a utility-maximizing set of rules. The agent should aim at maximizing his or her own happiness as well as other people's happiness. For the same reason it is best not to worry much about the needs of those not in our primary circle. Although we should be concerned about the needs of future and distant people, it actually would promote disutility for the average person to become preoccupied with these concerns. But, the utilitarian would remind us, we can surely do a lot more for suffering humanity than we now are doing—especially if we join together and act cooperatively.

Response to Problem 2

With regard to Problem 2, Ross's absurd-implications objection, utilitarians can agree that there is something counterintuitive in the calculus of equating an act of lying of one with honesty; but, they argue, we must be ready to change our culture-induced moral biases. What is so important about truth-telling or so bad about lying? If it turned out that lying really promoted human welfare, we'd have to accept it. But that's not likely. Our happiness is tied up with a need for reliable information (i.e., truth) on how to achieve our ends. So truthfulness will be a member of rule-utility's set. But where lying will clearly promote utility without undermining the general adherence to the rule, we simply ought to lie. Don't we already accept lying to a gangster or telling white lies to spare people's feelings?

With regard to Rubashov's utilitarian defense of the inhumanity of communism or the medieval defense of the Inquisition, the utilitarian replies that this abuse of utilitarianism only illustrates how dangerous the doctrine can be in the hands of self-serving bureaucrats. Any theory can be misused in this way.

Response to Problem 3

Let us turn to Problem 3, Williams' argument from integrity. The utilitarian can argue that (1) some alienation may be necessary for the moral life but (2) the utilitarian (even the act-utilitarian) can take this into account in devising strategies of action. That is, integrity is not an absolute that must be adhered to at all costs. Even when it is required that we sacrifice our lives or limit our freedom for others, we may have to limit or sacrifice something of what Williams calls our integrity. We may have to do the "lesser of evils" in many cases. If the utilitarian doctrine of negative responsibility is correct, we need to realize that we are responsible for the evil that we knowingly allow, as well as for the evil we commit.

But, as Peter Railton argues, a utilitarian may realize that there are important social benefits in having people who are squeamish about committing acts of violence, even those that preliminary utility calculations seem to prescribe. It may be that becoming certain kinds of people (endorsed by utilitarianism) may rule out being able to commit certain kinds of horrors—like Jim's killing of an innocent Indian. That is, utilitarianism recognizes the utility of good character and conscience, which may militate against certain apparently utility-maximizing acts.[16]

Response to Problem 4

We turn to the most difficult objection, Problem 4, the justice objection, the claim that utilitarianism permits injustice, as seen in the example of the sheriff framing the innocent derelict. The utilitarian counters that justice is not an absolute—mercy and benevolence and the good of the whole society sometimes should override it; but, the sophisticated utilitarian insists, it makes good utilitarian sense to have a principle of justice to which we generally adhere. It is not clear what the sheriff should do in the racially torn community. More needs to be known, but if we could be certain that it would not set a precedent of sacrificing innocent people, it may be right to sacrifice one person for the good of the whole. Wouldn't we all agree, the utilitarian continues, that it would be right to sacrifice one innocent person to prevent great evil?

Virtually all standard moral systems have a rule against torturing innocent people. But suppose a maniac is about to set off a nuclear bomb that will destroy New York City. He is scheduled to detonate the bomb in one hour. (Just in case you don't think New York City is worth saving, then imagine instead that the lunatic has a lethal gas that will spread throughout the globe and wipe out all life within a few weeks.) His psychiatrist knows the lunatic well and assures us that there is one way to stop him— torture his 10-year-old daughter and televise it. Suppose for the sake of the argument that there is no way to simulate the torture. Would you not consider torturing the child in this situation?

Is it not right to sacrifice one innocent person to stop a war or to save the human race from destruction? We seem to proceed on this assumption in wartime, in every bombing raid, especially in the dropping of the atomic bomb on Hiroshima and Nagasaki. We seem to be following this rule in our decision to drive automobiles and trucks even though we are fairly certain the practice will result in the death of thousands of innocent people each year.

On the other hand, the sophisticated utilitarian may argue that in the case of the sheriff framing the innocent derelict, justice should not be over-ridden by current utility concerns, for human rights themselves are out-comes of utility consideration and should not lightly be violated. That is, because we tend subconsciously to favor our own interests and biases, we institute the principle of rights to protect ourselves and others from capri-cious and biased acts that would in the long run have great disutility. So we must not undermine institutional rights too easily—we should not kill the bachelor in order to provide a heart, two lungs, a liver, and two kidneys to the five other patients—at least not at the present time, given people's expectations of what will happen to them when they enter hospitals. But neither should we worship rights! They are to be taken seriously but not given ultimate authority. The utilitarian cannot foreclose the possibility of sacrificing innocent people for the greater good of humanity. If slavery could be humane and yield great overall utility, utilitarians would accept it.

We see then that sophisticated, multilevel utilitarianism has responses to all of the criticisms directed toward it. For most people, most of the time, the ordinary moral principles should be followed, for they actually maximize long-term utility. But we should not be tied down to the rule, because "morality was made for man, not man for morality." The purpose of morality is to promote flourishing and to ameliorate suffering, and whenever these can be accomplished by sacrificing a rule, we should do so. Whether this is an adequate defense I leave for you to decide.

Response to Problem 5

Finally, with regard to Problem 5, the publicity objection, utilitarians have two responses. First they can counter that the objection only works against act-utilitarianism. Rule-utilitarianism can allow for greater public-ity, for it is not the individual act that is important but the set of rules that are likely to bring about the most good. But then the act-utilitarian may respond that this objection only shows a bias toward publicity (or even democracy). It may well be that publicity is only a rule of thumb to be overridden whenever there is good reason to believe that we can obtain more utility by not publicizing act-utilitarian ideas. I leave the plausibility of this response for your consideration.

Conclusion

We see then that sophisticated, multilevel utilitarianism has responses to all of the criticisms directed toward it. Whether they are adequate is another story, for that depends on certain factual claims—claims about human psychology, institutional feasibility, and so forth. Some ethicists—notably Kantians—might question the appropriateness of drawing conclusions about justice, human rights and responsibilities, and the like, based on claims that are themselves less certain than the moral claims that they are meant to support. Others hold that utilitarianism is the only theory that makes any sense. Perhaps it would be better to hold off making a final judgment until after you have read the next two chapters, wherein two other types of ethical theory are discussed.

NOTES

1. R. M. Hare, *The Language of Morals* (Oxford University Press, 1952), p. 60.

2. Sophocles, *Antigone,* trans. Robert Eagles (Penguin Classics), lines 204–214. I am indebted to an anonymous reviewer for this reference.

3. Jeremy Bentham, *An Introduction to the Principles of Morals and Legislation* (1789), Ch 1; reprinted in Louis Pojman, ed., *Ethical Theory* (Wadsworth, 1989) pp. 111–114.

4. John Stuart Mill, *Utilitarianism* (1863), Ch II; reprinted in Pojman, ed., *Ethical Theory,* p. 165.

5. Mill, *Utilitarianism,* in Pojman, ed., *Ethical Theory,* pp. 166–167.

6. Richard Brandt, "Towards a Credible Form of Utilitarianism," in H. Castaneda and G. Naknikian, eds., *Morality and the Language of Conduct* (Wayne State University Press, 1963), pp. 109–110.

7. Kai Nielsen, "Against Moral Conservatism," *Ethics* (1972), reprinted in Pojman, ed., *Ethical Theory.* Nielsen no longer holds the position espoused

in this article; J. J. C. Smart, "Outlines of a System of Utilitarian Ethics" in J. J. C. Smart and Bernard Williams, *Utilitarianism: For and Against* (Cambridge University Press, 1973).

8. See Anthony Quinton, *Utilitarian Ethics* (Macmillan, 1973), p. 49 f, for a good discussion of this and similar points. My discussion is indebted to Quinton.

9. Arthur Koestler, *Darkness at Noon* (Macmillan, 1941), p. 80.

10. Bernard Williams, "A Critique of Utilitarianism," in Smart and Williams, *Utilitarianism: For and Against,* p. 98 f.

11. This example and the trolley car example are found in Judith Jarvis Thomson, "The Trolley Problem," *Rights, Restitution and Risk* (Harvard University Press, 1986), pp. 94–116.

12. Dietrich von Nieheim, Bishop of Verden, *De Schismate Librii,* A.D. 1411, quoted in Koestler, *Darkness at Noon,* p. 76.

13. The famous utilitarian Henry Sidgwick, in his *The Methods of Ethics*

(Oxford, 1974), argues that utilitarians should keep their views a secret for the good of society.

14. The multilevel strategy was first developed by R. M. Hare in "Ethical Theory and Utilitarianism," in H. D. Lewis, ed., *Contemporary British Philosophy* (London: Allen and Unwin), p. 176. See also R. M. Hane, *Moral Thinking* (Oxford University Press,

1981); and Peter Railton, "Alienation, Consequentialism, and the Demands of Morality," *Philosophy and Public Affairs* 13 (1984), reprinted in Pojman, ed., *Ethical Theory.*

15. Thomson, "The Trolley Problem."

16. See Railton, "Alienation, Consequentialism, and the Demands of Morality," for an excellent defense of sophisticated utilitarianism on this point.

FOR FURTHER REFLECTION

1. Consider the three purposes of morality mentioned in Chapter 1: (1) to promote human flourishing, (2) to ameliorate human suffering, and (3) to resolve conflicts of interest justly. Which of these does utilitarianism fulfill and which does it fail to fulfill?

2. W. D. Ross has argued that utilitarianism is to be rejected because it is counterintuitive. Consider two acts, A and B, that will both result in 100 hedons (units of pleasure of utility). The only difference is that A involves telling a lie and B involves telling the truth. The utilitarian must maintain that the two acts are of equal value. Do you agree? Does more need to be known?

3. One criticism of utilitarianism is that it fails to protect people's rights. Consider five sadists who get a total of 100 hedons while torturing an innocent victim who is suffering 10 dolors (units of pain). On a utilitarian calculus this would produce a total of 90 hedons. If no other act would produce as many or more hedons, the utilitarian would have to endorse this act and argue that the victim has a duty to submit to the torture and that the sadists had a duty to torture the victim. What do you think of this sort of reasoning? How much does it count against utilitarianism?

4. With respect to the trolley car example in this chapter, many people agree that we ought to kill the one in order to save the five. But see how you feel about a similar case (given by Gilbert Harman): You are a doctor and have five needy patients all of whom are in danger of dying unless you get suitable organs within the day. One needs a heart transplant, two need kidneys, one needs a lung, and another needs a liver. A tramp who has no family walks into the hospital for a routine checkup. By killing him and using his organs for the first five you could save five persons, restoring them to health. If you don't kill the tramp, are you negatively responsible for the death of the five other patients? What is the difference, if any, between these two cases?

5. In his False-Analogy Argument, John Rawls maintains that utilitarianism errs in applying to society the principle of personal choice. That is, we all would agree that an individual has a right to forgo a present pleasure for a future good. I have a right to go without a new suit so that I can save the money for my college education or so that I can give it to my favorite charity. But utilitarianism prescribes that we demand that you forgo a new suit for someone else's college education or for the overall good of the community—whether you like it or not or whether you agree to it or not. That is, it extends the futuristic notion of agent-utility maximization to cover society in a way that violates individual rights. Is this a fair criticism?

6. Review Bernard Williams' arguments against utilitarianism. Do you agree that utilitarianism is unacceptable because its demands would undermine the agent's integrity? What if Jim's goal in life is to save as many people as possible from death? In that case would killing one person in order to save 19 be a violation of his integrity? Could the utilitarian argue that we all ought to have, as one of our goals, the saving of lives? Explain your answer.

7. A related example comes from Ursala Le Guin, "The Ones Who Walk Away from Omelas," *The Wind's Twelve Quarters* (Harper, 1975). Her short story describes the village of Omelas, wherein "mature, intelligent, passionate adults" were happy. Children were joyous and the elderly blessed. Technology was used only to satisfy necessary needs. For example, there were no cars in Omelas, but there was public transportation and "all kinds of marvelous devices...floating light-sources, fuelless power, a cure for the common cold." There was religion but no clergy, love but no guilt. There was no crime, no army, no hatred in Omelas. In sum, Omelas was a utilitarian Utopia.

   Well, Omelas was not quite perfect. One fact sullied its glory: In a locked room in the basement of one of its beautiful buildings sat a naked ten-year-old retarded child. "Its buttocks and thighs are a mass of festered sores, as it sits in its own excrement continually." It begged to be released, but its presence in public would corrupt the bliss of the city. The existence of this indescribably unhappy imbecile was the price of Omelas' happiness. Is the price worth paying?

   From time to time, an adolescent girl or boy went to see the imbecile and did not return home. He or she walked out of the basement and kept on walking out of the village. These adolescents left Omelas with all its glory and happiness, never to return. Would you leave Omelas?

8. Consider the following situation: You are an army officer who has just captured an enemy soldier who knows where a secret time bomb has been planted. Unless defused, the bomb will explode, killing thousands of people. Would it be morally permissible to torture the soldier to get him to reveal the bomb's location? Suppose you have also captured his children. Would it be permissible to torture them to get him to reveal the bomb's location? Discuss this problem in the light of utilitarian and deontological theories.

9. At the beginning of this chapter we quoted Francis Hutcheson: "The Greatest Happiness for the Greatest Number." Do you find anything puzzling about this motto? Notice that it has two superlatives. Let us repeat an example mentioned earlier in this chapter: I tell you that I am going to give a $1,000 prize to the person who runs the furthest distance in the least amount of time. Three people sign up and run. Here are the results.

Person	Distance	Time
John	7 miles	50 minutes
Joe	5 miles	31 minutes
Jack	1 mile	6 minutes

   Who should get the prize? Can you see how this could become a problem for utilitarian calculus? How does the utilitarian go about deciding how to distribute goods to different groups of people?

10. Suppose we have a situation involving three social policies that will divide up welfare among three equal groups of people. In Policy I, Group A will receive 75 units, Group B 45 units and Group C 25 units of welfare, for a total of 145 units. In Policy II, A will receive 50 units and B and C will receive 45 units each, for a total of 140 units. In Policy III, A will receive 100 units and B and C 25 each, for a total of 150 units (see Figure 2). Suppose that it is agreed that 30 units is necessary for a minimally acceptable social existence. Which policy should the utilitarian choose?

FIGURE 2 Units of Welfare

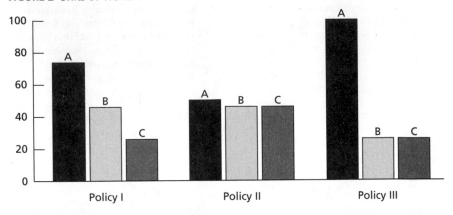

FOR FURTHER READING

Bentham, Jeremy. *Introduction to the Principles of Morals and Legislation,* ed. W. Harrison. Oxford University Press, 1948.

Brandt, Richard. "In Search of a Credible Form of Rule-Utilitarianism," in *Morality and the Language of Conduct,* ed. H. N. Castaneda and George Nakhnikian, Wayne State University Press, 1953. This oft-anthologized article is one of the most sophisticated defenses of utilitarianism.

Brandt, Richard. *A Theory of the Good and the Right.* Clarendon Press, 1979.

Brink, David. *Moral Realism and the Foundation of Ethics.* Cambridge University Press, 1989. Chapter 8 is an excellent discussion of utilitarianism.

Brock, Dan. "Recent Work in Utilitarianism," *American Philosophical Quarterly* 10 (Oct. 1973).

Hardin, Russell. *Morality Within the Limits of Reason.* University of Chicago Press, 1988. A cogent, contemporary defense of utilitarianism.

Hare, R. M. *Moral Thinking.* Oxford University Press, 1981.

Lyons, David. *Forms and Limits of Utilitarianism.* Oxford University Press, 1965.

Mill, John Stuart. *Utilitarianism.* Bobbs-Merrill, 1957.

Miller, Harlan B., and William Williams, eds. *The Limits of Utilitarianism.* University of Minnesota Press, 1982. Contains important but advanced articles.

Parfit, Derik. *Reasons and Persons.* Oxford University Press, 1984.

Railton, Peter. "Alienation, Consequentialism, and the Demands of Morality," in *Philosophy and Public Affairs* 13 (1984); reprinted in *Ethical Theory,* ed. Louis Pojman, Wadsworth, 1995.

Quinton, Anthony. *Utilitarian Ethics.* Macmillan, 1973. A clear exposition of classical utilitarianism.

Scheffler, Samuel. *The Rejection of Consequentialism.* Clarendon Press, 1982. A brilliant discussion, including an outline of a hybrid system between deontological and utilitarian theories.

Scheffler, Samuel, ed. *Consequentialism and Its Critics.* Oxford University Press, 1988. Contains important selections; many of

them refocus the debate between conse-
quentialists and deontologists.

Sen, Amartya, and Bernard Williams, eds.
Utilitarianism and Beyond. Cambridge
University Press, 1982. Contains
important readings.

Smart, J. J. C., and Bernard Williams.
Utilitarianism: For and Against. Cambridge University Press, 1973. A
classic debate on the subject.

Taylor, Paul. *Principles of Ethics.* Wadsworth, 1975.

7

Kantian and Deontological Systems

Kant's Groundwork of the Metaphysics of Morals *is one of the small books which are truly great: it has exercised on human thought an influence almost ludicrously disproportionate to its size. In moral philosophy it ranks with the* Republic *of Plato and the* Ethics *of Aristotle; and perhaps it shows in some respects a deeper insight even than these. Its main topic—the supreme principle of morality—is of the utmost importance to all who are not indifferent to the struggle of good against evil. Its message was never more needed than it is at present, when a somewhat arid empiricism is the prevailing fashion in philosophy.*

H. J. PATON, PREFACE TO KANT'S *GROUNDWORK OF THE METAPHYSIC OF MORALS*

TWO TYPES OF DEONTOLOGICAL SYSTEMS

What makes a right act right? The teleological answer to this question is that the good consequences make it right. Moral rightness and wrongness are determined by nonmoral values (e.g., happiness and utility). To this extent, the end justifies the means. The deontological answer to this question is quite the opposite. It is not the consequences that determine the rightness or wrongness of an act but certain features in the act itself or in the rule of which the act is a token or example. The end never justifies the means. For example, there is something right about truth-telling and promise-keeping, even when such actions may bring about some harm; and there is something wrong about lying and promise-breaking, even when such actions may bring about good consequences. Acting unjustly is wrong even if it will maximize expected utility. In our examples from Chapter 6, as a deontologist you would very likely keep your promise and give the $2 million to the Yankees, and you would either share the food on the raft or flip a coin to decide who gets the food.

Act-Deontological Theories

Deontological theories are of two kinds: act- and rule-deontological systems, or particularism and generalism. Act-deontologists see each act as a unique ethical occasion and believe that we must decide what is right or wrong in each situation by consulting our conscience or our intuitions or by making a choice apart from any rules. As this description suggests, there are two types of act-deontological ethics: intuitionism and decisionism. *Intuitionists* believe that we must consult our conscience in every situation in order to *discover* the morally right (or wrong) thing to do. *Decisionists,* sometimes called *existentialists,* believe there is no morally right answer until we choose for ourselves what is right and what is wrong: Nothing is right or wrong, but choosing makes it so. Existentialist Jean-Paul Sartre (1905–1980) held such a position. We have already examined and rejected this sort of radical relativism in Chapter 2, so we may concentrate here on act-intuitionism (to be distinguished from rule-intuitionism).

An expression of intuitional act-deontological ethics is in the famous moral sermons of the Bishop of Durham, Joseph Butler (1692–1752):

> [If] any plain honest man, before he engages in any course of action, ask himself, Is this I am going about right, or is it wrong? . . . I do not in the least doubt but that this question would be answered agreeably to truth and virtue, by almost any fair man in almost any circumstance.[1]

Butler believed that we each have a conscience that can discover what is right and wrong in virtually every instance. This is consistent with advice such as "Let your conscience be your guide." We do not need general rules to learn what is right and wrong; our intuition will inform us of those things. The judgment lies in the moral perception and not in some abstract, general rule.

Act-deontological systems have some serious disadvantages. First, it is hard to see how any argument could take place with an intuitionist:

Either you both have the same intuition about lying or you don't, and that's all there is to it. If I believe that a specific act of abortion is morally permissible and you believe it is morally wrong, then we may ask each other to look more deeply into our consciences, but we cannot argue about the subject. There *is* a place for deep intuitions in moral philosophy, I hasten to add, but intuitions must still be scrutinized by reason and corrected by theory.

Second, it seems that rules are necessary to all reasoning, including moral reasoning. As R. M. Hare says:

> To learn to do anything is never to learn to do an individual act; it is always to learn to do acts of a certain kind in a certain kind of situation; and this is to learn a principle.... Without principles we could not learn anything whatever from our elders.... Every generation would have to start from scratch and teach itself. But...self-teaching, like all other teaching, is the teaching of principles.[2]

You may test this by thinking about how you learn to drive a car, to do long division, or to type: Even though you may eventually internalize the initial principles as habits so that you are unconscious of them, one could still cite a rule that covers your action. For example, you may no longer remember the rules for accelerating a car, but there was an original experience of learning the rule, which you continue unwittingly to follow. Moral rules such as "Keep your promises" and "Don't kill innocent people" seem to function in a similar way.

Third, different situations seem to share common features, so it would be inconsistent for us to prescribe different moral actions. Suppose you believe that it is morally wrong for John to cheat on his math exam. If you also believe that it is morally permissible for you to cheat on the same exam, don't you need to explain what makes your situation different from John's? If I say that it is wrong for John to cheat on exams, am I not implying that it is wrong for anyone relevantly similar to John (including all students) to cheat on exams? That is, morality seems to involve a universal aspect, or what is called the *principle of universalizability:* If one judges that X is right (or wrong) or good (or bad), then one is rationally committed to judging anything relevantly similar to X as right (wrong) or good (bad). If this principle is sound, then act–deontological ethics are misguided.

Rule-Deontological Theories

Most deontologists have been of the rule variety. Rule-deontological systems accept the principle of universalizability as well as the notion that, in making moral judgments, we are appealing to principles or rules. Such rules as "We ought never to lie," "We ought always to keep our promises," and "We ought never to execute an innocent person" constitute a set of valid prescriptions regardless of the outcomes.

There are different types of rule-deontological systems. We may distinguish between rule-intuitionism and rule-rationalism and between objectivism and absolutism. W. D. Ross (1877–1971) is a good example of an objectivist rule-intuitionist. He defined *intuitions* as internal perceptions, and noted that, just as some people are better perceivers than others, so the moral intuitions of more reflective people count for more in evaluating our moral judgments. "The moral convictions of thoughtful and well-educated people are the data of ethics, just as sense-perceptions are the data of a natural science."[3] He believed that intuition both discovers the correct moral principles and applies them correctly. They have three main characteristics: (1) Although they cannot be proved, the moral principles are *self-evident* to any normal person upon reflection; (2) they constitute a plural set, which cannot be unified under a single overarching principle (e.g., utilitarianism); and (3) they are not absolute; every principle can be overridden by another in a particular situation. Ross wrote:

> That an act, *qua* fulfilling a promise, or *qua* effecting a just distribution of good . . . is *prima facie* right, is self-evident; not in the sense that it is evident . . . as soon as we attend to the proposition for the first time, but in the sense that when we have reached sufficient mental maturity and have given sufficient attention to the proposition it is evident without any need of proof, or of evidence beyond itself. It is evident just as a mathematical axiom, or the validity of a form of inference, is evident . . . . In our confidence that these propositions are true there is involved the same confidence in our reason that is involved in our confidence in mathematics . . . . In both cases we are dealing with propositions that cannot be proved, but that just as certainly need no proof.[4]

Ross spoke of two kinds of rules or duties: *prima facie* (Latin for "at first glance"), or conditional, duties and *actual* duties. Prima facie duties, although they are not actual duties, may become such, depending on the circumstances. Ross listed seven prima facie duties:

1. Promise-keeping
2. Fidelity
3. Gratitude for favors
4. Beneficence

5. Justice

6. Self-improvement

7. Nonmaleficence

If we make a promise, for example, we put ourselves in a situation in which the duty to keep promises is a moral consideration. It has presumptive force; and if no conflicting prima facie duty is relevant, then the duty to keep our promises automatically becomes an actual duty.

What about situations of conflict? For an absolutist, an adequate moral system can never produce moral conflict, nor can a basic moral principle be overridden by another moral principle. But Ross is no absolutist. He allowed for overridability of principles. For example, suppose you have promised your friend that you will help her with her ethics homework at 3:00 P.M. While you are on your way to meet her, you encounter a lost, crying child. There is no one else around to help the little boy, so you help him find his way home. But in doing so you miss your appointment. Have you done the morally right thing? Have you broken your promise?

It is possible to construe this situation as constituting a conflict between two moral principles:

1. We ought always to keep our promises.

2. We ought always to help people in need when it is not unreasonably inconvenient to do so.

In helping the child get home, you have decided that the second principle overrides the first. This does not mean that the first is not a valid principle—only that the "ought" in it is not an absolute "ought." The principle has objective validity, but it is not always decisive, depending on which other principles may apply to the situation. Although some duties are weightier than others—for example, nonmaleficence "is apprehended as a duty of a more stringent character...than beneficence"—the intuition must decide each situation on its own merits.

Although the idea of prima facie duties has merit, one can detach it from intuitionism, and rationalists and naturalists can appropriate it. The first objection against intuitionism (as mentioned earlier in this chapter) still has force. If we are thorough intuitionists, then we cannot use reason in arguing for or against various courses of action. You either "see" it or you don't. This desire to be able to build rational arguments has led many deontologists to opt for a rational form of deontological ethics. The most famous of these is Immanuel Kant's, which we now turn to.

KANT'S RULE-DEONTOLOGICAL SYSTEM

Immanuel Kant (1724–1804), the greatest philosopher of the German Enlightenment and one of the most important philosophers of all time, was both an absolutist and a rationalist. He believed that we could use reason to work out a consistent, nonoverridable set of moral principles.

To understand Kant's moral philosophy, it is helpful to understand a little about his life. Kant was born in Konigsberg, Germany, in 1724 and died there eighty years later, never having left the surroundings of the city. His father was a saddle maker. His parents were Pietists in the Lutheran church. The Pietists were a sect in the church, much like present-day Quakers, who emphasized sincerity, deep feeling, and the moral life rather than theological doctrine or orthodox belief. Pietism is a religion of the heart, not the head, of the spirit rather than of ritual. However, Kant, as an intellectual, emphasized the head as much as the heart, but it was a head concerned about the moral life, especially good will.

Kant was a short, quiet man and so methodical that, as tradition has it, the citizens of Konigsberg set their watches by his daily 3:00 P.M. walks. He never married. He devoted his life to the study and teaching of philosophy at the University of Konigsberg. His magnum opus, *The Critique of Pure Reason* (1781), was heralded in his own day as a monumental work, and his *The Fundamental Principles of the Metaphysics of Morals* (1785) is generally regarded as one of the two or three most important books in the history of ethics.

There were three strong influences on Kant's ethical thinking. The first was Pietism, already mentioned, which set a tone of deep sincerity to his views. It is not correct beliefs or results that really matter but inner goodness. The idea is that, if we live within our lights, we will be given more light and that God judges us not on how lucky or successful we are in accomplishing our tasks but on how earnestly we have lived according to our principles. This influence informs his notion of the good will as the sole intrinsic good in life.

The second influence was the work of Jean Jacques Rousseau (1712–1778) on human freedom, especially his *Social Contract,* and it was said that the only time Kant ever missed his afternoon walk was the day when he read that tome. Rousseau taught him the meaning and importance of human dignity, the primacy of freedom and autonomy, and the intrinsic worth of human beings apart from any functions they might perform.

The third influence was the debate between rationalism and empiricism, which took place in the seventeenth and eighteenth centuries. Rationalists, such as Rene Descartes, Baruch Spinoza, Gottfried Leibniz, and Christian Wolff, claimed that pure reason could tell us how the world is, independent of experience. We can know metaphysical truth such as the existence of God, the immortality of the soul, freedom of the will, and the universality of causal relations apart from experience (experience may be necessary to open our minds to these ideas, but essentially they are innate ideas, synthetic a priori truths). Empiricists, led by John Locke and David Hume, on the other hand, denied that we have any innate ideas and argued that all knowledge comes from experience. Our minds are a *tabula rasa,* an empty slate, upon which experience writes her lessons.

The rationalists and empiricists carried their debate into the area of moral knowledge. The rationalists claimed that our knowledge of moral principles is a type of metaphysical knowledge, implanted in us by God, and discoverable by reason as it deduces general principles about human nature. On the other hand, the Scottish empiricists, especially Francis Hutcheson, David Hume, and Adam Smith, argued that morality is founded entirely on the contingencies of human nature and based on desire. Morality concerns making people happy, fulfilling their reflected desires, and reason is just a practical means of helping them fulfill their desires. There is nothing of special importance in reason in its own right. It is mainly a rationalizer and servant of the passions ("a pimp of the passions"). As Hume said, "Reason is and ought only to be a slave of the passions and can never pretend to any other office than to serve and obey them." Morality is founded on our feeling of sympathy with other people's sufferings, on fellow feeling. For such empiricists then, morality is contingent upon human nature:

Human nature → Feelings and desires → Moral principles

If we had a different nature, then we would have different feelings and desires, and hence we would have different moral principles.

Kant rejected the ideas of Hutcheson, Hume, and Smith. He was outraged by the thought that morality should depend on human nature and be subject to the fortunes of change and the luck of empirical discovery. Morality is not contingent but necessary. It would be no less binding on us if our feelings were different than they are:

> Every empirical element is not only quite incapable of being an aid
> to the principle of morality, but is even highly prejudicial to the purity
> of morals; for the proper and inestimable worth of an absolutely good
> will consists just in this, that the principle of action is free from all
> influence of contingent grounds, which alone experience can furnish.
> We cannot too much or too often repeat our warning against this lax
> and even mean habit of thought which seeks for its principle amongst

empirical motives and laws; for human reason in its weariness is glad to rest on this pillow, and in a dream of sweet illusions it substitutes for morality a bastard patched up from limbs of various derivation, which looks like anything one chooses to see in it; only not like virtue to one who has once beheld her in her true form.[5]

No, said Kant, it is not our desires that ground morality but our rational will. Reason is sufficient for establishing the moral law as something transcendent and universally binding on all rational creatures.

THE CATEGORICAL IMPERATIVE

As we have noted, Kant wanted to remove moral truth from the zone of contingency and empirical observation and place it securely in the area of necessary, absolute, universal truth. Morality's value is not based on the fact that it has instrumental value, that it often secures nonmoral goods such as happiness. Rather, morality is valuable in its own right:

> Nothing can possibly be conceived in the world, or even out of it, which can be called good without qualification, except the Good Will. Intelligence, wit, judgment, and the other *talents* of the mind, however they may be named, or courage, resolution, perseverance, as qualities of temperament, as undoubtedly good and desirable in many respects; but these gifts of nature also may become extremely bad and mischievous if the will which is to make use of them, and which, therefore constitutes what is called *character* is not good.... Even if it should happen that, owing to special disfavor of fortune, or the stingy provision of a step-motherly nature, this Good Will should wholly lack power to accomplish its purpose, if with its greatest efforts it should yet achieve nothing, and there should remain only the Good Will,... then, like a jewel, it would still shine by its own light, as a thing which has its whole value in itself. Its usefulness or fruitfulness can neither add to nor take away anything from this value.[6]

The only thing that is absolutely good, good in itself and without qualification, is the good will. All the other intrinsic goods, both intellectual and moral, can serve the vicious will and thus contribute to evil. They are only *morally valuable* if accompanied by a good will. Even success and happiness are not good in themselves. Honor can lead to pride. Happiness without good will is undeserved luck, ill-gotten gain. Nor is utilitarianism plausible, for if we have a quantity of happiness to distribute, is it just to distribute it equally, regardless of virtue? Should we not distribute it discriminately, according to moral goodness? Happiness should be distributed in proportion to people's moral worth.

How good is Kant's argument for the good will? Could we imagine a world where people always and necessarily put nonmoral virtues to good use, where it is simply impossible to use a virtue such as intelligence for evil? Is happiness any less good simply because one can distribute it incorrectly? Can't one put the good will itself to bad use, as the misguided do-gooder might? As the aphorism goes, "The road to hell is paved with good intentions." Could Hitler have had good intentions in carrying out his dastardly programs? Can't the good will have bad effects?

While we may agree that the good will is a great good, it is not obvious that Kant's account is correct, that it is the only inherently good thing. For even as intelligence, courage, and happiness can be put to bad uses or have bad effects, so can the good will; and even as it doesn't seem to count against the good will that it can be put to bad uses, so it shouldn't count against the other virtues that they can be put to bad uses. The good will may be a necessary element to any morally good action, but whether the good will is also a *sufficient* condition to moral goodness is another question.

Nonetheless, perhaps we can reinterpret Kant so as to preserve his central insight. There does seem to be something morally valuable about the good will, apart from any consequences. Consider the following illustration. Two soldiers volunteer to cross enemy lines to contact their allies on the other side. Both start off and do their best to get through the enemy area. One succeeds; the other doesn't and is captured. But aren't they both morally praiseworthy? The success of one in no way detracts from the goodness of the other. Judged from a commonsense moral point of view, their actions are equally good; judged from a utilitarian or consequentialist view, the successful act is far more valuable than the unsuccessful one. Here we can distinguish the agent's worth from the value of the consequences and make two separate, nonconflicting judgments.

All mention of duties (or obligations) can be translated into the language of imperatives, or commands. As such, moral duties can be said to have imperative force. Kant distinguishes two kinds of imperatives: hypothetical and categorical. The formula for a *hypothetical imperative* is: "If you want A, then do B" (for example, "If you want a good job, then get a good education," or "If you want to be happy, then stay sober and live a balanced life"). The formula for a *categorical imperative* is simply: "Do B!" (that is, do what reason discloses to be the intrinsically right thing to do, such as "Tell the truth!"). Hypothetical, or means/ends, imperatives are not the kind of imperatives that characterize moral actions. Categorical, or unqualified, imperatives are the right kind of imperatives, for they show proper recognition of the imperial status of moral obligations. Such imperatives are intuitive, immediate, absolute injunctions that all rational agents understand by virtue of their rationality.

One must perform moral duty solely for its own sake ("duty for duty's sake"). Some people conform to the moral law because they deem it in their own enlightened self-interest to be moral. But they are not truly moral, because they do not act for the sake of the moral law. For example, a businessman may believe that "honesty is the best policy"; that is, he may judge that it is conducive to good business to give his customers correct change and high-quality products. But unless he performs these acts *because* they are his duty, he is not acting morally, even though his acts are the same ones they would be if he *were* acting morally.[7]

The kind of imperative that fits Kant's scheme as a product of reason is one that universalizes principles of conduct. He names it the *categorical imperative* (CI): "Act only according to that maxim by which you can at the same time will that it would become a universal law." He elaborates: You must act "as though the maxim of your action were by your will to become a universal law of nature," analogous to the laws of physics.[8] He gives this as the criterion (or second-order principle) by which to judge all other principles.

By "maxim" Kant means the general rule in accordance with which the agent intends to act, and by "law" he means an objective principle, a maxim that passes the test of universalizability. The categorical imperative is the way to apply the universalizability test. It enables us to stand outside our personal maxims and estimate impartially and impersonally whether they are suitable as principles for all of us to live by. If you could consistently will that everyone would act on a given maxim, then there is an application of the categorical imperative showing the moral permissibility of action. If you cannot consistently will that everyone would act on the maxim, then that type of action is morally wrong. The maxim must be rejected as self-defeated.[9] The formula looks like this:

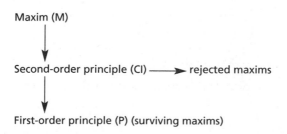

Maxim (M)

Second-order principle (CI) ⟶ rejected maxims

First-order principle (P) (surviving maxims)

In *Foundations of the Metaphysics of Morals,* Kant gives four examples of the application of this test: (1) making a lying promise, (2) suicide, (3) neglecting one's talent, and (4) refraining from helping others. Let us illustrate how the CI works by applying it to each of these maxims.

The Test for Making a Lying Promise

Suppose I need some money and am considering whether it would be moral to borrow the money from you and promise to repay it without ever intending to do so. Could I say to myself that everyone should make a false promise when he is in difficulty from which he otherwise cannot escape? The maxim of my act is M:

M. Whenever I need money, I should make a lying promise while borrowing the money.

Can I universalize the maxim of my act? By applying the universalizability test to M, we get P:

P. Whenever anyone needs money, that person should make a lying promise while borrowing the money.

But something has gone wrong, for if I universalize this principle of making promises without intending to keep them, I would be involved in a contradiction.

> I immediately see that I could will the lie but not a universal law to lie. For with such a law [i.e., with such a maxim universally acted on] there would be no promises at all.... Thus my maxim would necessarily destroy itself as soon as it was made a universal law.[10]

The resulting state of affairs would be self-defeating, for no one in his or her right mind would take promises as promises unless there was the expectation of fulfillment. So the maxim of the lying promise fails the universalizability criterion; hence it is immoral.

Now I consider the opposite maxim, one based on keeping my promise:

M1. Whenever I need money, I should make a sincere promise while borrowing it.

Can I successfully universalize this maxim?

P1. Whenever anyone needs money, that person should make a sincere promise while borrowing it.

Yes, I can universalize M1, for there is nothing self-defeating or contradictory in this. So, it follows, making sincere promises is moral; we can make the maxim of promise-keeping into a universal law.

The Test for Suicide

Some of Kant's illustrations do not fare as well as the duty to keep promises. For instance, he argues that the categorical imperative would prohibit suicide, for we could not successfully universalize the maxim of such an act. If we try to universalize it, we obtain the principle "Whenever it looks like one will experience more pain than pleasure, one ought to kill oneself," which, according to Kant, is a self-contradiction because it would go against the very principle of survival upon which it is based. But whatever the merit of the form of this argument, we could modify the principle to read: "Whenever the pain or suffering of existence erodes the quality of life in such a way as to make nonexistence a preference to suffering existence, one is permitted to commit suicide." Why couldn't this (or something close to it) be universalized? It would cover the rare instances in which no hope is in sight for terminally ill patients or for victims of torture or deep depression, but it would not cover the kinds of suffering and depression most of us experience in the normal course of life. Kant seems unduly absolutist in his prohibition of suicide.

The Test for Neglecting One's Talent

Kant's other two examples of the application of the CI are also questionable. In his third example he claims that we cannot universalize a maxim to refrain from developing our talents. But again, could we not qualify this and stipulate that under certain circumstances it is permissible not to develop our talents? Perhaps Kant is correct, in that if everyone selfishly refrained from developing talents, society would soon degenerate into anarchy. But couldn't one universalize the following maxim, M3?

M3. Whenever I am not inclined to develop a talent and this refraining will not seriously undermine the social order, I may so refrain.

The Test for Refraining from Helping Others

Kant's last example of the way the CI functions regards the situation of not coming to the aid of others whenever I am secure and independent. He claims that I cannot universalize this maxim because I never know whether I will need the help of others at some future time. Is Kant correct about this? Why could I not universalize a maxim never to set myself a goal whose achievement appears to require the cooperation of others? I would have to give up any goal as soon as I realized that cooperation with others was required. In what way is this contradictory or self-defeating? Perhaps it would be selfish and cruel to make this into a universal law, but there seems nothing contradictory or self-defeating in the principle itself. The problems with universalizing selfishness are the same ones we encountered in analyzing egoism, but it's dubious whether Kant's categorical imperative captures what is wrong with egoism. Perhaps he has other weapons that do elucidate what is wrong with egoism. We will return to this later.

Kant thought that he could generate an entire moral law from his categorical imperative. It seems to work with such principles as promise-keeping and truth-telling and a few other maxims, but it doesn't seem to give us all that Kant wanted. It has been objected that Kant's CI is both too wide and too unqualified.

The charge that it is too wide is based on the perception that it seems to justify some actions we might consider trivial or even immoral. Take, for example, principle P:

P. Everyone should always tie one's right shoe before one's left shoe.

Can we universalize P without contradiction? Why not? Just as we universalize that people should drive cars on the right side of the street rather than the left, we could make it a law that everyone should tie the right shoe before the left shoe. But it seems obvious that there would be no point to such a law—it would be trivial. But it is justified by the categorical imperative.

It may be objected that all this counterexample shows is that it may be permissible to live by the principle of tying the right shoe before the left, for we could also universalize the opposite maxim (tying the left before the right) without contradiction. That seems correct.

Another counterexample is offered by Fred Feldman.[11] Maxim M:

M. Whenever I need a term paper for a course and don't feel like writing one, I shall buy a term paper from Research Anonymous and submit it as my own work.

Now we universalize this maxim into a universal principle P:

P. Whenever anyone needs a term paper for a course and doesn't feel like writing one, one should buy one from a suitable source and submit it as one's own.

But this procedure seems to be self-defeating. It would undermine the whole process of academic work, for teachers wouldn't believe that research papers really represented the people who turned them in. Learning would not occur; grades would be meaningless, and so would transcripts; and the entire institution of education would break down—the whole purpose of cheating would be defeated.

But suppose that we made a slight adjustment to M and P, inventing M_1 and P_1:

M_1. When I need a term paper for a course and don't feel like writing one, and no change in the system will occur if I submit a store-bought one, then I shall buy a term paper and submit it as my own work.

P_1. Whenever anyone needs a term paper for a course and doesn't feel like writing it, and no change in the system will occur if one submits a store-bought paper, then one shall buy the term paper and submit it as one's own work.

Does P_1 pass as a legitimate expression of the categorical imperative? It might seem to satisfy the conditions, but Kantian students have pointed out that in order for a principle to be universalizable, or lawlike, one must ensure that it is public.

But if P_1 were public and everyone were encouraged to live by it, then it would be exceedingly difficult to prevent an erosion of the system. Teachers would take precautions against it. Would cheaters have to announce themselves publicly? In sum, the attempt to universalize even this qualified form of cheating would undermine the very institution that makes cheating possible. So P_1 may be a thinly veiled oxymoron: Do what will undermine the educational process in such a way that it doesn't undermine the educational process.

Another type of counterexample might be used to show that the CI refuses to allow us to do things that common sense permits. Suppose I need to flush the toilet. So I formulate my maxim M:

M. At time t_1 I would flush the toilet.

I universalize this maxim:

P. At time t_1 everyone should flush their toilet.

But I cannot will this if I realize that the pressure of millions of toilets flushing at the same time will destroy the nation's plumbing systems, and so I could not then flush the toilet.

The way out of this problem is to qualify the original maxim M to read M*:

M★. Whenever I need to flush the toilet and have no reason to believe that it will set off the impairment or destruction of the community's plumbing system, I may do so.

From this we can universalize to P★:

P★. Whenever anyone needs to flush the toilet and has no reason to believe that it will set off the destruction of the community's plumbing system, he or she may do so.

So Kant seems to be able to respond to some of the objections to his theory.

More serious is the fact that the categorical imperative appears to justify acts that we judge to be horrendously immoral. Suppose I hate people of a certain race, religion, or ethnic group. Suppose it is Americans that I hate and that I am not an American. My maxim is "Let me kill anyone who is American." By the universalizability test we get P2:

P_2. Always kill Americans.

Is there anything contradictory in this injunction? Could we make it into a universal law? Why not? Americans might not like it, but there is no logical contradiction involved in such a principle. Had I been an American when this command was in effect, I would not have been around to write this book, but the world would have survived my loss without too much inconvenience. If I suddenly discover that I am an American, I would have to commit suicide. But as long as I am willing to be consistent, there doesn't seem to be anything wrong with my principle, so far as its being based on the categorical imperative is concerned.

Of course, it would be possible to universalize the opposite—that no one should kill innocent people—but this only shows that either type of action is permissible.

Some may object that Kant presupposed that only rational acts could be universalized. But this won't work, for the CI is supposed to be the criterion for rational action. It may be that when we come to Kant's second formulation of the categorical imperative he will have more ammunition with which to defeat P_2.

Finally, Kant thought that the categorical imperative yielded unqualified absolutes. The rules that the categorical imperative generates are universal and exceptionless. He illustrates this point with regard to truth-telling: Suppose that an innocent man, Mr. Y, comes to your door, begging for asylum, because a group of gangsters is hunting him down in order to kill him. You take the man in and hide him in your third-floor attic. Moments later the gangsters arrive and inquire after the innocent man: "Is Mr. Y in your house?" What should you do? Kant's advice is to tell them the truth: "Yes, he's in my house."[12]

What is Kant's reasoning here? It is simply that the moral law is sacrosanct and exceptionless. It is your duty to obey its commands, not to reason about the likely consequences. You have done your duty: hidden an innocent man and told the truth when asked a straightforward question. You are absolved of any responsibility for the harm that comes to the innocent man. It's not your fault that there are gangsters in the world.

To many of us, this kind of absolutism seems counterintuitive. There are two ways in which we might alter Kant here. The first is simply to write in qualifications to the universal principles, changing the sweeping generalization "Never lie" to the more modest "Never lie, except in order to save an innocent person's life." The trouble with this way of solving the problem is that there seem to be no limits on the qualifications that would need to be attached to the original generalization—for example, "Never lie, *except* to save an innocent person's life (unless trying to save that person's life will undermine the entire social fabric)" or "Never lie, except to save an innocent person's life (unless this will undermine the social fabric) or when lying will spare people great anguish (such as telling a cancer patient the truth about her condition)." And so on. The process seems infinite and time-consuming and thus impractical.

A second way of qualifying the counterintuitive results of the Kantian program is to follow W. D. Ross (mentioned earlier in this chapter) and distinguish between actual and prima facie duties. The prima facie duty that wins out in the comparison is called the *actual duty* or the *all-things-considered duty*. We can apply this distinction to Kant's innocent-man example. First we have the principle L: "Never lie." Next we ask whether any other principle is relevant in this situation, and discover that that is principle P: "Always protect innocent life." But we cannot obey both L and P (we assume for the moment that silence will be a giveaway). We have two general principles; neither of them is to be seen as absolute or nonoverridable, but rather as prima facie. We have to decide which of the two overrides the other, which has greater moral force. This is left up to our considered judgment (or the considered judgment of the reflective moral community). Presumably, we will opt for P over L, meaning that lying to the gangsters becomes our actual duty.

Will this maneuver save the Kantian system? Well, it changes it in a way that Kant might not have liked, but it seems to make sense: It transforms Kant's absolutism into an objectivist system. But now we need to have a separate criterion to adjudicate the conflict between two objective principles.

We conclude, then, that even though the categorical imperative is an important criterion for evaluating moral principles, it still needs supplementation. In itself it is purely formal and leaves out any understanding about the content or material aspect of morality. The categorical imperative, with its universalizability test, constitutes a necessary condition for being a valid moral principle, but it does not provide us with a sufficiency criterion. That is, if any principle is to count as rational or moral, it must be universalizable, it must apply to everyone and to every case that is relevantly similar. If I believe that it's wrong for others to cheat on exams, then unless I can find a reason to believe that I am relevantly different from these others, it is also wrong for me to cheat on exams. If premarital heterosexual coitus is prohibited for women, then it must also be prohibited for men (otherwise, with whom would the men have sex—other men's wives?). But this formal consistency does not tell us whether cheating itself is right or wrong or whether premarital sex is right or wrong. That decision has to do with the material content of morality, and we must use other considerations to help us decide about that.

KANT'S OTHER FORMULATIONS OF THE CATEGORICAL IMPERATIVE

Kant offered three formulations of the categorical imperative. We have already discussed the first formulation; now we will consider the second.

The Principle of Ends

The second formulation, referred to as the *principle of ends,* is: "So act as to treat humanity, whether in your own person or in that of any other, in every case as an end and never as merely a means." Each person qua rational has dignity and profound worth, which entails that he or she must never be exploited or manipulated or merely used as a means to our idea of what is for the general good (or to any other end).

What is Kant's argument for viewing rational beings as having ultimate value? It goes like this: In valuing anything, I endow it with value; it can have no value apart from someone's valuing it. As a valued object, it has *conditional* worth, which is derived from my valuation. On the other hand, the person who values the object is the ultimate source of the object, and as such belongs to a different sphere of beings. We, as valuers, must conceive of ourselves as having *unconditioned* worth. We cannot think of our personhood as a mere thing, for then we would have to judge it to be without any value except that given to it by the estimation of someone else. But then that person would be the source of value, and there is no reason to suppose that one person should have unconditional worth and not another who is relevantly similar. Therefore, we are not mere objects. We have unconditional worth, and so must treat all such value-givers as valuable in themselves—as ends, not merely means. I leave it to you to evaluate the validity of this argument, but most of us do hold that there is something exceedingly valuable about human life.

Kant thought that this formulation, the principle of ends, was substantively identical with his first formulation of the categorical imperative, but most scholars disagree with him. It seems better to treat this principle as a supplement to the first, adding content to the purely formal categorical imperative. In this way, Kant would limit the kinds of maxims that could be universalized. Egoism and the principle P_2 (stated earlier) enjoining the killing of Americans would be ruled out at the very outset, since they involve a violation of the dignity of rational persons. The process would be as follows:

1. Maxim (M) formulated
2. Ends test (Does the maxim involve violating the dignity of rational beings?)
3. Categorical imperative (Can the maxim be universalized?)
4. Successful moral principles survive both tests.

Does the principle of treating persons as ends in themselves fare better than the original version of the categorical imperative? Three problems soon emerge. The first has to do with Kant's setting such a high value on rationality. Why does reason and only reason have intrinsic worth? Who gives this value to rational beings, and how do we know that they have this value? What if we believe that reason has only instrumental value?

Kant's notion of the high inherent value of reason will be more plausible to those who believe that humans are made in the image of God and who interpret that (as has the mainstream of the Judeo-Christian tradition) as entailing that our rational capabilities are the essence of being created in God's image: We have value because God created us with worth, that is, with reason. But even nontheists may be persuaded that Kant is correct in seeing rationality as inherently good. It is one of the things rational beings value more than virtually anything else, and it is a necessary condition to whatever we judge to be a good life or an ideal life (a truly happy life).

Kant seems to be correct in valuing rationality. It does enable us to engage in deliberate and moral reasoning, and it lifts us above lower animals. Where he may have gone wrong is in neglecting other values or states of being that may have moral significance. For example, he believed that we have no obligations to animals, since they are not rational. But surely the utilitarians are correct when they insist that the fact that animals can suffer should constrain our behavior toward them: We ought not cause unnecessary harm. Perhaps Kantians can supplement their system to accommodate this objection.

This brings us to our second problem with Kant's formulation. If we agree that reason is an intrinsic value, then does it not follow that those who have more of this quality should be respected and honored more than those who have less?

1. Reason is an intrinsic good.
2. The more we have of an intrinsically good thing, the better.[13]
3. Therefore, those who have more reason than others are intrinsically better.

Thus, by Kantian logic people should be treated in exact proportion to their ability to reason. So geniuses and intellectuals should be given privileged status in society (as Plato and Aristotle might argue). Kant could deny the second premise and argue that rationality is a threshold quality, but the objector could come back and argue that there really are degrees in ability to use reason, ranging from gorillas and chimpanzees all the way to the upper limits of human genius. Should we treat gorillas and chimps as ends in themselves while still exploiting small babies and severely senile people, since the former do not yet act rationally and the latter have lost what ability they had? If we accept Kantian principles, what should be our view on abortion?

There is a third problem with Kant's view of the dignity of rational beings. Even if we should respect them and treat them as ends, this does not tell us very much. It may tell us not to enslave them or not to act cruelly toward them without a good reason, but it doesn't tell us what to do in conflict situations. For example, what does it tell us to do about a terminally ill patient who wants us to help her die? What does it tell us to do in a war when we are about to aim our gun at an enemy soldier? What does it mean to treat such a rational being as an end? What does it tell us to do with regard to the innocent victim and the gangsters who have just asked us the whereabouts of the victim? What does it tell us about whether we should steal from the pharmacy to procure medicine we can't afford in order to bring healing to a loved one? It's hard to see how the notion of the kingdom of ends helps us much in these situations. In fairness to Kant, however, we must say that virtually every moral system has trouble with dilemmas, and that it might be possible to supplement Kantianism to solve some of them.

The Principle of Autonomy

The final formulation of the CI invokes the *principle of autonomy:* Every rational being is able to regard oneself as a maker of universal law. That is, we do not need an external authority—be it God, the state, our culture, or anyone else—to determine the nature of the moral law. We can discover this for ourselves. And, the Kantian faith proclaims, everyone who is ideally rational will legislate exactly the same universal moral principles.

The opposite of autonomy is *heteronomy:* The heteronomous person is one whose actions are motivated by the authority of others, whether it be religion, the state, his or her parents, or a peer group. The following illustration may serve as an example of the difference between these two states of being.

In the early 1960s Stanley Milgram of Yale University conducted a series of social psychological experiments aimed at determining the degree to which the ordinary citizen was obedient to authority. Volunteers from all walks of life were recruited to participate in "a study of memory and learning." Two people at a time were taken into the laboratory. The experimenter explained that one was to play the role of the teacher and the other the role of the learner. The "teacher" was put in a separate room from which he or she could see the "learner" through a window. The "teacher" was instructed to ask the "learner" to choose the correct correlate to a given word, and the learner was to choose from a set of options. If the "learner" got the correct word, then fine, they moved on to the next word. But if the learner chose the wrong word, he or she was punished with an electric shock. The "teacher" was given a sample shock of 45 volts just to get the feeling of the game. Each time the "learner" made a mistake the shock was increased by 15 volts (starting at 15 volts and continuing to 450 volts). The meter was marked with verbal designations: slight shock, moderate shock, strong shock, very strong shock, intense shock, extreme-intensity shock, danger: severe shock, and XXX.

As the experiment proceeded, the "learner" would generally be heard grunting at the 75-volt shock, crying out at 120 volts, begging for release at 150 volts, and screaming in agony at 270 volts. Around 300 volts there was usually dead silence.

Now, unbeknownst to the "teacher," the "learner" was not actually experiencing any shocks; the "learners" were really trained actors simulating agony.

The results of the experiment were astounding: Whereas Milgram and associates had expected that only a small proportion of citizens would comply with the instructions, actually 60 percent were completely obedient and carried out the experiment to the very end. Only a handful refused to participate in the experiment at all, once they discovered what it involved. Some 35 percent left at various stages. Milgram's experiments were later replicated in Munich, Germany, where 85 percent of the subjects were found to be completely "obedient to authority."

There are two ways in which the problems of autonomy and heteronomy are illustrated by this example. In the first place, the experiment seems to show that the average citizen acts less autonomously than we might expect. People are basically heteronomous, herd followers. But in the second place, there is the question about whether Milgram should have subjected people to these experiments. Was he violating their autonomy and treating them as means (rather than ends) in deceiving them in the way he did? Perhaps a utilitarian would have an easier time justifying these experiments than a Kantian.

In any case, for Kant it is our ability to use reason in universalizing the maxims of our actions that sets rational beings apart from nonrational beings. As such, rational beings belong to a kingdom of ends. Kant thought that each of us—as a fully rational, autonomous legislator—would be able to reason through to exactly the same set of moral principles, the ideal moral law.

KANT'S ETHICS AND RELIGION

Although Kant thought of ethics as fully autonomous, there is a deeply religious dimension to his system. Indeed, it is hard to separate Kant's system from the Judeo-Christian faith, which was his childhood heritage. His views of the unconditional worth and equal dignity of humanity, of natural purposes in nature and human nature, and of the ultimate justification of morality all seem deeply rooted in religious faith. We have already mentioned these first two points. Now let's consider briefly how religion provides an ultimate justification for the moral point of view.

First we must distinguish between the nature of ethics and its ultimate justification. With regard to the nature of ethics, Kant held to the doctrine of the autonomy of ethics. There could be no difference between valid religious ethics and valid philosophical ethics: Both God and humanity have to obey the same rational principles, and reason is sufficient to guide us to these principles.

Kant's system exalts ethics to an intrinsic good; indeed, we ought to do our duty for no other reason than that it is our duty. It constitutes the *summum bonum,* the supreme good. As such it is related to religion; it is our duty to God, since God desires that we attain to the highest good. God's commands are exactly those of morality, so there can be no conflict between morality and religion.

God loves the virtuous, and will finally reward the virtuous with happiness in proportion to their virtue. In fact, God and immortality are necessary postulates of ethics; without them ethics would not be fully justified.

Immortality is a necessary postulate in this way: We are commanded by the moral law to be morally perfect. Since "ought" implies "can," we must be *able* to reach moral perfection. But we cannot attain perfection in this life, for the task is an infinite one. So there must be an afterlife in which we continue to make progress toward this ideal.

God is a necessary postulate because there must be someone to enforce the moral law. That is, to be completely justified the moral law must end in a just recompense of happiness in accordance to virtue, what Kant refers to as the "complete good." From the standpoint of eternity, the complete good requires that happiness should be proportioned to virtue in such a way that those who deserve happiness receive it in proportion to their moral merit. Likewise, evil people must be punished with unhappiness in proportion to their vice. This harmonious correlation of virtue and happiness does not happen in this life, so it must happen in the next life. Thus, there must be a God, acting as judge and enforcer of the moral law, without which the moral law would be unjustified.

Kant is not saying that we can *prove* the existence of God or that we ought to be moral *in order* to be happy. Rather, the idea of God serves as a completion of our ordinary ideas of ethics.

Kant's moral theology has been criticized as being inconsistent with his overall system. Arthur Schopenhauer (1788–1860) thought Kant's moral theology was antithetical to Kant's idea of moral autonomy and the notion that morality is not prudence. If these religious notions are accepted, morality becomes the supreme act of prudence. Kant's defenders respond that criticisms such as Schopenhauer's miss the mark by confusing the reasons for actions with a total justification of the enterprise of morality. One should not take prudence into account in deciding what to do, but one must have faith in the divine harmony in order for the enterprise of morality to be fully justified.

Other critics point out that we can use Kant's argument against him. If his thesis is true, and the justification of morality depends on the existence of God, then if we find no convincing evidence for the existence of God, we are justified in rejecting morality! Yet many people are more confident of their moral beliefs than of their religious views, so that it would seem wiser to separate religion from morality and to free the justification of ethics from the necessity of religion. We shall examine this issue more fully in Chapter 10.

A RECONCILIATION PROJECT

In Chapters 6 and 7 we examined two radically different types of moral theories. Some people seem to gravitate to a deontological position and some to a utilitarian position, but many people find themselves dissatisfied with both positions. Though they see something valid in each type of theory, at the same time there is something deeply troubling about each. Utilitarianism seems to catch the spirit of the purpose of morality (human flourishing and the amelioration of suffering) but undercuts justice in a way that is counterintuitive. Deontological systems seem right in their emphasis on the importance of rules and the principle of justice but tend to become rigid or to lose focus on the central purposes of morality.

One philosopher, William Frankena of the University of Michigan, has responded to this sense of bifurcation by attempting to reconcile the two types of theories in an interesting way. He calls his position "mixed deontological ethics," for it is basically rule-centered but in such a way as to take account of the teleological aspect of utilitarianism.[14] Utilitarians are right about the purpose of morality: All moral action involves doing good or alleviating evil. However, utilitarians are wrong to think that they can measure these amounts or that they are always obligated to bring about the "greatest balance of good over evil," as articulated by the principle of utility.

In place of the principle of utility Frankena puts forth a near relative, the *principle of beneficence,* which calls on us to strive to do good without demanding that we be able to measure or weigh good and evil. Under the principle of beneficence he lists four hierarchically arranged subprinciples contained within the main principle:

1. One ought not to inflict evil or harm.

2. One ought to prevent evil or harm.

3. One ought to remove evil.

4. One ought to do or promote good.

In some sense, subprinciple 1 takes precedence over 2, 2 over 3, and 3 over 4, other things being equal. These are prima facie principles that may be overridden by the principle of justice.

The *principle of justice* is the second principle in Frankena's system. It involves treating every person with equal respect because that is what each is due. To quote John Rawls, "Each person possesses an inviolability founded on justice that even the welfare of society as a whole cannot override.... The rights secured by justice are not subject to political bargaining or to the calculus of social interests."[15] There is always a presumption of equal treatment, unless a strong case can be made for overriding this principle. So, even though both the principle of beneficence and the principle of justice are prima facie principles, the principle of justice enjoys a certain hegemony, a priority. All other duties can be derived from these two fundamental principles.

Of course, the problem with this kind of two-principle system is that we have no clear principle for adjudicating between them in cases of moral conflict. In such cases, Frankena opts for an intuitional approach: We need to use our intuition whenever the two rules conflict in such a way as to leave us undecided on whether beneficence should override justice. Perhaps we cannot decisively solve every moral problem, but we can solve most of our problems successfully and make progress toward refining our subprinciples in a way that will allow us progressively to reduce the undecidable areas. At least we have improved on strict deontological ethics by outlining a system that takes into account our intuitions in deciding complex moral issues.[16]

NOTES

1. Joseph Butler, *Five Sermons* (Liberal Arts Press, 1949), p. 45. Actually, Butler's position seems to be one of divine indirect utilitarianism: God designed us in such a way that by acting on conscience, independent of consequentialist considerations, we will actually bring about more happiness than if we sought directly to maximize happiness in the world. See Robert Louden, "Butler's Divine Utilitarianism" (unpublished manuscript), for a cogent defense of this interpretation of Butler.

2. R. M. Hare, *The Language of Morals* (Oxford University Press, 1952), p. 60 f.

3. W. D. Ross, *The Right and the Good* (Oxford University Press, 1930), pp. 39–41.

4. Ross, *The Right and the Good,* p. 21.

5. Immanuel Kant, *Fundamental Principles of the Metaphysics of Ethics,* trans. T. K. Abbott (London: Longman's, 1965), section 1, pp. 10–11. I have slightly revised the translation.

6. Kant, *The Right and the Good*, p. 6. An excellent example of a Kantian sense of duty comes from the Danish existentialist Soren Kierkegaard (1813–1855):

When I was five years old I was sent to school. I made my appearance at school, was introduced to the teacher, and then was given as my lesson for the following day the first ten lines of Balle's *Lesson Book* which I was to learn by heart. Every other impression was then obliterated from my soul, only my task stood out vividly before it. As a child I had a good memory, so I had soon learned my lesson. My sister had heard me recite it several times and affirmed that I knew it. I went to bed, and before I fell asleep I catechized myself once more; I fell asleep with the firm purpose of reading the lesson over the following morning. I awoke at five o'clock, got dressed, got hold of my lesson-book, and read it again. At this moment everything stands as vividly before my eyes as if it had occurred yesterday. To me it was as if heaven and earth might collapse if I did not learn my lesson, and on the other hand as if, even if heaven and earth were to collapse, this would not exempt me from doing what was assigned to me, from learning my lesson. . . . I had only one duty, that of learning my lesson, and yet I can trace my whole ethical view of life to this impression. [Soren Kierkegaard, *Either/Or,* Vol. II, trans. Walter Lowrie (Anchor Books, 1959), pp. 271 f].

7. Kant, *Fundamental Principles,* p. 46.

8. Kant, *Fundamental Principles,* p. 46.

9. A note on consequences in Kant: Universal principles may be known a priori, independent of their consequences. This does not mean that Kant entirely ignores consequences— he doesn't. We may take them into account in order to apply a maxim (to see if it qualifies as a moral law), but not in order to establish the validity of the principle or to make an exception to it. We should not ask what the consequences of this particular principle would be, but rather what the consequences of everyone's acting on this principle would be. This would show whether the law somehow yielded a self-defeating state or an impossible situation. If it did, the principle was proscribed; if it didn't, it was permitted.

10. Kant, *Fundamental Principles,* p. 19.

11. Fred Feldman, *Introductory Ethics* (Prentice Hall, 1978), pp. 114 f.

12. Immanuel Kant, "On a Supposed Right to Lie from Altruistic Motives" (1797), in *Immanuel Kant: Critique of Practical Reason and Other Writings in Moral Philosophy,* ed. Lewis Beck White (Garland Press, 1976).

13. One of my students, Scott Morris, has pointed out that the proposition "The more of a good thing, the better" is not a necessary truth. Food and sex are good, but you can have too much of these good things. This is true, but the proposition seems to work better with intrinsic goods, such as love, happiness, knowledge, health, and reason. Though even here we might argue that if the intrinsically good thing were to crowd out another intrinsically good thing, it would serve a bad purpose (e.g., in our quest for knowledge or aesthetic excellence we might neglect our duties to family or friends).

14. William Frankena, *Ethics,* 2nd ed. (Prentice-Hall, 1973), pp. 43–53.

15. John Rawls, *A Theory of Justice* (Harvard University Press, 1971), p. 3.

16. See Robert Louden, *Morality and Moral Theory* (Oxford University Press, 1991) for a sophisticated contemporary account of morality that integrates Frankena's insights into a Kantian framework. My thanks to Ed Langerack, Robert Louden and Walter Schaller for their helpful critical comments on an earlier version of this chapter.

FOR FURTHER REFLECTION

1. Why does Kant believe that the good will is the only thing that is good without qualification? What are his supporting reasons? Do you agree with him? Can you see any problems with his theory at this point?

2. Do you think that the Kantian argument that combines the categorical imperative with the notion of the principle of ends is successful? Is the notion of the principle of ends clear enough to be significantly action-guiding? Does it cover some intelligent animals but not severely retarded people? Are fetuses and infants included in it? Why or why not?

3. Note the comments of anti-Kantian Richard Taylor:

   If I were ever to find, as I luckily never have, a man who assured me that he really *believed* Kant's metaphysical morals, and that he modeled his own conduct and his relations with others after those principles, then my incredulity and distrust of him as a human being could not be greater than if he told me he regularly drowned children just to see them squirm. [Richard Taylor, *Good and Evil* (Macmillan, 1970), p. xii].

   He and others have criticized Kant for being too rigid. Many people use the idea of moral duty to keep themselves and others from enjoying life and showing mercy. Do you think that there is a basis for this criticism?

4. Kant has been criticized for stifling spontaneous moral feelings in favor of the deliberate will, so that the person who successfully exercises the will in overcoming a temptation is superior to the person who isn't tempted at all but acts rightly spontaneously. For example, the person who, through a strenuous act of the will, just barely resists the temptation to shoplift would be, by this criterion, morally superior to the person who isn't tempted to shoplift at all. Based on your analysis of Kant, do you think this is a fair interpretation of Kant? If so, does it undermine his ethics?

5. Many people besides Richard Taylor have a negative reaction to Kant's moral theory. Evaluate the following quotation from Oliver Wendell Holmes, Jr:

   From this it is easy to proceed to the Kantian injunction to regard every human being as an end in himself and not as a means. I confess that I rebel at once. If we want conscripts, we march them up to the front with bayonets in their rear to die for a cause in which perhaps they do not believe. The enemy we treat not even as a means but as an obstacle to be abolished, if so it may be. I feel no pangs of conscience over either step, and naturally am slow to accept a theory that seems to be contradicted by practices that I approve. [Oliver Wendell Holmes, Jr., *Collected Legal Papers* (Harcourt, Brace and Jovanovich, 1920), p. 340]

6. Review the section on the principle of autonomy. What do you make of the Milgram experiments? Would a Kantian condemn such experiments as treating individuals "merely as means" rather than as ends in themselves? Do you think that the information derived from the experiments justified the experiments?

7. Evaluate Frankena's reconciliation project. How plausible is his attempt to reduce morality to two fundamental intuitions? Can you exercise moral reasoning without appeal to intuitions at some point in your deliberations? Explain your answer.

FOR FURTHER READING

Acton, Harry. *Kant's Moral Philosophy.* Macmillan, 1970.

Baier, Kurt. *The Moral Point of View.* Cornell University Press, 1958.

Broad, C. D. *Five Types of Ethical Theory.* Routledge & Kegan Paul, 1930.

Donagan, Alan. *The Theory of Morality.* University of Chicago Press, 1977. A comprehensive deontological account of ethical theory.

Feldman, Fred. *Introductory Ethics.* Prentice-Hall, 1978, Chapters 7 and 8. A clear and critical exposition.

Gewirth, Alan. *Reason and Morality.* University of Chicago Press, 1978. Important but advanced.

Harris, C. E. *Applying Moral Theories.* Wadsworth, 1986, Chapter VII. An excellent exposition of contemporary deontological theories, especially of Gewirth's work.

Kant, Immanuel. *Critique of Practical Reason,* trans. Lewis White Beck. Bobbs-Merrill, 1956.

Kant, Immanuel. *Foundations of the Metaphysics of Morals,* trans. Lewis White Beck. Bobbs-Merrill, 1959.

Kant, Immanuel. *Lectures on Ethics,* trans. Louis Infield. Harper Torchbooks, 1963.

Louden, Robert. *Morality and Moral Theory* (Oxford University Press, 1991). A sophisticated contemporary account combining Kantian and virtue-based ethics.

O'Neill, Onora. *Acting on Principle: An Essay on Kantian Ethics.* Columbia University Press, 1975.

O'Neill, Onora. *Constructions of Reason.* Cambridge University Press, 1989.

Raphael, D. D. *Moral Philosophy.* Oxford University Press, 1981, Chapter 6.

Ross, W. D. *Kant's Ethical Theory.* Clarendon Press, 1954.

Ward, Keith. *The Development of Kant's Views of Ethics.* Blackwell's, 1972.

Wolff, Robert P. *The Autonomy of Reason: A Commentary on Kant's "Groundwork of the Metaphysics of Morals."* Harper & Row, 1973.

8

Virtue-Based
Ethical Systems

Suppose, however, that in articulating the problems of morality the ordering of evaluative concepts has been misconceived by the spokesman of modernity and more particularly of liberalism; suppose that we need to attend to virtues in the first place in order to understand the function and authority of rules.

ALASDAIR MACINTYRE, *AFTER VIRTUE*

Morality is internal. The moral law ... has to be expressed in the form "be this," not in the form "do this." ... [T]he true moral law says "hate not," instead of "kill not." ... [T]he only mode of stating the moral law must be as a rule of character.

LESLIE STEPHENS, *THE SCIENCE OF ETHICS*

John hears that 100,000 people are starving in Ethiopia. He feels deep sorrow about this and sends $100 of his hard-earned money to a famine relief project in Ethiopia. Joan hears the same news but doesn't feel anything. However, out of a sense of duty she sends $100 of her hard-earned money to a famine relief project in Ethiopia.

Jack and Jill each have the opportunity to embezzle $1 million from the bank at which they work. Jill never even considers embezzling; the possibility is not an option for her. Jack wrestles valiantly with the temptation, almost succumbs to it, but through a grand effort of will finally succeeds in resisting the temptation.

Who, if anyone, in each of these cases is more moral?

Whereas most ethical theories have been either duty-oriented or action-oriented, that is, either deontological (from the Greek for "duty") or teleological, there is a third tradition, which goes back to Plato and, especially, Aristotle, and which receives support in the writings of the Epicureans, the Stoics, and members of the early Christian Church. I refer to the *virtue-based systems,* sometimes called *aretaic ethics* (from the Greek *arete,* which we translate "excellence" or "virtue"). Rather than seeing the heart of ethics in actions or duties, virtue ethics centers in the heart of the agent—in his or her character. Whereas action-governed (rule-governed) ethics emphasizes *doing,* virtue (agent) ethics emphasizes *being,* being a certain type of person who will no doubt manifest his or her being in actions or nonactions. For traditional duty-based ethics the question is: What should I do? For virtue ethics the question is: What sort of person should I become?

Virtue ethics seeks to produce excellent persons, who act well out of spontaneous goodness and serve as examples to inspire others. It seeks to create people like Moses, Confucius, Socrates, Jesus, Buddha, St. Francis, Abraham Lincoln, John Stuart Mill, Albert Schweitzer, Mohandas Gandhi, and Mother Teresa—people who light up our moral landscape as jewels who shine in their own light. There is a teleological aspect in virtue ethics, but it differs from the kind usually found in utilitarianism, which asks what sort of action will maximize happiness or utility. The aretaic concept of teleology focuses, rather, on the *goal* of life: living well and achieving excellence.

In this chapter we will examine the nature of the virtues and the possibility of a virtue-based ethic within the context of the ongoing battle between deontic and virtue ethics. First we will look at four charges brought against rule-governed ethics by the aretaic camp. Then we will examine the nature of virtue ethics. And finally we will address the question of the relationship between deontic systems and aretaic systems: Do virtue ethics supplement action-based ethical systems, or can they be entirely accounted for by action-based systems?

THE ARETAIC CRITIQUE OF ACTION-BASED (DEONTIC) ETHICAL SYSTEMS

Virtue ethics has reemerged as a major ethical theory, largely due to a dissatisfaction with rule-governed (action-centered) ethical systems. Since 1958 philosophers such as Elizabeth Anscombe, Philippa Foot, Alasdair Mac-Intyre, Bernard Mayo, Edmund Pincoffs, and Richard Taylor have become disenchanted with the promises of the mainstream of the modern ethical tradition and have argued for a return to a virtue-based theory.[1] Four specific criticisms have been lodged against rule-governed ethics: (1) they lack a motivational component; (2) they are founded on a theological-legal model that is no longer appropriate; (3) they ignore the spiritual dimension of morality; and (4) they overemphasize the principle of autonomy and neglect the communal context of morality. Virtue ethics are thought to make up for these deficiencies. Let us look more closely at these charges.

Action-Based Ethics Lack a Motivational Component

Critics claim that action-based ethics are uninspiring, even boring—and largely negative. They fail to motivate or inspire to action. Ethics becomes a sort of mental plumbing, moral casuistry, a set of hair-splitting distinctions that somehow loses track of the purpose of morality altogether. But what good are such rules without the dynamo of character that propels the rules to action?

That deontological systems may be uninspiring is illustrated by their largely negative nature. Most of the commandments and rules in such systems are inherently negative: "Thou shalt not _____!" As John Stuart Mill complained about the so-called Christian morality of the Victorian Age:

> Christian morality (so-called) has all the characters of a reaction; it is, in great part, a protest against Paganism. Its ideal is negative rather than positive, passive rather than active; Innocence rather than Nobleness; Abstinence from Evil, rather than energetic Pursuit of the Good; in its precepts "Thou shalt not" predominates unduly over "Thou shalt." Whatever exists of magnanimity, highmindedness, personal dignity, even the sense of honor, is derived from the purely human, not the religious part of our education, and never could have grown out of a standard of ethics in which the only worth, professedly recognized, is that of obedience.[2]

There is something unsatisfactory about a morality that is so disproportionately defined in terms of "Thou shalt nots," stressing innocence rather than an "energetic Pursuit of the Good." Deontological and contractual systems (such as Hobbes') focus on an egoistic, minimal morality whose basic principles seem to be more preventive than positive. The only sure principle is a reciprocal duty to do no harm. This sort of theory places a very low value on morality, judging it primarily as a necessary evil. The aretaist rejects this judgment, seeing morality as an intrinsically worthwhile activity.

Action-Based Ethics Are Founded on a Theological-Legal Model That Is No Longer Appropriate

Moral language in traditional schemes usually has a structure that resembles that of law. Typically, the notions of right and wrong occur within the structure of a legal context in which there is a clear authority. Traditional, natural law ethics used this model with integrity, for it saw moral principles as analogous to law and God as analogous to the sovereign. Now, however, ethics has been detached from its theological moorings. It has become an autonomous activity, leaving the legal model without an analogue, so that it is now an incoherent metaphor. The virtue ethicist rejects this model. Rather than spend time on moral hair-splitting and puzzle-solving, ethics should help us develop admirable characters that will generate the kinds of insights needed for the exigencies of life.

In this regard, the legalistic bent of modern moral theory has the effect of undermining the spirit of morality: "Morality was made for man, not man for morality." Rules often get in the way of kindness and spontaneous generosity. An illustration of this is the following passage from Mark Twain's *Huckleberry Finn,* in which Huck sees that his duty is to obey the law and turn in his black friend, the runaway slave Jim. Huck's principles tell him to report Jim to the authorities:

> Conscience says to me: "What had poor Miss Watson done to you, that you could see her nigger go off right under your eyes and never say one single word? What did that poor old woman do to you, that you could treat her so mean?" I got to feeling so mean and miserable I most wished I was dead. . . . My conscience got to stirring me up hotter than ever, until at last I says to it: "Let up on me—it ain't too late, yet—I'll paddle ashore at first light and tell."

Huck intends to report Jim, and soon has the opportunity when two slave-hunters ask him whether the man on his raft is black. But something in his character prevents Huck from turning Jim in. Virtue ethicists point out that Huck does the right thing because of his character, not because of his principles, and that sometimes, at least, our moral principles actually militate against deeper moral action that arises out of character.[3]

Action-Based Ethics Often Ignore the Spiritual Dimension of Ethics

Action-based ethics reduce all moral judgment to judgments about actions ("deontic judgments") and neglect the spiritual qualities of gratitude, self-respect, sympathy, having one's emotions in proper order, and aspiring to become a certain kind of person.

Consider the case of Jack and Jill mentioned at the beginning of this chapter. Both have the opportunity to embezzle. For Jack it is a strenuous effort of the will that enables him to resist the temptation to embezzle, whereas for Jill the temptation does not even arise. She automatically rejects the fleeting thought as out of range of her character. Now, it might be said that Jack has the important virtue of considerable strength of will, but lacks the virtue of deep integrity that Jill possesses. Whereas stringent action-based ethics (such as Kant's which puts the emphasis on conscientiousness, or doing one's duty for duty's sake) would say that Jack is the only one of the two who is moral, virtue ethics would say that Jill is the superior moral being. She has something good about her character that Jack lacks.

Or consider the case of John and Joan also mentioned at the chapter's opening. Both send money to charity, but John does it with a deep feeling of sorrow for the famine victims, whereas Joan does it simply out of a sense of duty. The virtue ethicist would argue that John has the right moral feelings, whereas Joan is merely a cold, calculating moral machine who lacks the appropriate warmth of judgment toward the starving.

Virtue ethicists often cite Kant's theory (see Chapter 7) as a paradigm of an antivirtue ethics. They point out that an examination of Kant's extreme action-centered approach highlights the need for a virtue alternative. For Kant, natural goodness is morally irrelevant. The fact that you actually want to help someone (because you like them or just like doing good deeds) is of no moral importance. In fact, because of the emphasis put on the good will (doing duty for duty's sake), it seems that Kant's logic would force him to conclude that you are actually moral in proportion to the amount of temptation that you have to resist in performing your duty: For little temptation you receive little moral credit; if you experience great temptation, you receive great moral credit for overcoming it.

To virtue ethicists this is preposterous. Taken to its logical conclusion, the homicidal maniac who always just barely succeeds in resisting his perpetual temptation to kill is actually the most glorious saint, surpassing the "natural saint" who does good just because of a good character. True goodness is to spontaneously, cheerfully, and enjoyably do what is good. As Aristotle said,

> We may even go so far as to state that the man who does not enjoy performing noble actions is not a good man at all. Nobody would call a man just who does not enjoy acting justly, nor generous who does not enjoy generous actions, and so on.[4]

It is not the hounded neurotic who barely manages to control himself before each passing temptation, but the natural saint—the one who does good out of habit and from the inner resources of good character—who is the morally superior person.

Action-Based Ethics Overemphasize Autonomy and Neglect the Communal Context of Ethics

This criticism, set forth by Alasdair MacIntyre in *After Virtue* (1981), claims that rule-governed ethics is a symptom of the Enlightenment, which exaggerated the principle of autonomy, that is, the ability of each person to arrive at a moral code by reason alone. In fact, all moral codes are rooted in practices that themselves are rooted in traditions or forms of life. We do not make moral decisions as rational atoms in a vacuum, and it is sheer ideological blindness that allows this distorted perception. MacIntyre does not want to embrace relativism. We can discover better ways of living, but they will probably be founded on an account of what the good life is and what a good community is.

It is in communities that such virtues as loyalty, natural affection, spontaneous sympathy, and shared concerns arise and sustain the group. It is out of this primary loyalty (to family and friends and community) that the proper dispositions arise that flow out to the rest of humanity. Hence, moral psychology is more important than traditional ethics has usually recognized. Seeing how people actually learn to be moral and how they are inspired to act morally is vital to moral theory itself, and this, it seems, has everything to do with the virtues.

In sum, rule-governed systems are uninspiring and unmotivating, negative, improperly legalistic, neglectful of the spiritual dimension, overly rationalistic, and atomistic. Against this background of dissatisfaction with traditional moral theory, virtue ethics has reasserted itself as offering something that captures the essence of the moral point of view.

THE NATURE OF VIRTUE ETHICS

Virtue ethics says that it is important not only to do the right thing, but also to have the requisite dispositions, motivations, and emotions in being good and doing right. It is important that normally we are not even tempted to steal, lie, or cheat and that normally we enjoy doing good because we are good. Virtue ethics is not only about action but about emotions, character, and moral habit. As Richard Taylor puts it, it is an ethics of aspiration rather than an ethics of duty.[5] It calls us to aspire to be an ideal person.

The virtues are excellences of character, trained behavioral dispositions that result in habitual acts. Traditionally, they have been divided into two types: moral and nonmoral virtues, the criterion of difference being whether they are intuitive or whether they are tied to moral principles.[6]

1. *Moral virtues:* honesty, benevolence, nonmalevolence, fairness, kindness, conscientiousness, gratitude, and so forth

2. *Nonmoral virtues:* courage, optimism, rationality, self-control, patience, endurance, industry, musical talent, cleanliness, wit, and so forth

The exact classification of various virtues is debatable. Courage is sometimes in the "moral" category and virtues such as kindness (as opposed to impartial benevolence) might fit into either category. The moral virtues are more closely associated with what has been deemed essential for the moral life and incompatible with the immoral life; but the distinction seems rough and inexact, for many of the "moral" virtues could be used for bad purposes (e.g., the benevolent person who has a penchant for making things worse). The nonmoral virtues generally are considered as contributing to the moral life but also as more easily expropriated for immoral purposes (e.g., the courageous criminal who is more dangerous than the cowardly one).

Although most virtue systems do not deny that there are principles of action that serve as action guides (at least as rules of thumb), these entities are not the essence of morality. Likewise, even though it is sometimes appropriate to reason about what to do, such reasoning or deliberating should also give significant attention to feelings such as sympathy and loyalty. The primary focus is not on abstract reason but on ideal types of persons or on actual ideal persons. Discovering the proper moral example and imitating that person or ideal type thus replace casuistic reason as the most significant aspects of the moral life. Eventually, the apprenticelike training in virtue gained by imitating the ideal model results in a virtuous person who spontaneously does what is good.

Let us look more closely at this *exemplar model* of virtue ethics. As just mentioned, there are two different ways this comes into focus: either through an examination of ideal types of persons or through following someone who is an ideal type. We shall examine each of these in turn.

The Ideal Type: Aristotle's *Nicomachean Ethics*

In Aristotle's classic work on the virtues, written more than three centuries before Christ, the virtues are simply those characteristics that enable individuals to live well in communities. In order to achieve a state of well-being (*eudaimonia,* meaning "happiness" or "human flourishing"), proper social institutions are necessary. Thus the moral person cannot really exist apart from a flourishing political setting that enables him or her to develop the requisite virtues for the good life. For this reason ethics is considered a branch of politics.

For Aristotle, humanity has an essence, or function. Just as it is the function of a doctor to cure the sick and restore health, the function of a ruler to govern society well, and the function of a knife to cut well, so it is the function of humans to use reason in pursuit of the good life (*eudaimonia*). The virtues indicate the kind of moral–political characteristics necessary for people to attain happiness.

After locating ethics as a part of politics, Aristotle explains that the moral virtues are different from the intellectual ones. Whereas the intellectual virtues may be taught directly, the moral ones must be lived in order to be learned. By living well we acquire the right habits. These habits are in fact the virtues. The virtues are to be sought as the best guarantee to the happy life. But, again, happiness requires that we be lucky enough to live in a flourishing state. The morally virtuous life consists in living in moderation, according to the "Golden Mean." By the "Golden Mean" Aristotle means that the virtues are a mean between excess and deficiency (e.g., courage is the mean between cowardice and foolhardiness; liberality is the mean between stinginess and unrestrained giving):

> We can experience fear, confidence, desire, anger, pity, and generally any kind of pleasure and pain either too much or too little, and in either case not properly. But to experience all this at the right time, toward the right objects, toward the right people, for the right reason, and in the right manner—that is the mean and the best course, the course that is the mark of virtue.[7]

Aristotle himself was an elitist who believed that people have unequal abilities to be virtuous: Some are endowed with great ability, but others lack it altogether; some people are worthless, natural slaves.[8] External circumstances could prevent even those capable of developing moral dispositions from reaching the goal of happiness. The moral virtues are a necessary but not a sufficient condition for happiness. One must, in addition to being virtuous, be healthy, wealthy, wise, and have good fortune.

What seems so remarkable to contemporary ethicists is that Aristotle hardly mentions principles. It wasn't that he thought them unnecessary; they are implied in what he says. For example, his condemnation of adultery may be read as a principle ("Thou shalt not commit adultery").

Aristotle seems to think that such activities are inherently and obviously bad, so that it is laboring the point to speak of a rule against adultery or against killing innocent persons. What is emphasized in place of principles is the importance of a good upbringing, of good habits, of self-control, of courage and character, without which the ethical life is impossible.[9] A person of moral excellence cannot help doing good—it is as natural as the change of seasons or the rotation of the planets.

The Ideal Individual

Most of us learn by watching others and imitating them; this is a hallmark of virtue ethics. Rules cut up moral reality in fragmented and unnatural ways, but lives exhibit appropriate attitudes and dispositions in holistic fashion. The lives of Socrates, Jesus, Gandhi, and Mother Teresa provide examples of possibilities of moral excellence and inspire us to become ideal types.

In an influential article, philosopher Susan Wolf has argued that moral saints are unattractive because they lack the "ability to enjoy the enjoyable in life" and are so "very, very nice" that they must be "dull-witted or humorless or bland." Their lives are "strangely barren."[10] But I find nothing "dull-witted or humorless or bland" about the lives of Jesus, Gandhi, Martin Luther King, Jr., and Mother Teresa. I see nothing "strangely barren" about Jesus' embodying the spirit of love, putting high altruism to practice as never before seen, accepting the pariahs of society and bringing out their innate dignity; about Gandhi's fearlessly confronting the British Empire in the name of justice, his "quiet and determined voice" saying to the Indian people, "Be not afraid," and giving them courage; about Martin Luther King, Jr.—who for all his venality comes close to sainthood—standing quietly and courageously praying for his enemies while they are about to unleash police dogs on him and his followers; about those incredible (often unnamed) prisoners of Auschwitz who shared their food and precious possessions and who refused to be dehumanized by Nazi barbarities; about the Catholic priest who—when every other victim had been crushed by the brainwashing and torture of a Chinese Communist attempt to recondition people—alone survived, a peaceful, praying paragon of virtue; or about Mother Teresa, who spent her days healing the wounds and saving the lives of disease-ridden homeless in the stench-filled slums of Calcutta. These are people who have reached a deeper way of living, who embody the Good in ways that far surpass our ordinary expressions of morality, as the sun's light outshines that of a flickering candle.

Wolf says the saints are boring when compared to such "interesting" and "attractive" people as Katherine Hepburn, Paul Newman, Fred Astaire, and Nasta Rostov. But perhaps what we find interesting or boring is more a function of our moral education and development or appreciation than it is attributable to any saints or moral heroes. Is it not our own fault if we do not see their inherent beauty? And yet these saints and moral heroes do more than merely inspire our admiration. In them we have living proof that a higher way of life is available to each of us. They shame us for being satisfied with our spiritual mediocrity. They challenge us to aspire to moral heights. The lesson of the exemplars is: "If these humans can overcome temptation and live a deeply moral life, then so can I."

Perhaps no figure has served as an exemplar for more people in Western culture than Jesus of Nazareth.[11] An example of how his image has helped form the moral conscience of individuals is related in the biography of agnostic ethicist G. E. Moore. As Moore's biographer, Paul Levy, puts it:

> The habit of examining one's conscience by asking oneself "What would Jesus do?" is conducive to the frame of mind required to enable one to ask oneself "What is the right (or the good) thing to do?" And it is only a short step from asking oneself what Jesus would do, to the realization that one is not asking an historical question such as "What in fact did Jesus do?", but a question that means "What would Jesus have done in these circumstances?" In the end...he is appealing to the idea of Jesus as a perfectly moral human being to give him ethical standards.[12]

The saints and moral heroes are the salt by which the world is preserved.

TYPES OF RELATIONSHIPS BETWEEN VIRTUE ETHICS AND ACTION ETHICS

There are three basic relationships between principles and virtues in the history of ethical theory. All of them are positions held today. In this section and the following we will examine these positions. After each relationship listing I have set the names of some contemporary philosophers who might be interpreted as espousing the position in question.[13]

1. **Pure Aretaic Ethics.** The virtues are dominant and have intrinsic value. Moral principles or duties are derived from the virtues. For example, if we claim that we have a duty to be just or beneficent, we must discover the virtues of fairness and benevolence in the good person.

This view, attributed by some to Aristotle, is held by Philippa Foot, Alasdair MacIntyre, and Richard Taylor.

2. **The Standard Deontic View: Subordinate Nonaretaic Ethics.** Action-guiding principles are the essence of morality. The virtues are derived from the principles and are instrumental in performing right action. For each virtue there is a corresponding principle that is the important aspect of the relationship. This view can be found in the works of William Frankena, Bernard Gert, Alan Gewirth, John Rawls, and Geoffrey Warnock.

3. **Complementarity Ethics.** Also called *pluralistic ethics,* this holds that both deontic and aretaic models are necessary for an adequate or complete system. Neither the virtues nor principles are primary; they complement each other, and both may have intrinsic value. Robert Louden, Walter Schaller, and Gregory Trianosky are among those holding this view.

Pure Aretaic Ethics

Even though the formula for pure aretaic ethics sometimes accurately describes how a moral act is generated (that is, we sometimes act spontaneously out of a good heart), it hardly seems to cover all ethical actions. Sometimes we do use rules and moral reasons in order to decide what to do. The question is whether these rules are really irrelevant to what morality is getting at. As of now, no one has worked out a complete, pure aretaic account, so it is hard to know whether it can be done. It seems to suffer from two major types of problems: epistemological and practical. We turn to these problems.

Epistemological Problems   What habits and emotions are genuine or proper virtues? How do you know which ones these are? Who is the virtuous person? Suppose you ask me, "What is the right thing to do?" I answer, "Do what the virtuous person would do!" But you counter, "Who is the virtuous person?" To which I reply, "The man who does the right thing." The reasoning is circular. As Frankena has stated, "Virtues without principles are blind." We need something to serve as a criterion for the virtues.

Related to this epistemological problem is the problem of virtue relativism: What counts as a virtue changes over time and place. Whereas Aristotle valued pride as a special virtue, Christians see it as a master vice. An ancient caveman facing a herd of mastodons with a spear would be thought by his community to have "excessive" fear if he abandoned his fellow tribesmen and fled; whereas contemporary society would make no such judgment. Capitalists view acquisitiveness as a virtue, whereas Marxists see it as a vice.[14]

We now turn to the second criticism of virtue systems.

The Problem of Moral Direction   One of the perennial criticisms of virtue-based ethical systems is that such theories provide no guidance on how to resolve an ethical dilemma.[15] In Aristotle's *Nicomachean Ethics,* precious little is said about what we are supposed to *do.* One would think that ethics should be, at least to some extent, action-guiding. Aristotle's answer seems to be: Do what a good person would do. But, the question arises, who is the good person, and how shall we recognize him or her? Furthermore, even if we could answer that question without reference to kinds of actions or principles addressed by nonvirtue-oriented ethicists, it is not always clear what ideal persons would do in our situations. Sometimes Aristotle writes as though the right action is that intermediate, or "golden" mean between two extremes; but it is often hard, if not impossible, to determine how to apply this. As J. L. Mackie says:

> As guidance about what is the good life, what precisely one ought to do, or even by what standard one should try to decide what one ought to do, this is too circular to be very helpful. And though Aristotle's account is filled out with detailed descriptions of many of the virtues, moral as well as intellectual, the air of indeterminacy persists. We learn the names of the pairs of contrary vices that contrast with each of the virtues, but very little about where or how to draw the dividing lines, where or how to fix the mean. As Sidgwick says, he "only indicates the whereabouts of virtue."[16]

In sum, virtue ethics has a problem of application: It doesn't tell us what to do in particular instances in which we most need direction.

We turn now to rule-governed systems that incorporate the virtues: the standard deontic view and the complementarity view.

The Standard Deontic View: The Correspondence Thesis

The standard deontic view asserts three theses:[17]

1. Moral rules require persons to perform or omit certain actions, and these actions can be performed by persons who lack the various virtues as well as by those who possess them. (For example, both the benevolent and those who lack benevolence can perform beneficent acts such as giving to charity.)

2. The moral virtues are dispositions to obey the moral rules, that is, to perform or omit certain actions. (For example, the virtue of benevolence is a disposition to carry out the duty to perform beneficent acts.) According to the correspondence theory of virtues, each virtue corresponds to an appropriate moral principle.

3. The moral virtues have no intrinsic value but do have instrumental and derivative value. (Agents who have the virtues are more likely to do the right acts, i.e., obey the rules.) The virtues are important only because they motivate right action.

By the standard view, it is important to make two different but related assessments within the scope of morality: We need to make separate evaluations of the agent and the act. Both are necessary to a full ethical assessment, but it is the act that is logically prior in the relationship. Why is this?

It has to do with the nature of morality. If we agree that the general point of morality is to promote human flourishing and to ameliorate suffering, then we may judge that it is good or right kinds of acts that are, in the end, of utmost importance. But if we agree that there is a general tendency in human affairs for social relations to run down due to natural inclinations toward self-interest, then we can see that special forces have to be put in motion in order to countervail natural selfishness. One of these forces is the external sanctions produced by the law and social pressure. But a deeper and more enduring force is the creation of dispositions in people to do what is morally commendable. As Geoffrey Warnock says,

> It is necessary that people should acquire, and should seek to ensure that others acquire, what may be called *good dispositions,* that is, some readiness on occasion voluntarily to do desirable things which not all human beings are just naturally disposed to do anyway, and similarly not to do damaging things.[18]

Warnock identifies four such countervailing virtues that are necessary for social well-being. Since in the competitive struggle for goods we have a natural tendency to inflict damage on others (especially those outside the circle of our sympathies), there is a need for the virtue of nonmaleficence. But we will all do better if we are not simply disposed to leave each other alone, but are positively disposed to help each other whenever social cooperation is desirable. Thus, we should cultivate the virtue of beneficence. There is also a natural tendency to discriminate in favor of our loved ones or our own interests, so we must train ourselves to be just, impartial judges who give each person his or her due: We must acquire the virtue of fairness. Finally, there is a natural temptation to deceive in our own interest; we lie, cheat, and give false impressions when it is to our advantage. But this deception tends to harm society at large, generating suspicion, which in turn undermines trust and leads to the breakdown of social cooperation. So we must cultivate the disposition to honesty or truthfulness, and we must value and praise those who have the right dispositions and safeguard ourselves against those who lack these virtues.

Duty-based ethical theorists who hold to the standard account do not deny the importance of character. But they claim that the nature of the virtues can only be derived from right actions or good consequences. To quote Frankena once more, "Traits without principles are blind."[19] Whenever there is a virtue, there must be some possible action to which the virtue corresponds and from which it derives its virtuousness. For example, the character trait of truthfulness is a virtue because telling the truth, in general, is a moral duty. Likewise, conscientiousness is a virtue because we have a general duty to be morally sensitive. There is a correspondence between principles and virtues, the latter being derived from the former, as the following suggests:

The Correspondence Theory of Virtues

The Virtue — derived from — *The Principle* (prima facie)

Nonmaleficence	Duty not to harm
Truthfulness	Duty to tell the truth
Conscientiousness	Duty to be sensitive to one's duty
Benevolence	Duty to be beneficent
Faithfulness	Duty to be loyal or faithful
Fairness	Duty to be just
Love	Duty to do what promotes another's good

Although derived from the right kind of actions, the virtues are nonetheless very important for the moral life: They provide the dispositions that generate right action. In a sense, they are motivationally indispensable. To extend the Frankena passage quoted earlier, "Traits without principles are blind, but principles without traits are impotent." Frankena modifies this position, distinguishing two types of virtues: (1) the standard moral virtues, which correspond to specific kinds of moral principles, and (2) nonmoral virtues, such as natural kindliness or gratefulness, industry, courage, and intelligence or rationality, which are "morality-supporting." They are sometimes called "enabling virtues" because they make it possible for us to carry out our moral duties. The relationship looks something like this:

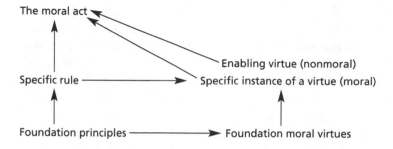

For example, take a situation in which you have an obligation to save a drowning child in spite of some risk to your own life. The specific rule of "Always come to the aid of drowning people" is grounded in a foundational principle of general beneficence, which in turn generates the foundation virtue of benevolence. In this case, it gives rise to a tendency to try to save the drowning child. But whether or not you actually dive into the lake may depend on the enabling (nonmoral) virtue of courage. Courage itself is not a moral virtue, as are benevolence and justice, for it is the kind of virtue that enhances and augments both virtues and vices (for example, think of the courageous murderer).

The Standard Deontic View's Responses to the Aretaic Critique

Can the correspondence theory answer the objections leveled against it earlier in this chapter? Let's consider the kinds of initial responses available to it.

(1) To the charge that it lacks an adequate motivational component (p. 159), philosophers such as Warnock would insist that we can bring up children to prize the correct principles and to embody them in their lives. Moral psychology will help us develop the necessary virtues in such a way as to promote human flourishing.

A deontic (action-centered) ethicist can honor the virtues and use them wisely without distorting their role in life. Sophisticated deontic ethicists can even insist that we have a duty to obtain the virtues as the best means to achieving success in carrying out our duties, and that we have a special duty to inculcate in ourselves and others the virtue of conscientiousness (the disposition to do one's duty), which will help us achieve all our other duties. This kind of thinking shows that the story of Huck Finn's conscience (discussed earlier) is not really a good counterexample to deontic ethics. Sometimes our character is ahead of our principles, but that has nothing to do with the essential relationship between virtue and rule.

(2) To the charge that action ethics is based on an improper theologi-cal–legal model (p. 160), action-based ethicists respond that we can separate the rational decision-making procedures from the theological ones without violating those procedures. To the charge that this still leaves us with a skewed process of casuistry, or hair-splitting, they answer that it is impor-tant to come as close as possible to working out a consistent system, for we want to have all the guidance for our actions that is possible. Appropriate modesty will inform us of our limits in this respect, but at least we have rules as guides—unlike the extreme aretaist, who only has dispositions.

(3) To the charge that deontic ethics neglects the spiritual dimension of morality (p. 160), the action ethicist responds that we can honor the virtues without making them into a religion. It is better to have a virtue (such as benevolence) than not to have it, because having the virtue gives us the best chance of acting rightly. However, there is no intrinsic value in the virtue. What really is important is *doing* the right act. This is not to deny that there may be aesthetic value in having correct attitudes or virtues besides their morally instrumental value, but we ought not to con-fuse ethical value with aesthetic value. In our opening example in this chapter, there is something satisfying about John's feeling sorrow over the starving Ethiopians, but it is an aesthetic satisfaction. Note the language describing deeply altruistic people: They are, to paraphrase Kant, "jewels who shine in their own light." The very metaphor should signal the fact that beyond their moral worth (in the actions they perform) we find something aesthetically attractive in their virtuous lives.

(4) Finally, to MacIntyre's criticism that morality emerges in communi-ties and cultures (p. 162), action ethicists respond that if this is taken as the whole story, it implies ethical relativism, in which case the virtues have no objective status either. On the other hand, if MacIntyre allows that we can discover the Good for man in the context of an Aristotelian naturalism, then we can derive a core set of principles as well as the right virtues.

Complementarity (Pluralistic) Ethics

The aretaic ethicist will not be satisfied with the correspondence theory, because it is still reductionistic, treating the virtues like second-class citi-zens, like servants of the master rules. While agreeing that aretaic ethics cannot stand alone, the aretaist will not accept reductionism. There must be true complementarity, a recognition of the importance of both rules and virtues in ways that do not exhaust either. Some instances of carrying out the rule may be done without a virtue, and some virtues will be prized for their own sake even without any correspondence to a moral duty. Let us examine the virtue ethicist's response to the three theses of the standard deontic view. Recall the three theses:

1. Moral rules require persons to perform or omit certain actions, and these actions can be performed by persons who lack the various virtues as well as by those who possess them.
2. The moral virtues are dispositions to obey the moral rules, that is, to perform or omit certain actions. According to the correspondence theory of virtues, each virtue corresponds to an appropriate moral principle.
3. The moral virtues have no intrinsic value but do have instrumental and derivative value. The virtues are important only because they motivate right action.

The virtue ethicist rejects all three theses of the standard deontic view: the action-nature of the rules thesis, the reductionist thesis, and the instrumental value thesis. The complementarity ethicist still holds to the essential Aristotelian idea that the virtues are excellences that have value in their own right, not merely *instrumental* to, but *constitutive* of the good life. The virtues are not wholly derivative, but partly intrinsic; their value is at least partially independent of the rightness of the actions to which they are related. And, finally, sometimes the rules require not action but the right kind of sentiments or attitudes.

Let us look at these points in greater detail, beginning with the first thesis of the standard deontic views:

1. Moral rules require persons to perform or omit certain actions, and these actions can be performed by persons who lack the various virtues as well as by those who possess them.

There are two problems with this thesis from the point of view of the virtue ethicist. First of all, it neglects the close causal link between virtue and action. Doing right without the requisite disposition is like a person who has never before played baseball hitting a home run against a leading major-league pitcher: He may have luck this time, but he shouldn't count on it. Likewise, without the virtues we shouldn't expect right conduct, even though we may occasionally be surprised both by the right act of the nonvirtuous and by the wrong act of the virtuous. Because of the close causal connection, it is statistically improbable that the good will do wrong and the bad or indifferent will do right.

But second, the thesis fails to point out that we have moral obligations to be certain kinds of people—that is, to have the requisite dispositions and attitudes for their own sake. It specifies only rules requiring action, but there are other types of moral rules as well—those requiring virtue.

We turn to the second thesis of the standard deontic view, the *reductionist thesis:*

2. The moral virtues are dispositions to obey the moral rules, that is, to perform or omit certain actions. According to the correspondence theory of virtues, each virtue corresponds to an appropriate moral principle.

What is at issue here is whether the virtues are more than just dispositions to act—whether they include attitudes that may not involve action.

Kant pointed out that love (in the passional or emotional sense) could not be a moral duty because it could not be commanded, since we have no direct control over our emotions. While the moral law may require me to give a part of my income to feed the poor, I don't have to like them; I give my money because it is right to do so.

The virtue ethicist rejects this kind of thinking. While we don't have direct control over our emotions, we do have indirect control over them. We cannot turn our dispositions on and off like water faucets, but we can take steps to inculcate the right dispositions and attitudes. If we recognize the appropriateness of certain emotions in certain situations, we can use meditation, sympathetic imagination, and therapy (and, if one is religious, prayer) in order to obtain those attitudes in the right way. We are responsible for our character. We must not only *be* good, but we must love the good. As Aristotle said, "There must first be a disposition to excellence, to love what is fine and loathe what is base."[20]

Consider two people, John and Joan, whose actions are equally correct. However, there is a difference in their attitudes. John tends to rejoice in the success of others and to feel sorrow over their mishaps. Joan, on the other hand, tends to feel glee at their mishaps and to envy their success. So long as their outward actions (and their will to do right) are similar, the action ethicist regards them as equally moral. But not the virtue ethicist: John has, but Joan lacks, the requisite moral attitude—and Joan has a moral duty to change that attitude.

Thomas Hill tells the story of a deferential wife who always does what is morally right or permissible but does it out of a motive borne of low self-esteem.[21] She doesn't respect herself but defers to her husband and children with an attitude of self-deprecation. Self-respect doesn't appear to be easily dissected into separate action types; yet it seems plausible to believe that it is a virtue, one we have a duty to inculcate (assuming that we are intrinsically worthy qua rational beings). If this is correct, then the duty to respect oneself is yet another counterexample to the second thesis.

There are reactive attitudes or emotions, such as grief, gratitude, respect, and sensitivity, that in many situations seem appropriate for their own sake, regardless of whether they can be acted upon. The action view neglects this feature of morality; it reduces morality to actions.

Let us examine the last thesis of the standard deontic position:

3. The moral virtues have no intrinsic value but do have instrumental and derivative value. The virtues are important only because they motivate right action.

This instrumental view of the virtues is rejected by the aretaist: The virtues have intrinsic value and are not merely derivative but part of what constitutes the good life. The Good is not simply good for others but is good for you as well. The virtues are an inextricable part of what makes life worth living—having the right dispositions and attitudes to the right degree expressed in the right way. John is a better person for grieving with the suffering and rejoicing with the successful. He has an appropriate attitude, whereas Joan doesn't, and this reflects on the quality of their happiness. It is not enough to do the right thing—even to do the right thing for the right reason; it is also important to do it with the right attitude and to have the right attitude and dispositions even when no action is possible.

The difference between the standard deontic view and the pluralist aretaic view is this: Both recognize that the promotion of human flourishing is an essential goal of morality, but the action ethicist thinks that morality only has to do with the kinds of actions that produce this state of affairs, whereas the virtue ethicist believes that the virtues are constitutive of what human flourishing is, and hence partly define the state of affairs we ought to be trying to produce by our actions. For the virtue ethicist the unvirtuous (virtue-indifferent or vicious) life is not worth living.

Conclusion

It is doubtful whether the action ethicist will be satisfied with the complementarity thesis of virtues as just set forth, but we must leave the matter here—exactly where it is in the contemporary debate. If nothing else, virtue ethicists have been successful in drawing attention to the importance of the virtues. There is a consensus in moral philosophy that the virtues had been neglected and that it is now important to work them into one's moral perspective. There is also some consensus that a pure virtue ethic cannot stand alone without a strong deontic component. Principles of action are important largely in the way deontological and utilitarian accounts have said they were. The question is not whether these accounts were wrong in what they said but whether they said enough. The present debate centers on whether the virtues can be successfully incorporated into an actional account, or whether they are worth pursuing for their own sake as well as for the external benefits they bring. The debate is likely to go on, and you are challenged to come to your own judgment in this matter.

NOTES

1. See "For Further Reading" for books and articles by the authors mentioned.

2. John Stuart Mill, *Essay on Liberty* (Penguin Books, 1974), p. 112.

3. See Jonathan Bennett, "Conscience of Huckleberry Finn," *Philosophy* (1974), pp. 123–134.

4. Aristotle, *Nicomachean Ethics,* trans. Martin Ostwald (Bobbs-Merrill, 1962), 1099a.

5. Richard Taylor, *Ethics, Faith and Reason* (Prentice-Hall, 1985).

6. Contemporary virtue ethicists want to reorganize this classification, but as far as I know, no complete theory has been forthcoming. This may be due partly to the fact that virtue ethicists often applaud their piecemeal, anti-theoretical approach to ethics. See Edmund Pincoffs, *Virtues and Quandaries* (University of Kansas Press, 1986). I am indebted on this subject to Robert Louden, *Morality and Moral Theory: A Reappraisal* (Oxford University Press, 1992), Part II.

7. Aristotle, *Nicomachean Ethics,* 1099a.

8. Aristotle's elitist and functional view of human nature includes: (a) the necessity of a political base where the virtues ensure a flourishing quality of life; (b) the centrality of the moral-political domain wherein most people are judged as worthless, natural slaves who should not play a dominant role in the political process; (c) the idea that the highest form of life is the life

of pure reason, of contemplation; and (d) the idea that the ideal life is that of the great-souled man (*megalopsychos*), who is proud, patronizing, and indifferent to ordinary hardship to himself or others.

9. See "A Concluding Reflection" at the end of this book for a discussion of moral character.

10. Susan Wolf, "Moral Saints," *Journal of Philosophy* 79: 8 (August 1982), pp. 419–439. This essay and my reply to it are reprinted in Louis Pojman, ed., *Ethical Theory: Classical and Contemporary Readings* (Wadsworth, 1995).

11. An example of the exemplar model is found in Sidney Lanier's encomium to Jesus:

But Thee, O sovereign Seer of Time,
But Thee, O poet's Poet, Wisdom's
    Tongue,
But Thee, O man's best Man, O love's
    best Love,
O perfect life in perfect labor writ,
O all men's Comrade, Servant, King
    or Priest—
What if and yet, what mole, what
    flaw, what lapse,
What least defect or shadow of defect,
What rumor, tattled by an enemy,
Of inference loose, what lack of
    grace
Even in torture's grasp, or sleep's or
    death's—
Oh, what amiss may I forgive in Thee,
Jesus, good Paragon, thou Crystal
    Christ?

Closer to our own time is Mohandas Gandhi. Gandhi's teachings represent a different type of virtue ethics, drawn more from the Hindu tradition but influenced by the New Testament Gospels and the writings of Leo Tolstoy. Gandhi's ideals are summed up in the 15th-century Hindu song *Vaishna Janas,* which embodies the virtues of the "devotee of God" (the *Vaishnava*):

He is the true devotee who knows and
    feels another's woes as his own.
    Ever ready to serve, he never boasts.
He bows to everyone and despises no
    one, keeping his thoughts, words
    and deeds pure. . . .
He looks upon all with an equal eye.
    He has rid himself of lust. . . .
His tongue would fail him if he at-
    tempted to utter an untruth.
He covets not another's wealth. . . .
He has conquered greed, hypocrisy,
    passion and anger.

Gandhi was deeply influenced by the *Vaishna Janas* and took it as his model for living. It characterizes the heart of his nonviolent approach to life (*ahimsha*). By prayer, meditation, self-discipline, and abstinence he strove to be a person who felt the sufferings of other people, who was humble and despised no one, who was pure in thought, word, and deed. He strove to conquer his lust, covetousness, greed, hypocrisy, passion, and anger. His ascetic practices—celibacy and fasting—were a means to self-mastery.

Sometimes Gandhi is made out to be primarily a liberator of India, his main goal being to secure freedom from England's colonial power. His biographer, Robert Payne, writes, "By purifying himself and subjugating the flesh he would increase the powers of the soul and thus acquire the strength to dominate events" [*The Life and Death of Mahatma Gandhi* (Dutton, 1969), p. 557]. But the goal of dominating events in the world was secondary to Gandhi. His primary goal was to dominate himself, to be pure, to achieve a vision of God. His sec-

ondary goal of political liberation can be seen as a result of the primary goal, religious and moral purification. In fact, for Gandhi political liberation without spiritual liberation was still a form of slavery, slavery to the passions. Gandhi was inspired by ideas of saintliness and virtue, but he himself represents the second way of understanding virtue ethics—that of imitating the virtuous person.

12. Paul Levy, *Moore* (Oxford University Press, 1979) pp. 41 f.

13. See the works listed under the various authors in "For Further Reading." This schema is an oversimplification, meant only to indicate the general direction of the position held by each author.

14. See Gregory Pence, "Recent Work on Virtues," *American Philosophical Quarterly* 21 (1984), pp. 282f, for a good discussion of this point.

15. For an excellent discussion of the problems connected with virtue ethics, see Robert Louden, "Some Vices of Virtue Ethics," *American Philosophical Quarterly* 21 (1984); reprinted in Pojman, ed., *Ethical Theory,* pp. 311–320.

16. J. L. Mackie, *Ethics: Inventing Right and Wrong* (Penguin Books, 1977), p. 186.

17. I am indebted to Walter Schaller, "Are Virtues No More Than Dispositions to Obey Moral Rules?" *Philosophia* 20 (July 1990), pp. 559–573, for these theses, which I have altered slightly. Schaller illustrates them from the work of Gert, Gewirth, and Rawls.

18. Geoffrey Warnock, *The Object of Morality* (Methuen, 1971), p. 76.

19. William Frankena, *Ethics,* 2nd ed. (Prentice-Hall, 1973); reprinted in Pojman, ed., *Ethical Theory,* pp. 305–310.

20. Aristotle, *Nicomachean Ethics.*

21. Thomas Hill, "Servility and Self-Respect," *The Monist* (1973), pp. 87–104; reprinted in Thomas Hill, *Autonomy and Self-Respect* (Cambridge University Press, 1991).

FOR FURTHER REFLECTION

1. Examine the four criticisms of traditional ethics discussed at the beginning of this chapter (pp. 158–162). How valid are they? How would such moral philosophers as Frankena and Warnock, who hold to a correspondence theory of virtues, reply to them?

2. Consider again Aristotle's statement: "There must first be a disposition to excellence, to love what is fine and loathe what is base." Virtue ethicists maintain that it is not enough habitually to do the right act in order to be counted a virtuous person; one must also have the proper emotions. Are there moral emotions? Is it important not only to act kindly to people in distress but also to feel sympathy for them? Is it morally significant not simply to do good but also to take pleasure in doing good—to enjoy it? And, conversely, is a lack of proper emotions in the right amount at the right time a sign of weak character?

3. Is moral character, as described by virtue ethicists, really an aesthetic, rather than a moral, category? Note the language of the aretaic philosopher: The good person "is a jewel who shines in his own light." Is it at best only accidental that certain habits and emotions are connected with doing the morally right act? Or is there something necessary about the connection between the right act and good habits and appropriate emotions? (See "A Concluding Reflection" at the end of this book for a further discussion on the importance of moral character.)

4. Robert Fulghum has written that the rules are fairly basic and simple, and most of us have learned them in kindergarten:

Wisdom was not at the top of the graduate school mountain, but there, in the sandbox at nursery school. These are the things I learned: Share everything... Play fair... Don't hit people... Put things back where you found them... Clean up your own mess... Don't take things that aren't yours... Say you're sorry when you hurt somebody... Wash your hands before you eat... Flush... Warm cookies and cold milk are good for you... Live a balanced life... Learn some and think some and draw and paint and sing and dance and play and work some every day... Take a nap every afternoon... When you go out into the world, watch for traffic, hold hands and stick together... Be aware of wonder. [*All I Really Need to Know I Learned in Kindergarten* (Villard Books), 1988, p. 6]

Do you agree with Fulghum? What implications does this have for the action/virtues debate?

FOR FURTHER READING

Anscombe, Elizabeth. "Modern Moral Philosophy," *Philosophy* 33 (1958).

Blum, Lawrence A. *Friendship, Altruism and Morality*. Routledge & Kegan Paul, 1980. A pioneering work in contemporary virtue theory, including a sustained critique of both utilitarian and Kantian ethics.

Foot, Philippa. *Virtues and Vices*. Blackwell, 1978. A collection of articles by one of the foremost virtue ethicists.

Frankena, William. *Ethics*. Prentice-Hall, 1973.

French, Peter, Theodore Uehling, Jr., and Howard K. Wettstein, eds. *Midwest Studies in Philosophy*, Vol. XIII

("Ethical Theory: Character and Virtue"). University of Notre Dame Press, 1988.

Gert, Bernard. *The Moral Rules,* 2nd ed. Harper & Row, 1988. Ch. 9.

Gewirth, Alan. "Rights and Virtues," *Review of Metaphysics* 38 (1985), pp. 739–762.

Hardie, W. F. R. *Aristotle's Ethical Theory.* Clarendon Press, 1968.

Hill, Thomas. *Autonomy and Self-Respect.* Cambridge University Press, 1991.

Kruschwitz, Robert, and Robert, Roberts, eds. *The Virtues.* Wadsworth, 1987. Contains excellent readings and bibliography.

Louden, Robert. "Some Vices of Virtue Ethics," *American Philosophical Quarterly* 21 (1984).

Louden, Robert. *Morality and Moral Theory: A Reappraisal and Reaffirmation.* Oxford University Press, 1992.

MacIntyre, Alasdair. *After Virtue.* University of Notre Dame Press, 1981.

Mayo, Bernard. *Ethics and the Moral Life.* Macmillan, 1958.

Murdoch, Iris. *The Sovereignty of Good.* Schocken Books, 1971.

Pence, Gregory. "Recent Work on Virtues," *American Philosophical Quarterly* 21 (1984).

Pincoffs, Edmund. *Quandaries and Virtues.* University of Kansas Press, 1986.

Roberts, Robert. "Willpower and the Virtues," *Philosophical Review* 93 (1984).

Taylor, Richard. *Ethics, Faith and Reason.* Prentice-Hall, 1985.

Trianosky, Gregory. "Supererogation, Wrongdoing and Vice: On the Autonomy of the Ethics of Virtue," *Journal of Philosophy* 83 (1986), pp. 26–40.

Trianosky, Gregory. "Virtue, Action and the Good Life: A Theory of the Virtues," *Pacific Journal of Philosophy* (1988).

Wallace, James. *Virtues and Vices.* Cornell University Press, 1978.

Warnock, Geoffrey. *The Object of Morality.* Methuen, 1971.

9

Why Should I
Be Moral?

The question [why be moral] is on a par with the hazards of love; indeed, it is simply a special case. Those who love one another, or who acquire strong attachments to persons and to forms of life, at the same time become liable to ruin: their love makes them hostages to misfortune and the injustice of others. Friends and lovers take great chances to help each other; and members of families willingly do the same. . . . Once we love we are vulnerable.

JOHN RAWLS, *A THEORY OF JUSTICE*

The Good is good for you.

(STATEMENT OF SOCRATIC ETHICS)

"Why should people in general be moral?"

"Why should I be moral?"

These two questions should not be confused. The first question asks for a justification for the institution of morality, whereas the second asks for reasons why one personally should be moral even when it does not appear to be in one's interest. I once knew a student, call him Joe, who cheated his way into medical school. Had he not cheated, he probably would not have been admitted into medical school, and, hence, would not have become a physician. For Joe, morality and self-interest were clearly at odds, and he chose self-interest. Was he correct to do so?

Thomas Hobbes' account of the "state of nature" in the *Leviathan,* as we noted in Chapter 4, offers a plausible answer to our first question, supplying a minimal justification of morality in general. Unless there is a general adherence to a basic moral code that protects basic values, society itself would be impossible. Without that minimal morality that contains rules against killing the innocent, rape, robbery, the violation of agreements, and the like, we would exist in a "state of nature," deprived of common laws, reliable expectations, and security of person and possessions. There would be no incentive for mutual trust or cooperation, but only chaotic anarchy as egoists tried to maximize personal utility. The result would be a "war of all against all" in which individual life is "solitary, poor, nasty, brutish and short."

Morality serves as an antidote to this state of nature and allows self-interested individuals to fulfill their needs and desires in a context of peace and cooperation. As such, morality is a mechanism for social control. It is in all of our interests to have a moral system that is generally adhered to so that we can maximize our individual life plans. Unless there is general adherence to the moral point of view, society will break down. Many sociologists have come to the same conclusion: Without a minimal morality society will break down.[1]

This minimalist model of morality may not be the whole picture of morality, nor a very inspiring one, but it is certainly part of the picture, the part with which virtually everyone agrees. Whether morality also has intrinsic value, whether it is, as Kant said, "a jewel that shines by its own light," is another matter, one that has to do with the second question about morality.

The second question is "Why should I be moral?" Actually, this question may also be divided into two questions: "Why should I accept the moral point of view at all?" and "Why should I be moral all of the time, that is, even on those rare occasions when I can greatly profit from breaking the moral code?" We'll examine both of these questions in this chapter.

Why shouldn't I *appear* to be moral and to promote morality in society, so that I can profit egoistically from the docility of the stupid public? Paul Taylor calls this the "Ultimate Question":

> There is one problem of moral philosophy that perhaps deserves, more than any other, to be called the Ultimate Question. It is the question of the rationality of the moral life itself. It may be expressed thus: Is the commitment to live by moral principles a decision grounded on reason or is it, in the final analysis, an arbitrary choice?[2]

Is the choice of a moral way of life a rational choice or simply an arbitrary one? The question was first raised over two millenia ago in Plato's dialogue, the *Republic,* in which Plato's brother, Glaucon, asks Socrates whether justice or moral goodness is something that is only a necessary evil. That is, he wants to know whether it would be better if we could have complete freedom to indulge ourselves as we wish or whether, since others could do the same, it would be better to compromise and limit our acquisitive instincts. Glaucon tells the story of a shepherd named Gyges who comes upon a ring that at his behest makes him invisible. Gyges uses it to escape the external sanctions of society, its laws and censure, and to serve his greed to the fullest. He kills the king, seduces his wife, and becomes king himself. Glaucon asks whether we all wouldn't do likewise.

In order to sharpen his case, Glaucon offers us a thought-experiment that in contemporary terms goes like this: Suppose there were two brothers, Jim and Jack. Jim was a splendid fellow, kind and compassionate, almost saintly, always sacrificing for the poor, helping others (including Jack, with his homework and chores). In fact, he was too good to be true. As a young man, he was framed by Jack for a serious crime, was imprisoned, gang-raped, and constantly harassed and tortured by the guards and prisoners. When released, he was unable to secure employment and was forced to beg for his food. Now he lives as a street-person in a large city, in poor health, without a family, and without shelter. People avoid him whenever they can, for he looks dangerous. Yet, in truth, his heart is as pure as the driven snow.

Jack, Jim's older brother and the man who framed him, is as evil as Jim is good. He also is as "successful" as Jim is "unsuccessful." He is the epitome of respectability and civic virtue. He is a rising and wealthy corporate executive who is praised by all for his astuteness and integrity (the latter of which he lacks completely). He is married to the most beautiful woman in the community, and his children all go to the best boarding schools. Jack's wife is not too smart, so she is completely taken in by his performance; and his children, being away at boarding school, hardly know him, but love him. He is an elder in his church, a member of his denomination's board of directors, and a prominent supporter of its work (he can afford to be, as a millionaire who pays no taxes, thanks to tax write-offs). Last year he was voted the Ideal Citizen of his city. Teachers use him as an example of how one can be both morally virtuous and a successful entrepreneur. He is loved and honored by all. Yet he has attained all his success and wealth by ruthlessly destroying people who trusted him. He is an evil man.

So, Glaucon wants to know, if you had to make a choice between living either of these lives, which life would you choose: that of the unjust man who seems just and is incredibly successful, *or* that of the just man who seems unjust and is incredibly unsuccessful? Is it better to be bad but seem good than to be good but to seem bad? Which would *you* choose?[3]

I don't know which you would choose, but let us consider two initial reasons for opting to live the life of the seemingly unjust *but* good man, Jim. The first is Socrates' answer to Glaucon—that, in spite of appearances, we should choose the life of the "unsuccessful" just person because it's to our advantage to be moral. He draws attention to the idea of the harmony of the soul and argues that immorality corrupts the inner person, whereas virtue purifies the inner person, so that one is happy or unhappy in exact proportion to one's moral integrity. Asking to choose between being morally good and immoral is like asking to choose between being healthy and sick. Even if the immoral person has material benefits, he cannot enjoy them in his awful state, whereas the good person may find joy in the simple pleasures in spite of poverty and ill fortune.

But is Socrates correct? Is the harm that Jim suffers compensated by the innate goodness of his soul? And is the good that Jack experiences outweighed by the evil of his heart? Perhaps we don't know enough about the hearts of people to be certain who is better off, Jim or Jack. But perhaps we know of (or can imagine) people like Jack who seem to flourish in spite of their wickedness. They may not fool us completely, but they seem satisfied with the lives they are living, moderately happy in their business and personal triumphs. And perhaps we know of some people like Jim who are really very sad in spite of their goodness. They wish they had meaningful work, a loving family, friends, and shelter; but they don't, and their virtue is insufficient to produce happiness. Some good people are unhappy and some bad people seem to be happy. So the Socratic answer on the health–sickness analogy may not be correct.

The second answer to Glaucon is the religious response: God will reward or punish people on the basis of their virtue or vice. The promise is of eternal bliss for the virtuous and hard times for the vicious. God sees all and rewards with absolute justice according to individual moral merit. Accordingly, in spite of what may be their differing fates here on earth, Jim is infinitely better off than Jack. If ethical monotheism of this sort is true, it is in our self-interest to be moral. The good is really good for us. The religious person has good reason to choose the life of the destitute saint.

We will take up the relationship of religion to morality in the next chapter, but we can say this much about the problem: Unfortunately, we do not know for certain whether there is a God or life after death. Many sincere people doubt or disbelieve religious doctrines, and it is not easy to prove them wrong. Even the devout have doubts and probably cannot be sure of the truth of the doctrine of life after death and the existence of God. In any case, millions of people are not religious, and the question of the relationship between self-interest and morality is a pressing one. Can a moral philosopher give a secular answer to secularists as to why they should choose to be moral all of the time?

THE PARADOX OF MORALITY
AND SELF-INTEREST

Initially we seem to run into a paradox when trying to discuss this issue. By many contemporary accounts of moral duty, we only have a duty to do some act A if there is sufficient reason to do it. But this seems to generate a paradox of asking for self-interested reasons as to why we should prefer morality when it conflicts with our self-interest. What David Gauthier has called the Paradox of Morality and Advantage[4] goes like this:

> If it is morally right to do an act, then it must be reasonable to do it.
> If it is reasonable to do the act, then it must be in my interest to do it.
> But sometimes the requirements of morality are incompatible with the requirements of self-interest. Hence, we have an apparent contradiction: It both must be reasonable and need not be reasonable to meet our moral duties.

Since morality is not always in our self-interest, we must wonder if it is not simply a delusion, an artifice to keep us in place. If it is a delusion, then the rational person will be an egoist and promote morality for everyone else but will violate it whenever he or she can safely do so.

In order to get started in our attempt to solve this puzzle, consider the case of the Prisoner's Dilemma: The secret police in another country have arrested two of our spies, Sam and Sue. They both know that if they adhere to their agreement to keep silent, the police will be able to hold them for four months, but if they violate their agreement and confess that they are spies, they will each get six years in prison. However, if one adheres and the other violates, the one who adheres will get nine years and the one who confesses will be let go immediately. We might represent their plight with the following matrix (let the figures on the left represent the amount of time Sam will spend in prison under the various alternatives and let the figures on the right represent the amount of time that Sue will spend in prison under those alternatives):

The Prisoner's Dilemma

Sue

		Adheres	Violates
Sam	Adheres	4 months, 4 months	9 years, 0 time
	Violates	0 time, 9 years	6 years, 6 years

Initially Sam reasons that either Sue will adhere to the agreement or she will violate it: If Sue adheres, then I should violate; if Sue violates, then violate it. If Sue adheres, then I should violate. If Sue violates, then I should still violate. Therefore I should violate. But Sue reasons exactly the same way about Sam; that is, either he will adhere or he will violate: If he adheres, I should violate; if he violates, then I should still violate. Therefore, I should violate. But if both reason in this way they will obtain the second-worst position, six years each, which we know to be pretty awful. If they could only come to an agreement, they could each do better—get off with only four months. But how can they do that?

If it is only a one-time choice, it is difficult to be sure that the other person will cooperate. But suppose we switch to an *iterated* version of the Prisoner's Dilemma. Recently Robert Axelrod developed such a game.[5] In it there are two players and a banker who pays out money or fines the players. Each player has two cards, labeled *Cooperate* and *Cheat*. Each move consists of both players simultaneously laying down one of their cards. Suppose you and I are playing "against" one another. There are four possible outcomes:

Outcome I: We both play *Cooperate*. The banker pays each of us $300. We are rewarded nicely.

Outcome II: We both play *Cheat*. The banker fines each of us $10. We are punished for mutual defection.

Outcome III: You play *Cooperate* and I play *Cheat*. The banker pays me $500 (Temptation money) and you are fined $100 (a Sucker fine).

Outcome IV: I play *Cooperate* and you play *Cheat*. The banker fines me $100 and pays you $500. This is the reverse of Outcome III.

See the payoff matrix on page 186.

The game continues until the banker calls it quits. Theoretically, I could win a lot of money by always cheating. After 20 moves I could hold the sum of $10,000—that is, if you are sucker enough to continue to play *Cooperate,* in which case you will be short $2,000. If you are rational, you won't do that. If we both continually cheat, we'll each end up minus $200 after 20 rounds.

What you do

	Cooperate	Cheat
Cooperate	Fairly good **REWARD** (for mutual cooperation) e.g., $300	Very bad **SUCKER'S PAYOFF** e.g., $100 fine
Cheat	Very good **TEMPTATION** (to cheat) e.g., $500	Fairly bad **PUNISHMENT** (for mutual cheating) e.g., $10 fine

What I do

So suppose that we—like the Grudgers described in Chapter 4—act on the principle "Always cooperate if the other fellow does and cheat only if he cheats first." If we both adhere to this principle, we'll each end up with $6,000 after our 20 rounds—not a bad reward! And we have the prospects of winning more—if we continue to act rationally, that is, like Grudgers.

We may conclude that rational self-interest over the long run would demand that Sam and Sue (and you and I) adhere to their agreement. It may not be the optimal choice for each (exploiting the situation would bring that about—however, rational people won't stand for that), but it is a very good second best. As David Gauthier puts it, "Morality is a system of principles such that it is advantageous for everyone if everyone accepts and acts on it, yet acting on the system of principles requires that some persons perform disadvantageous acts."[6] The Prisoner's Dilemma illustrates that morality is the dues we each have to pay to keep the minimal good we have in a civilized society. We have to bear some disadvantage in loss of freedom (analogous to paying membership dues in an important organization) so that we can have both protection from the onslaughts of chaos and promotion of the good life. Since an orderly society is no small benefit, the egoist will allow his or her freedom to be limited. So there is no real paradox between morality and self-interest in this sense. We allow some disadvantage in order to reap an overall, long-run advantage.

Still, it may be conceded that this is not quite the same as accepting the moral point of view, for the prudent person will still break the moral code whenever he or she can do so without getting detected and unduly undermining the whole system. The clever amoralist takes into account the overall consequences on the social system and cheats whenever a careful cost-benefit analysis warrants it. With the proceeds of such embezzlement, this amoralist will perhaps give a tithe to moral education so that more people will be more dedicated to the moral code, which in turn will allow him or her to cheat with greater impunity.

So although the Prisoner's Dilemma informs us that even the amoralist must generally adhere to the moral code, it doesn't tell us why he—or I—should be moral all of the time, why I should not act egoistically when it is in my self-interest to do so. Let us look more closely, then, at Gauthier's Paradox of Morality and Advantage, sketched earlier.

> If it is morally right to do an act, then it must be reasonable to do it.
> If it is reasonable to do the act, then it must be in my interest to do it.
> But sometimes the requirements of morality are incompatible with the requirements of self-interest. Hence, we have a seeming contradiction: It both must be reasonable and need not be reasonable to meet our moral duties.

The problematic premise seems to be the second sentence, which we will label *SI,* to stand for the thesis that reasons for acting have to appeal to self-interest.

SI: If it is reasonable to do act A, then it must be in my interest to do A.

Might we not doubt SI? Could we not have good reasons for doing something that goes against our interest? Suppose Lisa sees a child about to get run over by a car and, intending to save the child, hurls herself at the child, fully aware of the danger to herself. Lisa's interest is in no way tied up with the life of that child, but she still tries to save its life at great risk to her own. Isn't this a case of having a reason to go against one's self-interest?

I think that it is such a reason. SI seems unduly based on the doctrine of psychological egoism, which we showed to be false in Chapter 4. Sometimes we have reasons to do things that go against our perceived self-interest. For example, the nonreligious person who gives away needed funds to help the poor or hungry does so; and so apparently does the student who refrains from cheating when he knows that he could easily escape detection. Being faithful, honest, generous, and kind often requires us to act against our own interest.

But you may object to this reasoning by saying "It is perhaps *against* our immediate or short-term interest to be faithful, honest, generous, or kind. But in the long run it really is likely to be in our best interest, for the moral and altruistic life promises benefits and satisfactions that are not available to the immoral and stingy."

There seems merit in this response. The basis of it seems to be a plausible view of moral psychology that stipulates that character formation is not like a bathroom faucet that you can turn on and off at will. To have the benefits of the moral life—friendship, mutual love, inner peace, moral pride or satisfaction, and freedom from moral guilt—one has to have a certain kind of reliable character. All in all, these benefits are eminently worth having. Indeed, life without them may not be worth living. So we may assert that for every rational being, qua rational being, the deeply moral life is the best sort of life that he or she can live. Hence it follows that it is prudent to develop such a deeply moral character—or to continue to develop it (since our upbringing partly forms it for most of us).

Those raised in a normal social context will feel deep psychic distress at the thought of harming others or doing what is immoral, and deep psychic satisfaction in being moral. For such persons the combination of internal and external sanctions may well bring prudence and morality close together. But this situation may not apply to persons not brought up in a moral context. Should this dismay us? No. As Gregory Kavka says, we should not perceive "an immoralist's gloating that it does not pay him to be moral...as a victory over us. It is more like the pathetic boast of a deaf person that he saves money because it does not pay him to buy opera records."[7] He is a Scrooge who takes pride in not having to buy Christmas presents because he has no friends.

We want to say, then, that the choice of the moral point of view is not an arbitrary choice, but a rational one. Some kinds of lives are better than others: A human life without the benefits of morality is not an ideal or fulfilled life; it lacks too much that makes for human flourishing.

The occasional acts through which we sacrifice our self-interest within the general flow of a satisfied life are unavoidable risks that reasonable people will take. For although you can lose by betting on morality, you are almost certain to lose if you bet against it.

So SI must be restated as SI_M (self-interest modified):

SI_M: If it is reasonable to choose a life plan L, which includes the possibility of doing act A, then it must be in my interest (or at least not against it) to choose L, even though A itself may not be in my self-interest.

Now there is no longer anything paradoxical in doing something not in one's interest, for while the individual moral act may occasionally conflict with one's self-interest, the entire life plan in which the act is embedded and from which it flows is not against the individual's self-interest. For instance, though you might be able to cheat a company or a country out of some money that would leave you materially better off, it would be contrary to the *form of life* to which you have committed yourself and that has generally been rewarding.

Furthermore, character counts, and habits harness us to predictable behavior. Once we obtain the kind of character necessary for the moral life—once we become *virtuous*—we will not be able to turn morality on and off like a faucet. When we yield to temptation, we will experience alienation in going against this well-formed character. The guilt will torment us, greatly diminishing any ill-gotten gains.

Thus the paradox is resolved, and Glaucon's question has been successfully answered: Not only is it sometimes reasonable to act for reasons that do not immediately involve our self-interest, but, more importantly, a life without such spontaneous or deliberate altruism may not be worth living.

Of course, there's no guarantee that morality will yield success and happiness. Jim, in our story at the beginning of this chapter, is not happy. In a sense morality is a rational gamble. It doesn't guarantee success or happiness. Life is tragic. The good fail, and the bad—the Jacks of life— seem to prosper. Yet the moral person is prepared for this eventuality. John Rawls sums up the vulnerability of the moral life this way:

> A just person is not prepared to do certain things, and so in the face
> of evil circumstances he may decide to chance death rather than to act
> unjustly. Yet although it is true enough that for the sake of justice a
> man may lose his life where another would live to a later day, the just
> man does what all things considered he most wants; in this sense he is
> not defeated by ill fortune, the possibility of which he foresaw. The
> question is on a par with the hazards of love; indeed, it is simply a
> special case. Those who love one another, or who acquire strong at-
> tachments to persons and to forms of life, at the same time become
> liable to ruin: their love makes them hostages to misfortune and the
> injustice of others. Friends and lovers take great chances to help each
> other; and members of families willingly do the same. . . . Once we love
> we are vulnerable.[8]

But we can take steps to lessen the vulnerability by working together for a more moral society, by bringing up our children to have keener moral sensitivities and good habits so that there are fewer Jacks around. We can establish a more just society so that people are less tempted to cheat and more inclined to cooperate, once they see that we are all working together for a happier world, a mutual back-scratching world, if you like. In general, the more just the political order, the more likely it will be that the good will prosper, the more likely that self-interest and morality will converge.

NOTES

1. See Steven Lukes, *Emile Durkeim: His Life and Work* (Harper & Row, 1972), Ch. 21, and Brigette and Peter Burger, *The War Over the Family* (Doubleday, 1983).

2. Paul Taylor, *Problems of Moral Philosophy* (Wadsworth, 1978), p. 483.

3. In case you think this story is far-fetched, let me cite a quote (given to me by an anonymous reviewer) from Joseph Kennedy on the prospects of his son, John F. Kennedy, becoming a congressman. When the elder Kennedy's daughter expressed doubt that John could ever be a successful congressman, he replied, "You must always remember, it isn't what you are, but what people *think* you are, that counts." In Peter Collier and David Horowitz, *The Kennedys* (Summit Books, 1984).

4. David Gauthier, "Morality and Advantage," *Philosophical Review* 76 (1967), pp. 460–475; reprinted in Louis Pojman, ed., *Ethical Theory* (Wadsworth, 1995).

5. Robert Axelrod, *The Evolution of Cooperation* (Basic Books, 1984); and Robert Axelrod and William Hamilton, "The Evolution of Cooperation," *Science* 211 (1981), pp. 1390–1396.

6. Gauthier, "Morality and Advantage."

7. Gregory Kavka, "Reconciliation Project," in *Morality, Reason and Truth,* ed. D. Copp and D. Zimmerman (Rowmand and Allenheld, 1984); reprinted in Pojman, ed., *Ethical Theory.* In this article, Kavka attempts to resolve the paradox and to reconcile prudence with morality. Beginning with an analysis of a Hobbesian approach to the problem (one similar to Gauthier's), Kavka argues that this sort of approach, though illuminating and partially correct, "cannot take us far enough" and ultimately is invalid because of its assumption of psychological egoism (cf. Chapter 4 of this volume), which assumes that all motivation must be self-interested. What needs to be added to the Hobbesian picture is an account of internal sanctions, the kind of in-built constraints that are an important part of socialization.

8. John Rawls, *A Theory of Justice* (Harvard University Press, 1971), p. 573. Rawls goes on to add that "in a well-ordered society, being a good person (and in particular having an effective sense of justice) is indeed a good for that person" (p. 577).

FOR FURTHER REFLECTION

1. Consider the following situation proposed by John Hospers in *Human Conduct* (Harcourt Brace Jovanovich, 1961), p. 174:

Suppose someone whom you have known for years and who has done many things for you asks a favor of you which will take considerable time and trouble when you had planned on doing something else. You have no doubt that helping out the person is what you ought to do, but you ask yourself all the same *why* you ought to do it. Or suppose you tell a blind news vendor that it's a five-dollar bill you are handing him, and he gives you four dollars and some coins in change, whereas actually you handed him only a one-dollar bill. Almost everyone would agree that such an act is wrong. But some people who agree may still ask, "Tell me why I shouldn't do it just the same."

What would you say to such people?

2. Hospers believes that the question "Why should I be moral?" can only be answered by the response "Because it's right." Self-interested answers just won't do, for they come down to asking for self-interested reasons for going against my self-interest, which is a self-contradiction. Is Hospers correct about this, or is there something more we can say about being moral?

3. At the opening of this chapter I described a student who cheated his way into medical school. Would you want to be one of his patients? What does this tell you about the reasons to be moral?

4. Whether you believe that there are always self-interested reasons for being moral will largely depend on whether and to what degree you believe that some forms of life are objectively better than others, as we discussed in Chapter 4. Can you see how this goes back to the question of whether values are subjective or objective?

5. Could a person understand that something was his or her duty and yet not be motivated to do it? What is the connection between having a duty and being motivated to do it? If there is no necessary connection, then Kant would seem to be wrong when he wrote that "ought implies can." According to Kant's formula, if I *cannot* do act A, I have no duty to do A. Kant seems to have a point: It does seem odd to say that I have a duty to do what it is impossible for me to do. On the other hand, if I must be motivated to do X before I can be said to have an obligation to do X, why don't I always do my duty? Is there a way out of this paradox?

FOR FURTHER READING

Baier, Kurt. *The Moral Point of View.* Cornell University Press, 1959.

Frankena, William. *Thinking About Morality.* University of Michigan Press, 1980.

Gauthier, David, ed. *Morality and Rational Self-Interest.* Prentice-Hall, 1970.

Gauthier, David. *Morals by Agreement.* Clarendon Press, 1986.

Hospers, John. *Human Conduct: An Introduction to the Problems of Ethics.* Harcourt Brace Jovanovich, 1961.

Kavka, Gregory. "A Reconciliation Project," in *Morality, Reason and Truth,* ed. D. Copp and D. Zimmerman. Rowman and Allanheld, 1984.; reprinted in Louis Pojman, ed., *Ethical Theory.* Wadsworth, 1995.

Nielsen, Kai. "Is 'Why Should I Be Moral?' an Absurdity?" *Australasian Journal of Philosophy* 36 (1958).

Nielsen, Kai. "Why Should I Be Moral?" *Methodos* XV (1963). This comprehensive article appears in several anthologies.

Phillips, D. Z. "Does It Pay to Be Good?" *Proceedings of the Aristotelian Society* 65 (1964–1965).

Richards, David. *A Theory of Reasons for Action.* Oxford University Press, 1971.

Taylor, Richard. *Good and Evil.* Macmillan, 1970. See especially Chapter 5.

10

Religion
and Ethics

Does God love goodness because it is good, or is it good because God loves it?

PARAPHRASE OF SOCRATES' QUESTION IN PLATO'S EUTHYPHRO

*The attempts to found a morality apart from religion are like the attempts of
children who, wishing to transplant a flower that pleases them, pluck it from
the roots that seem to them unpleasing and superfluous, and stick it rootless into
the ground. Without religion there can be no real, sincere morality, just as without
roots there can be no real flower.*

LEO TOLSTOY, "RELIGION AND MORALITY," FROM HIS SELECTED ESSAYS

Adam and Eve disobeying God in the Garden of Eden and bringing
suffering and death upon themselves and all people for all time; Moses
receiving the Ten Commandments from the hand of God and delivering
them to the people of Israel as laws to be obeyed on pain of death; the
prophets Amos, Hosea, Isaiah, and Jeremiah warning the people that to
disobey God's laws is to ensure doom and destruction; Jesus' Sermon on
the Mount, Golden Rule, parable of the Good Samaritan, his teaching us
to love God with all our hearts, our neighbor as ourself, and extend that
love even to our enemy; visions in the Apocalypse of the Last Judgment,

wherein God shall reward every man and woman according to his or her deeds on earth; the hope of heaven and the fear of hell—all these religious landmarks have profoundly affected conscious life and moral behavior for almost two millennia. For Western civilization, as for most of humanity throughout the ages, morality has been identified with adherence to religion, immorality with sin, and the moral law with the command of God, so that the moral life is seen as a personal relationship with a heavenly parent. To act immorally is essentially to disobey God. David, after committing adultery with Bathsheba and arranging for the death of her husband, Uriah, can say to God without being misunderstood, "Against Thee only have I sinned" (Ps. 51).

Whether it be the poor Calcutta harijan (untouchable) accepting degradation as his or her karma, the Shiite Muslim fighting a jihad in the name of Allah, the Jew circumspectly striving to keep kosher, or the Christian giving to charity in the name of Christ, religion has so dominated the moral landscape as to be virtually indistinguishable from it. There have been exceptions, to be sure: Confucianism in China is essentially a secular system; there are nontheist versions of Buddhism; and the ancient Greek philosophers contemplated morality independently of religion. But for the most part, throughout most of our history, most people have identified morality with religion, with the commands of God.

The question remains whether the equation is valid. Is morality essentially so tied to religion so that the term *secular ethics* is an oxymoron, a contradiction in terms? Can morality survive without religion? Is it so, as Tolstoy declares in the opening quotation of this chapter, that to separate morality from religion is like cutting a flower from its roots and transplanting it, rootless, into the ground? Is Dostoevsky's character Ivan Karamazov correct when he proclaims that "If God doesn't exist, everything is permissible"?

Essentially, our inquiry comes down to addressing two questions: (1) does morality depend on religion? and (2) is religious ethics essentially different from secular ethics?

DOES MORALITY DEPEND ON RELIGION?

The first question is whether moral standards themselves depend on God for their validity, or whether there is an autonomy of ethics, so that even God is subject to the moral order. This question first arises in Plato's dialogue the *Euthyphro,* in which Socrates asks the pious Euthyphro, "Do the gods love holiness because it is holy, or is it holy because the gods love it?"[1] Changing the terms but still preserving the meaning, we want to know whether God commands what is good because it is good, or whether the good is good because God commands it. According to one theory, called the *Divine Command Theory* (DCT), ethical principles are simply the commands of God. They derive their validity from God's commanding them, and they *mean* "commanded by God." Without God, there would be no universally valid morality. Here is how theologian Carl F. H. Henry states this view:

> Biblical ethics discredits an autonomous morality. It gives theonomous ethics its classic form—the identification of the moral law with the Divine will. In Hebrew-Christian revelation, distinctions in ethics reduce to what is good or what is pleasing, and to what is wicked or displeasing to the Creator-God alone. The biblical view maintains always a dynamic statement of values, refusing to sever the elements of morality from the will of God. . . . The good is what the Creator-Lord does and commands. He is the creator of the moral law, and defines its very nature.[2]

We can analyze the DCT into three separate theses:

1. Morality (i.e., rightness and wrongness) originates with God.
2. *Moral rightness* simply means "willed by God," and *moral wrongness* means "being against the will of God."
3. Since morality essentially is based on divine will, not on independently existing reasons for action, no further reasons for action are necessary.

Modified versions of the DCT (one of which I examine in Appendix 1) omit or qualify one or more of these three theses, but the strongest form includes all three theses. We may characterize that position as follows:

> Necessarily, for any person S and for all acts A, if A is forbidden (required) of S, then God commands that not-A (A) for S. Likewise, if A is permitted for S, then God has commanded neither A nor not-A for S.

Bringing out the implications of this position, we may list four propositions:

1. Act A is wrong if and only if it is contrary to the command of God.
2. Act A is right (required) if and only if it is commanded by God.
3. Act A is morally permissible if and only if it is permitted by the command of God.
4. If there is no God, then nothing is ethically wrong, required, or permitted.

We may summarize the Divine Command Theory this way: Morality not only originates with God, but *moral rightness* simply means "willed by God" and *moral wrongness* means "being against the will of God." That is, an act is right *in virtue* of being permitted by the will of God, and an act is wrong *in virtue* of being against the will of God. Since morality essentially is based on divine will, not on independently existing reasons for action, no further reasons for action are necessary. As Ivan Karamazov asserts, "If God doesn't exist, everything is permissible." Nothing is forbidden or required. Without God we have moral nihilism. If there is no God, then nothing is ethically wrong, required, or permitted.

The opposing viewpoint, which we will call the *autonomy thesis* (standing for the independence of ethics), denies the DCT theses and asserts the following:

1. Morality does not originate with God (although the way God created us may affect the specific nature of morality).

2. Rightness and wrongness are not based simply on God's will.

3. Essentially, there are reasons for acting one way or the other, which may be known independently of God's will.

In sum, ethics is autonomous, and even God must obey the moral law, which exists independently of himself—as the laws of mathematics and logic do. Just as even God cannot make a three-sided square or cause himself not to have existed, so even God cannot make what is intrinsically evil good or make what is good evil.

Theists who espouse the autonomy thesis may well admit some epistemological advantage to God: God knows what is right—better than we do. And since he is good, we can always learn from consulting him. But in principle we act morally for the same reasons that God does: We too follow moral reasons that are independent of God. We are against torturing the innocent, because it is cruel and unjust, just as God is against torturing the innocent, because it is cruel and unjust. By this account, if there is no God, then nothing changes; morality remains intact, and both theists and nontheists have the very same moral duties.

The attractiveness of the DCT lies in its seeming to do justice to God's omnipotence or sovereignty. God somehow is thought to be less sovereign or necessary to our lives if he is not the source of morality. It seems inconceivable to many believers that anything having to do with goodness or duty could be "higher" than or independent of God, for he is the supreme Lord of the believer's life, and what the believer means by *morally right* is that "The Lord commands it—even if I don't fully understand it."

When the believer asks what God's will is, this question is a direct appeal to a personal will, not to an independently existing rule.

There are two problems that proponents of the DCT must face. One problem is that the DCT would seem to make attributing "goodness" to God redundant. When we say "God is good," we think we are ascribing a property to God; but if *good* simply means "what God commands or wills," then we are not attributing any property to God. Our statement "God is good" merely means "God does whatever he wills to do" or "God practices what he preaches," and the statement "God commands us to do what is good," is merely the tautology "God commands us to do what God commands us to do."

The other problem is that the DCT seems to make morality into something arbitrary. If God's fiat is the sole arbiter of right and wrong, then it would seem to be logically possible for such heinous acts as rape, murder, and gratuitous cruelty to become morally good actions—if God suddenly commanded us to do these things. A classic statement by William of Occam has set forth the radicality of the DCT:

> The hatred of God, theft, adultery, and actions similar to these actions according to common law, may have an evil quality annexed, in so far as they are done by a divine command to perform the opposite act. But as far as the sheer being in the actions is concerned, they can be performed by God without any evil condition annexed; and they can even be performed meritoriously by an earthly pilgrim if they should come under divine precepts, just as now the opposite of these in fact fall under the divine command.[3]

The implications of this sort of reasoning seem far-reaching. If there are no constraints on what God can command, no independent measure or reason for moral action, then anything can become a moral duty, and our moral duties can change from moment to moment. Could there be any moral stability? The proponent of the DCT may object that God has revealed his will in his word, the sacred Scriptures. But the fitting response is: How do you know that God isn't lying? For if there is no independent criterion of right and wrong except what God happens to will, then how do we know God isn't willing to make lying a duty (in which case believers have no reason to believe the Bible)?

When I was a teenager, I read in the newspaper of a missionary in Africa who put a knife through the hearts of his wife and five children. Upon his arrest for murder, he claimed God had commanded him to kill his family, and he was only obeying God. The missionary might ask, "Didn't God command Abraham to kill his son Isaac?" How do we know that God didn't command the missionary to do this horrible deed? He would only be sending his family to heaven a bit sooner than normal. Insane asylums are filled with people who have heard the voice of God commanding them to do what we normally regard as immoral: rape, steal, embezzle, and kill. If the DCT is correct, then perhaps we are calling these people insane simply for obeying God.

If God could make what seems morally heinous morally good simply by willing it, wouldn't that reduce morality to the right of the powerful— Nietzsche's "Might makes right"? Indeed, what would be the difference between the devil and God if morality were simply an arbitrary command? Suppose we had two sets of commands, one from the devil and one from God. How would we know which set was which? Could they be identical? What would make them different? If there is no independent criterion by which to judge right and wrong, then it's difficult to see how we could know which was which; the only basis for comparison would be who won. God is simply the biggest bully on the block (granted, it is a pretty big block—covering the entire universe).

Furthermore, the Scriptures speak of God being love: "Beloved, let us love one another, for love is of God, and he who loves is born of God and knows God. He who does not love does not know God; for God is love" (I John 4:7–8). Could you truly love people and at the same time rape, kill, or torture them? Could a loving God command you to torture them? If so, then I suppose that Auschwitz could be considered God's loving act toward the Jews.

The opponent of the DCT denies that God's omnipotence includes an ability to make evil actions good. Just as God's power does not enable him to override the laws of logic (e.g., he cannot make a contradiction true or make two plus two equal five), so too God cannot make rape, murder, and torture into good deeds. The objective moral law, which may be internal to God's nature, is a law that even God must follow, if he is to be a good God.

Some philosophers and theologians acknowledge that God cannot change the moral law any more than he can change the laws of logic, but they claim that he is, nevertheless, the source of the moral law. I recently heard the Christian philosopher William Lane Craig set forth the following argument:

1. If there is no God, then no moral absolute values exist.
2. Evil exists (which is a negative absolute value and implies that the good exists as an absolute positive value).
3. Therefore, God exists.[4]

Craig assumes that, unless God is the ultimate source and authority of morality, it cannot have absolute or objective status. But if what we have argued in Chapters 1 through 3 is correct, then objective moral principles exist regardless of whether God exists. Such principles enable human beings to flourish, to make life more nearly a heaven than a hell. Rational beings can discover these principles independently of God or revelation, by using reason and experience alone.

More sophisticated versions of the DCT exist. If you are interested in my analysis of the leading version, you can consult Appendix 1, "An Analysis of the Modified Divine Command Theory."

IS RELIGIOUS ETHICS ESSENTIALLY DIFFERENT FROM SECULAR ETHICS?

The second problem related to religion and morality concerns the relationship between religion and secular morality. Are they essentially compatible or incompatible? We can divide this question into two subquestions: (1) does religion actually do moral harm and detract from deep morality? and (2) does religion provide, and do secular systems fail to provide, ethics with the necessary motivation to be deeply moral?

Immanuel Kant, who espoused the autonomy thesis, thought that no difference could exist between valid religious ethics and valid philosophical ethics. God and humanity must both obey the same rational principles, and reason is sufficient to guide us to these principles:

> [Christianity] has enriched philosophy with far more definite and purer concepts than it had been able to furnish before; but which, once they are there, are freely assented to by Reason and are assumed as concepts to which it could well have come of itself and which it could and should have introduced. . . . Even the Holy One of the Gospels must first be compared with our ideal of moral perfection, before we can recognize him as such.[5]

Kant's system exalts ethics to an intrinsic good; indeed, doing one's duty for no other reason but that it is one's duty is the highest good. As such, it is related to religion; it is our duty to God. God loves the virtuous and finally will reward the virtuous with happiness in proportion to their virtue. In fact, God and immortality are necessary postulates of ethics. Immortality is necessary in this way: According to Kant, the moral law commands us to be morally perfect. Since *ought* implies *can,* we must be *able* to reach moral perfection. But we cannot attain perfection in this life, for the task is infinite. So there must be an afterlife in which we continue progressing toward this ideal.

God is a necessary postulate in that someone must enforce the moral law. That is, in order for the moral law to be completely justified, there must finally be a just recompense of happiness in accordance with virtue. The good must be rewarded by happiness in proportion to their virtue, and the evil must be punished in proportion to their vice. This harmonious correlation of virtue and happiness does not happen in this life, so it must happen in the next life. Thus there must be a God, acting as judge and enforcer of the moral law, without which the moral law would be unjustified.

Kant is not saying that we can *prove* that God exists or that we ought to be moral *in order* to be happy. Rather, the idea of God serves as a completion of our ordinary ideas of ethics. Is Kant right about this?

IS RELIGION IRRELEVANT OR EVEN INIMICAL TO MORALITY?

Many secularists, such as Bertrand Russell and Kai Nielsen, have argued against both the stronger claim of the Divine Command Theory (that religion is the basis of ethics) and the weaker, Kantian claim (that religion completes ethics). They contend that morality has no need of God: One can be moral and, within the limits of thoughtful stoic resignation, even happy. The world may well be a product of blind evolutionary striving, ultimately absurd, but this doesn't remove our duty to fill our lives with meaning and goodness. As Russell put it:

> Nature, omnipotent but blind, in the revolutions of her secular hurryings through the abysses of space, has brought forth at last a child, subject still to her power, but gifted with sight, with knowledge of good and evil, with the capacity of judging all the works of his unthinking Mother.[6]

This conscious power of moral evaluation makes the child superior to his omnipotent mother. He is free to think, evaluate, create, and live committed to ideals. So in spite of suffering, despair, and death, humans are free. Life has the meaning that we give it, and morality will be part of any meaningful life.

But theists may counter that secularists like Russell are "whistling in the dark." Christian philosopher George Mavrodes has criticized Russell's secular view as puzzling.[7] If there is no God, then doesn't secular ethics suffer from a certain inadequacy? Mavrodes argues that the Russellian world of secular morality can't satisfactorily answer the question "Why should I be moral?" for, on its account, the common goods that morality in general aims at, are often just those that we sacrifice in carrying out our moral obligations. Why should we sacrifice our welfare or self-interest for our moral duty?

Another oddity about secular ethics, according to Mavrodes, is that it is superficial and not deeply rooted. It seems to lack the necessary metaphysical basis afforded by a Platonic worldview (i.e., the view that reality and value essentially exist in a transcendent realm) or a Judeo-Christian worldview:

> Values and obligations cannot be deep in such a [secular] world. What is deep in a Russellian world must be such things as matter and energy, or perhaps natural law, chance, or chaos. If it really were a fact that one had obligations in a Russellian world, then something would be laid upon man that might cost a man everything but that went no further than man. And that difference from a Platonic world seems to make all the difference.[8]

Of course, the secularist will continue the debate. If what morality seeks is the good, as I have argued, then secular morality based on a notion of the good life is inspiring in itself, for it promotes human flourishing and can be shown to be in everyone's interest, whether or not God exists. A religious or Platonic metaphysical orientation may not be necessary for a rational, secular, commonsense morality. To be sure, there will be differences in the exact nature of the ethical codes—religious ethics will be more likely to advocate strong altruism, whereas secular codes will emphasize reciprocal altruism—but the core morality will be the same.

Some secularists—let us call them antireligious secularists—go even further than Russell or Nielsen. They claim that religious and secular morality are dissimilar, but religious morality is an inferior brand of morality that actually prevents deep moral development. P. H. Nowell-Smith and James Rachels have argued that religion is (or gives rise to) an inferior morality.[9] Both base their contention on the notion of autonomy. Nowell-Smith's argument is based on psychologist Jean Piaget's research on child development: Very small children must be taught to value rules. When they do, they tend to hold tenaciously to those rules, even when games or activities would seem to call for suspending the rules. For example, suppose ten children are to play baseball on a rectangular lot that lacks a right field. Some children might object to playing with only five on a side and no right field, because that violates the official rules. Religious morality, in being deontologically rule-governed, is analogous to the children who have not understood the wider purposes of the rules of games; it is an infantile morality.

Rachels's argument alleges that believers relinquish their autonomy in worship and so are immoral. Using Kant's dictum that "kneeling down or groveling on the ground, even to express your reverence for heavenly things, is contrary to human dignity," he argues that, since we have inherent dignity, no one deserves our worship. But since the notion of *God* implies "being worthy of worship," God cannot exist. Rachels writes:

1. If any being is God, he must be a fitting object of worship.
2. No being could possibly be a fitting object of worship, since worship requires the abandonment of one's role as an autonomous moral agent.
3. Therefore, there cannot be any being who is God.[10]

Are Nowell-Smith's and Rachels's arguments sound? They seem to contain problems. Consider Nowell-Smith's contention that religious morality is infantile. Perhaps some religious people and some secularists as well are rigidly and unreasonably rule-bound, but not all religious people are. Indeed, Jesus himself broke the rule about healing on the Sabbath day, saying, "The Sabbath was made for man, not man for the Sabbath." Doesn't the strong love motif in New Testament religious morality indicate that the rules are seen as serving a purpose—the human good?

Premise 2 of Rachels's argument seems false. In worshipping God, you need not give up your reason, your essential autonomy. Doesn't a rational believer need to use reason to distinguish the good from the bad, the holy from the unholy? A mature believer does not (or need not) sacrifice his or her reason or autonomy in worship; rather, these traits are part of what worship entails. The command to love God means to love him with one's whole *mind* as well as one's heart and strength. If there is a God, then he must surely want us to be intelligent, discriminating, and sensitive in all our deliberations. Being a religious worshipper in no way entails or condones intellectual suicide.

Of course, a believer may subordinate his or her judgment to God's when there is good evidence that God has given a judgment. If this is sacrificing one's autonomy, then it only shows that autonomy is not an absolute value but rather a significant prima facie value. If I am working in a physics laboratory with Albert Einstein, whom I have learned to trust as a competent authority, and he advises me to do something different from what my amateur calculations dictate, then I am likely to defer to his authority. But I don't thereby give up my autonomy. I freely and rationally judge that, in this particular matter, I ought to defer to Einstein's judgment on the grounds that it is more likely to be correct. Functioning autonomously is not the same as deciding each case from scratch, nor does it require self-sufficiency in decision-making. Autonomy is *higher-order* reflective control over one's life; a considered judgment that, in certain cases, another's opinion is more likely to be correct than one's own is an *exercise* of autonomy rather than an abdication of it.[11] Similarly, the believer may submit to God whenever the believer judges God's authority to override his or her own finite judgment. It seems eminently rational to give up that kind of autonomy. To do otherwise would be to make autonomy a foolhardy fetish.

DOES RELIGION ENHANCE
THE MORAL LIFE?

Contrary to philosophers like Nowell–Smith and Rachels (and even Russell and Nielsen), theism may offer some morally relevant advantages. Theists argue that religion may enrich morality in at least five ways:

1. **If God exists, then good will win out over evil.** We're not fighting alone—God is on our side in the battle. Neither are we fighting in vain—we'll win eventually. As William James (1842–1910) said:

   If religion be true and the evidence for it be still insufficient, I do not wish, by putting your extinguisher upon my nature, to forfeit my sole chance in life of getting upon the winning side—that chance depending, of course, on my willingness to run the risk of acting as if my passional need of taking the world religiously might be prophetic and right.[12]

   This thought of the ultimate victory of goodness gives us confidence to keep fighting against injustice and cruelty when others calculate that the odds against righteousness are too great to oppose. Whereas the secularist may embrace a noble stoicism, resigned to fate as Russell asserts, the believer lives in faith, confident of the final triumph of God's kingdom on earth.

2. **If God exists, then cosmic justice reigns in the universe.** The scales are perfectly balanced so that all people will eventually get what they deserve, according to their moral merit. It is true that, in most religious traditions, God forgives the repentant sinner his or her sins— in which case divine grace goes beyond what is strictly deserved. It's as though a merciful God will never give us *less* reward than we deserve,

but if we have a good will, then he will give us more than we deserve. Nonetheless, the idea that "whatsoever a man sows, that will he also reap" (Gal. 6:7) is emphasized in Judaism, Islam, Christianity, and most other world religions. In Hinduism it is carried out with a rigorous logic of karma (that is, what you are now is a direct result of what you did in a previous life, and what you do with your present life will determine what kind of life you inherit in the next life).

The question that haunts secular ethics (which we discussed in the preceding chapter)—"Why should I be moral, when I can get away with being immoral?"—has a ready answer: I will not get away with immorality. God is the perfect judge who will bring my works to judgment, so that my good works will be rewarded and my bad works punished.

3. **If theism is true, then moral reasons always override non-moral reasons.** In Chapter 1, we cited overridingness (i.e., that moral reasons always override nonmoral reasons) as an important trait of moral principles, but recognized that it was the most controversial one. Let me illustrate why. I once argued with my teacher Philippa Foot, of Oxford University, about Gauguin's abandonment of his family. I argued that, all things considered, Gauguin had done wrong. However, to my amazement, Foot argued that, although Gauguin did what was morally wrong, he did what was right, all things considered, for sometimes nonmoral reasons override moral ones. From a secular perspective, Foot's argument seems plausible: Why should moral reasons always override nonmoral ones? It is true that philosophers like R. M. Hare build overridingness into the definition of a moral principle but then stipulate that we are free to choose our principles. Here is the dilemma for secular ethics: *either* overridingness *or* objectivity, but not both. If we believe in moral realism (the idea that moral principles are universally valid whether or not anyone recognizes them), then the secularist faces the question, "Why should I adhere to a given moral principle when I can get away with violating it?" If we believe in overridingness (the idea that moral reasons are always motivating reasons, the best reasons when all things are considered), then we will probably adopt some sort of agent relativity with regard to morals. From a religious perspective, however, the world is so ordered that the question "Why be moral?" can hardly be taken seriously: To be moral is to function properly, the way God intended us to live, and he will see that the good are ultimately rewarded and the wicked punished. God ensures the supremacy of morality.[13]

4. **If theism is true, then God loves and cares for us—his love inspires us.** A sense of gratitude pervades the believer's life so that he or she is ready to make greater sacrifices for the good of others. That is, the believer has an *added reason* to be moral, beyond the ones a secular person already has, beyond even rewards and punishments: He or she wants to please a perfect God.

5. **If God created us in his image, then all persons are of equal worth.** Theism claims that God values us all equally. If we are all his children, then we are all brothers and sisters; we are family and ought to treat each other benevolently, as we would treat family members of equal worth. Indeed, modern secular moral and political systems often assume the equal worth of the individual without justifying it. But without the parenthood of God, it makes no sense to say that all persons innately possess positive equal value. What gives us animals, the products of the survival of the fittest, any value at all, let alone equal value? From a perspective of intelligence and utility, Aristotle and Nietzsche seem to be right; there are enormous inequalities, and why shouldn't the superior persons take advantage of the baser types? In this regard, secularism, in rejecting inegalitarianism, seems to be living off the interest of a religious capital that it has relinquished.

In sum, if theism is false, then it may be doubtful whether all humans have equal worth, or any worth at all, and it may be more difficult to provide an unequivocal response to the question "Why be moral even when it is not in my best interest?" If there is no sense of harmony and objective purpose in the universe, then many of us will conclude that we are sadder and poorer because of it.

Add to this the fact that theism doesn't deprive us of any of the autonomy that we have in nontheistic systems. If we are equally free to choose the good or the evil regardless of whether God exists (assuming that the notions of good and evil make sense in a nontheistic universe), then it seems plausible to assert that, in some ways, the theist's world is better and more satisfying than a Godless world. It could also be that revelation affords the theist access to deeper moral truths that are not available to the secularist.

Of course, two important points may be made on the other side. First, a lot of evil has been done by religious people in the name of religion. We have only to look at our sordid history of heresy hunts, religious bigotry, and religious wars, some of which are still being fought. Religion may be used as a powerful weapon for harming others. Second, we don't know for sure whether a benevolent God exists. The arguments for God's existence are not obviously compelling. Furthermore, even if a divine being exists, we lack compelling evidence to prove that our interpretation of God's will and ways is the right one. Religion is based largely on faith rather than on hard evidence, so it behooves believers to be modest about their policies. It would seem that most of us are more certain about the core of our morality than about the central doctrines of theology. So it is ill-advised to require society to give up a morality based on reason for some injunctions based on revelation. Sometimes a religious authority puts forth a command that conflicts with our best rational judgments, giving rise to the kind of confrontation that can rip society apart.

The medieval Crusades and Inquisition, the religious wars of the Reformation, the present conflict in Northern Ireland between Roman Catholics and Protestants, devastation in the former Yugoslavia because Christians and Muslims are killing each other, the Hindu-Muslim massacres in India, and the Ayatollah Khoumeni's order to kill Salman Rushdie for writing the allegedly blasphemous *Satanic Verses* rightly cause apprehension in many fair-minded people. Religion can be a force for good or evil, but dogmatic and intolerant religion deeply and rightly worries the secularist, who sees religion as a threat to society.

Our hope in solving such problems rests in working out an adequate morality on which theists and nonthesists alike can agree. If there is an ethics of belief, as I have argued elsewhere, then we can apply rational scrutiny to our religious beliefs, as well as to all our other beliefs, and work toward a better understanding of the status of our belief systems.[14] It is a challenge that should inspire the best minds, for perhaps neither science nor technology, but rather deep, comprehensive ethical theory and moral living, will not only save our world but solve its perennial problems and produce a state of flourishing.[15]

NOTES

1. Plato, *Euthyphro,* trans. William Jowett (Charles Scribner's Sons, 1889).

2. Carl F. Henry, *Christian Personal Ethics* (Eerdmans, 1957), p. 210.

3. William of Occam, quoted in J. M. Idziak, ed., *Divine Command Morality* (Mellon, 1979).

4. William Lane Craig set forth this argument in a debate with Paul Draper at the United States Military Academy, West Point, New York, September 30, 1997.

5. Immanuel Kant, *Critique of Judgment,* trans. J. Bernard (Haefner, 1951) p. 410, and *Fundamental Principles of the Metaphysics of Ethics,* trans. T. K. Abbott (Longmans, Green, 1898).

6. Bertrand Russell, "A Free Man's Worship," in Louis Pojman, ed., *Ethical Theory* (Wadsworth, 1995). Note also the comment of my student Laura Burrell (University of Mississippi):

God is like a cosmic gardener—he tends and protects individual morality, he nourishes it and helps it bloom. Some people, like a hothouse orchid or a fancy rose, do seem to need religion for their morality to have a purpose or justification. Others are like the Queen Anne's Lace (QAL)—able to withstand almost anything on their own. And many are borderline QAL, who need just that extra bit of fertilizer to break into bloom—and God provides it. But mankind could do as well. The relationship between God and morality is as simple as that—God is a parent, gardener, etc. He strengthens and cushions individual morality, he gives motivation (in the form of the outcomes: heaven or hell) and justice and order in a sometimes extremely chaotic world. But morality exists apart from God, and as hard as it is for some to accept it, could survive and even flourish in a world without God.

7. George Mavrodes, "Religion and the Queerness of Morality," in Pojman, ed., *Ethical Theory.*

8. Mavrodes, "Religion and the Queerness of Morality," p. 539.

9. Patrick H. Nowell-Smith, "Morality: Religious and Secular," in Pojman, ed., *Ethical Theory.*

10. James Rachels, "God and Human Attitudes," in *Religious Studies* 7 (1971); reprinted, with a reply by Philip Quinn, in Paul Helm, ed., *Divine Commands and Morality* (Oxford University Press, 1979).

11. For a fuller defense of this thesis, see Arthur Kuflik, "The Inalienability of Autonomy," *Philosophy & Public Affairs* (Fall 1984). Kuflik's work here has influenced my ideas.

12. William James, *The Will to Believe* (Longmans, Green, 1897).

13. For a fuller account of the differences between religious and secular morality, see Louis Pojman, "Ethics: Religious and Secular," in *The Modern Schoolman* LXX (November 1992), pp. 1–30.

14. See Louis P. Pojman, "Believing, Willing and the Ethics of Belief," in *The Theory of Knowledge* (Wadsworth, 1993), pp. 525–543. Samuel Scheffler in *Human Morality* (Oxford University Press, 1992), like Foot, rejects the overridability thesis.

15. I am indebted to Michael Beaty, Arthur Kuflik, and two anonymous reviewers for criticisms of an earlier draft of this chapter.

FOR FURTHER REFLECTION

1. Evaluate the quotation from Leo Tolstoy that appears at the beginning of this chapter.

2. In your judgment, how important is religion for a meaningful moral life? What would a secularist say about the five ways that religion may enrich morality? Do you think that religion really does enhance the moral life?

3. Karl Marx said that religion was the opium of the people (today, the metaphor might better be changed to "cocaine" or "crack"): Religion deludes them into thinking that all will be well with the world, leading to passive acceptance of evil and injustice. Is there some truth in Marx's dictum? How would a theist respond to it?

4. Imagine that a superior being appears to you and says, "I am God and I am good; therefore, obey me when I tell you to torture your mother." (In case you don't think that a religious tradition would set forth such a message, read Genesis 22, in which God commands Abraham to kill his son Isaac as a sacrifice to God.) How would a DCT proponent deal with this problem?

5. Discuss the problems connected with religious revelation and rational morality. What if one's religion prohibits certain types of speech and requires the death of those who disobey, such as when the Ayatollah Khoumeni called for the assassination of Salman Rushdie? Some religious people believe that abortion or homosexual behavior is morally wrong, on the basis of religious authority. How should a secular ethicist who accepts these practices argue with the believer? Can there be a rational dialogue?

FOR FURTHER READING

Adams, Robert M. "A Modified Divine Command Theory of Ethical Wrongness" in his *The Virtue of Faith*. Oxford University Press, 1987.

Hare, John. *The Moral Gap*. Oxford University Press, 1996.

Helm, Paul, ed. *The Divine Command Theory of Ethics*. Oxford University Press, 1979. Contains valuable articles by Frankena, Rachels, Quinn, Adams, and Young.

Kant, Immanuel. *Religion Within the Bounds of Reason Alone,* trans. T. M. Greene and H. H. Hudson. Harper & Row, 1960.

Kierkegaard, Soren. *Fear and Trembling,* trans. Howard and Edna Hong. Princeton University Press, 1983.

Mitchell, Basil. *Morality: Religious and Secular.* Oxford University Press, 1980.

Mouw, Richard. *The God Who Commands.* University of Notre Dame Press, 1990.

Nielsen, Kai. *Ethics Without God*. Pemberton Books, 1973. A very accessible defense of secular morality.

Outka, Gene, and J. P. Reeder, eds. *Religion and Morality: A Collection of Essays.* Anchor Books, 1973. Contains Robert M. Adams's "A Modified Divine Command Theory of Ethical Wrongness."

Pojman, Louis, ed. *Ethical Theory: Classical and Contemporary Readings.* Wadsworth, 1998. Part XI contains important essays by Immanuel Kant, Bertrand Russell, George Mavrodes, and Kai Nielsen.

Pojman, Louis. "Ethics: Religious and Secular," *The Modern Schoolman* LXX (November 1992), pp. 1–30.

Quinn, Philip. *Divine Commands and Moral Requirements.* Clarendon Press, 1978.

Robinson, Richard. *An Atheist's Values.* Clarendon Press, 1964.

Ward, Keith. *Ethics and Christianity.* Allen & Unwin, 1970.

11

The Fact-Value Problem: Metaethics in the 20th Century

I cannot forbear adding to these reasonings an observation, which may, perhaps, be found of some importance. In every system of morality which I have hitherto met with, I have always remarked, that the author proceeds for some time in the ordinary way of reasoning, and establishes the being of a God, or makes observations concerning human affairs; when of a sudden I am surprised to find, that instead of the usual copulations of propositions, is, and is not, I meet with no proposition that is not connected with an ought, or an ought not. This change is imperceptible; but is, however, of the last consequence. For as this ought, *or* ought not, *expresses some new relation or affirmation, it is necessary that it should be observed and explained; and at the same time that a reason should be given, for what seems altogether inconceivable, how this new relation can be a deduction from others, which are entirely different from it. But as authors do not commonly use this precaution, I shall presume to recommend it to the readers; and am persuaded, that this small attention would subvert all the vulgar systems of morality, and let us see that the distinction of vice and virtue is not founded merely on the relations of objects, nor is perceived by reason.*

DAVID HUME, A TREATISE ON HUMAN NATURE

In this classic quotation from David Hume's work on philosophical anthropology, the question of the relationship of *is* to *ought*—of facts to values—is raised. Hume suggests that there is something illicit in arguing from facts to values. This illicitness is sometimes referred to as "Hume's Fork" or the "naturalistic fallacy."

In this chapter we will consider various 20th-century responses to Hume's question. We want to know whether values are essentially different from facts or whether they are derived from facts, and whether value statements can be true and false like factual statements are. Ultimately, we want to understand the nature of moral language and of moral justification. So we are trying to understand how to think about ethics itself. Sometimes this second-order reflection is called *metaethics,* as opposed to normative ethics. Whereas ethics is a philosophical examination of morality, metaethics is philosophizing about ethics—that is, about the very terms and structure of ethical theory.

To get us started in our inquiry, consider the following situation: Jill is presently getting a D in her philosophy course and sees an opportunity to raise her grade by cheating on an exam. She would like to get a higher grade, for if she doesn't do better, her father will very likely take away her automobile, and her chances of getting into professional school will be severely diminished. So Jill considers cheating. Yet she is troubled by the thought of cheating. Ought she to cheat? The statement "Jill wants to cheat" is a factual one. But is it a fact that she *ought* to cheat? Where does the value term *ought* come in? What if her boyfriend, Jack, asserts that "Jill ought not to cheat"? How could we decide who is right? Does an action-guiding directive—an obligation either to cheat or not to cheat—follow from some descriptions of Jill, for example, that she desperately needs to get a higher grade in her philosophy course? Given the premises:

1. Jill is in need of a B in her philosophy course.

2. Jill can get a B in her philosophy course by cheating.

can we infer the following conclusion?

3. Jill ought to cheat in her philosophy course.

Or given the premise:

1a. Jack wants Jill to refrain from cheating in her philosophy course because it will undermine the integrity of the academic process.

can we infer the following conclusion?

2a. Jill ought not to cheat in her philosophy course.

What is the relationship between facts and values and between descriptive statements and prescriptive judgments?

In this part of our inquiry we will consider several 20th-century responses to Hume's question concerning the relationship of facts to values: naturalism, intuitionism, noncognitivism (emotivism and prescriptivism), and neonaturalism (descriptivism). Essentially, *naturalism* is the theory that value statements can be defined in terms of factual statements. By *fact* we refer to what is signified by empirically verifiable statements—for example, that Jill cheated on her exam. By *value* we refer to what is signified by an evaluative sentence—for example, "Cheating is wrong." When we claim that something is a fact, we imply that some object or state of affairs exists. When we make a value judgment, we are evaluating or appraising something.

According to naturalism, from the factual statement about Jill's situation (1 or 1a) and a major premise stating a naturalist principle, we can derive a conclusion, (either 3 or 2a). The other theories (intuitionism, emotivism, and prescriptivism) deny this, whereas neonaturalism seeks an innovative compromise, asserting that values can sometimes be derived from facts; that is, certain facts entail values. The history of ethical theory in the 20th century is largely the history of the development of these theories as responses to the fact/value problem.

NONNATURALISM

In 1903 one of the most influential books in the history of ethics was published: G. E. Moore's *Principia Ethica*.[1] It inaugurated a sustained inquiry about the meaning of ethical terms and the relation of facts to values that was to dominate moral philosophy in the 20th century. This mode of inquiry was later to be known as "metaethics"—the philosophizing *about* the very terms of ethics and considering the structure of ethics as an object of inquiry. Whereas philosophers before Moore mainly set forth systematic attempts to describe the correct moral theory, philosophers since Moore have been concerned with the functions of ethical terms, the status of moral judgments, and the relation of ethical judgments to nonethical factual statements (the *is/ought* problem). Normative concerns (for example, Is it possible to fight a just war?) were replaced by logical and epistemological concerns. The central questions became: What, if anything, is the meaning of the terms *good* and *right?* How, if at all, can we justify our moral beliefs? Although these questions were raised prior to Moore, they became as a result of his work the sum and substance of moral philosophy for over two generations. It is worth our while to outline Moore's argument here.

Moore begins *Principia Ethica* by announcing that philosophers have been muddled about ethical problems largely because they have not first clearly defined the province of ethics and limited the kinds of questions that philosophers were able to ask and answer. Philosophers must first determine the exact domain of ethics before they can deal with the further implications of ethics: "That province may indeed be defined as the whole truth about that which is at the same time common to all such judgments and peculiar to them."

Ultimately, Moore was interested in making ethics a science with clear decision-making procedures, and getting clear on the domain of ethics is but the first step in this direction. Moore thought that the way to understand the "right," as in "right action"—which has often been the subject matter of ethics—is first to discover what is the meaning of the term *good.* At first glance this seems odd, for we generally think of the domain designated by the term *good* to be the general area of axiology (including aesthetics and prudence as well as ethics). Moore may have been broadening the concept of *ethics* to be coterminous with axiology, or else he thought that axiology was the door to ethics; he did not make this clear.

The philosopher, qua philosopher, is not concerned with morality—right and wrong behavior—but with the meaning of fundamental terms:

> There are far too many persons, things, and events in the world, past, present, or to come, for a discussion of their individual merits to be embraced in any science. Ethics, therefore, does not deal at all with facts of this nature, facts that are unique, individual, absolutely particular...and, for this reason, it is not the business of the ethical philosopher to give personal advice or exhortation.

On the contrary, Moore explains, the sole task of ethics proper is to define the term *good:*

> That which is meant by "good" is, in fact, except its converse "bad," the only simple object of thought which is peculiar to Ethics.... Unless this first question be fully understood, and its true answer clearly recognized, the rest of Ethics is as good as useless from the point of view of systematic knowledge.

Good, Moore concludes, must be a simple notion like yellow, and, just as you cannot explain to anyone who does not already know it what yellow is, so you cannot explain what *good* is. No further analysis is possible, for analysis always is the making of the complex simpler; but the Good is already a simple fact and the sort of atomic fact that we use to build up more complex ideas. Here, Moore contrasts the notion of *good* with that of *horse,* which is complex and in need of further analysis.

We come to the heart of Moore's argument against naturalism. Moore's argument may be compared to David Hume's version of the naturalistic fallacy in the passage quoted at the beginning of this chapter. Hume believed that naturalists confuse facts with values. His point is that we cannot go from fact statements (*is* statements) to value statements (*ought* statements) without including a value statement as one of our premises. He is criticizing those who argue in the following manner:

A. 1. Jill wants to cheat in order to realize an important goal.

    2. Therefore, Jill ought to cheat.

or

B. 1a. Cheating will undermine the integrity of the academic enterprise.

    2a. Therefore, Jill ought not to cheat.

or

C. 1b. God has commanded us to love our neighbor.

    2b. Therefore, we ought to love our neighbor.

According to Hume all of these arguments are invalid because they commit the naturalistic fallacy of moving from a factual statement to a value statement without including a value statement in the premises. They have the form:

1. *Fact*

2. Therefore, *value*

or

1. *Is*

2. Therefore, *ought.*

This is an invalid form, because in order to get a value in the conclusion, we need to have one in at least one of the premises.

But Moore means more than simply this,[2] for Hume could still allow that ethical terms could be reduced to nonethical ones. He could fill out the preceding arguments by adding a second premise that includes a value statement in the following way:

A. 1. Jill wants to cheat in order to realize an important goal.

   2. Anyone who wants to cheat in order to get an important goal ought to cheat.

   3. Therefore, Jill ought to cheat.

and

C. 1b. God has commanded us to love our neighbor.

   2b. We ought to do what God commands.

   3b. Therefore, we ought to love our neighbor.

A Humean could define *good* in terms of a natural property, such as meeting human need (or desire) or obedience to God; that is, a Humean could be a self-reflective naturalist—one who answers in the affirmative his own question about whether one can derive an *ought* from an *is.*

But Moore would not accept this reasoning. His views are more radical than Hume's, for according to Moore's interpretation of the naturalistic fallacy, we cannot reduce ethical (normative) terms to nonethical (natural) terms. Ethical characteristics are different in kind from nonethical ones, and hence we cannot deduce ethical propositions from nonethical ones in the way that many Humeans would allow (for many followers of Hume would allow, but Moore would not, that ethical terms are definable by nonethical terms).

In order to expose the naturalist's error and show that all forms of naturalism are false, Moore set forth what he called "the open-question argument." He asks us to imagine some naturalistic definition for *good,* such as Bertrand Russell's suggestion that "*good* means that which we desire to desire." But when we analyze this statement carefully, we find a problem: We can still ask, "Is it good to desire to desire X?," which reduces to "Is the desire to desire X one of the things which we desire to desire?" or to "Do we desire to desire to desire to desire X?," which seems ridiculous and not at all equivalent to the question "Is X good?," which seems to be a simple question, not at all complex.

Stated formally, the argument goes as follows: First we define the term *good* by a natural property, F: (1) Good = df★ F. We can still always ask (2) "Are Fs good?." But by substitution for *good* in (2) we get a tautology (3) "Are Fs F?," which is not a meaningful question. So, presumably, *good* cannot be identified with F. Equivalently,

---

★ "=df" means "equals the definition of."

1. Good = df* F.

2. X is F.

3. X is F, but is X good?

4. By substitution 1, statement 3 becomes "X is good, but is X good?," which is a tautology.

5. But statement 3 is not a tautology, so statements 3 and 4 are not equivalent.

6. Therefore, statement 1 is false and we cannot define *good* in terms of a natural property.

Let's illustrate this. Suppose you say, "Pleasure is good" and I respond, "Torturing children gives me pleasure, but is it good?" I seem to have a counterexample to your claim. If we say, "Jogging is pleasant, but is it pleasant?," we see that the sentence makes no sense, for we are asking a tautological question (of the form: X is F, but is it F?); but if we say, "Jogging is pleasurable, but is it good?," we have asked a meaningful question—something nontautological—which it would be if *good* meant "that which gives pleasure." We can apply this test to any candidate for a definition of *good,* and Moore would contend that the result will be the same: We will find that we cannot define *good.*

Moore's conclusion is that because the Good cannot be defined, there are only two alternatives: Either it is a simple, indefinable property, or it doesn't refer to anything at all (and, hence, there is no subject of ethics). Because he was convinced that ethics is not an illusion, he inferred that the subject matter of ethics—*good*—"is a simple, indefinable, unanalyzable object of thought."

One may ask whether Moore was right about all this. Does the open-question test show that *good* is entirely an indefinable, nonnatural property? A tradition going back at least as far as Aristotle had viewed the Good as a natural property in terms of either the object of desire or some psychological state (such as pleasure or, more complexly, happiness).

To Moore's open question—"X has F, but is it good?"—could not the naturalist respond, "Yes"? When Moore points out that this substitution leads to a tautology ("X is good, but is it good?"), the naturalist might point out that this difference in meaning doesn't affect the essential referent. Consider the following:

D. 1. This is Venus, but is it the Morning Star?

by Moorean substitution:

D. 2. This is Venus, but is it Venus?

or

E. 1. This is the 42nd President of the United States, but is it Bill Clinton?

by Moorean substitution:

E. 2. This is Clinton, but is it Clinton?

In both cases adequate information convinces us that the answer to both questions is "yes," even though statements 1 and 2 in each case may not mean the same thing. Likewise, might not the naturalist respond in a similar way to the open-question argument? For example, naturalists might say that *good* means or includes as part of its meaning "being an object of positive interest" or "the flourishing of rational (or sentient) beings."

Whether this sort of move is adequate to save naturalism will be considered toward the end of this chapter. During the first half of the twentieth century, the prospects of naturalism looked bleak.

EMOTIVISM

According to Moore, intuitionism was the only satisfactory ethical theory. If *good* could not be identified with a natural property, it must be definable ostensibly as a nonnatural one, resembling a Platonic form (for example, the Good), that we all know by intuition.[3] It is by adhering to our intuitions, then, that morality "gets off the ground"—that we know its nature and become moral people. The influence of Moore on subsequent ethics cannot be overemphasized. On the one hand, it inspired intuitionism to new endeavors; on the other hand, those who were skeptical of nonnatural properties—forms of the Good and other ideals—were nevertheless convinced by his open-question argument that ethical terms could not be defined by natural properties.

Recall that Moore said that there were three possibilities with regard to the meaning of *good:* It was either (1) a complex natural property; (2) a simple, unanalyzable, nonnatural property; or (3) not a property at all, in which case ethics was not a reality at all. Those who accepted the open-question argument against naturalism but rejected Moore's Platonism were forced to accept the third possibility—the death of ethical truth. Because there was no subject matter for ethics, they concluded that ethics is only about emotions (hence the school's name, *emotivism*).

It may be helpful at this point to put the matter into a schema. Moore's intuitionism includes four theses:

1. **The Humean Thesis:** *Ought* statements cannot be derived from *is* statements.

2. **The Platonic Thesis:** Basic value terms, including moral statements, refer to nonnatural properties.

3. **The Cognitive Thesis:** Moral statements are either true or false; that is, they are objective, putative claims about reality, which can be known.

4. **The Intuition Thesis:** Moral truths are discovered by the intuition; they are self-evident upon reflection.

Moore held only thesis 3, the cognitive thesis, in common with the naturalist.

We can best understand emotivism, which was a reaction to intuitionism, as a rigorously empirical analysis of these four theses. Emotivists accept thesis 1 but deny theses 3 and 4; thesis 2 is the crucial thesis. Emotivists agree that evaluative statements *claim* to refer to a nonnatural world, but because there is no way to find out whether there is a nonnatural world, there is no way to know whether they refer to anything at all. Because meaningful discourse, according to the emotivists, is made up of either analytic statements or empirical statements that can be verified, we must reject evaluative language as meaningless or, as C. L. Stevenson (1908–1979) did, give it a separate, noncognitive meaning (that is, use the term *meaning* in a way that does not depend on whether a sentence is true or false).[4] For the classical emotivist, value sentences are neither true nor false; they are without a clear sense, and there is no reason to think that intuition will save us here. Intuitive speculation is unverifiable and thus a form of nonsense.

Perhaps the purest example of an ethical emotivist is Oxford University philosopher A. J. Ayer (1910–1989). In the 1930s Ayer went to Vienna to study with a group of philosophers called the "Logical Positivists," who believed that the meaning of a sentence is found in its method of verification. All meaningful sentences must be either tautologies (of the form "A is A," or reducible to such statements) or empirically verifiable (for example, observations about the world, such as "The book is red"). Value statements are neither tautologies nor verifiable statements; hence they are meaningless. Theological statements were also meaningless—neither true nor false but simply a form of nonsense—because we cannot state the manner in which they could be verified.

Compare the empirical statement (1) "There are cobwebs in the northwest corner of your dorm room" with (2) "Cheating is wrong" and (3) "A benevolent, omnipotent being is guiding your life." We have a pretty good idea what can verify statement 1. But what kinds of observations could verify statements 2 and 3? It seems difficult to say. So only statement 1 is meaningful, and statements 2 and 3 are nonsense. To the emotivist all value and religious and metaphysical utterances are seen as meaningless.

Here is how two of the earliest emotivists put the matter:

> "Good" is alleged to stand for a unique, unanalyzable concept...
> [which] is the subject matter of ethics. This peculiar ethical use of
> 'good' is...a purely emotive use. When so used the word stands
> for nothing whatever.... Thus, when we so use it in the sentence,
> "This is good," we merely refer to *this,* and the addition of "is good"
> makes no difference whatever to our reference... It serves only as
> an emotive sign expressing our attitude to *this,* and perhaps evoking
> similar attitudes in other persons, or inciting them to action of one
> kind or another.[5]

In 1935 Ayer wrote that:

> the fundamental ethical concepts are unanalyzable, inasmuch as there
> is no criterion by which one can test the validity of the judgments
> in which they occur.... The reason why they are unanalyzable is that
> they are mere pseudo-concepts. The presence of an ethical symbol
> in a proposition adds nothing to its factual content. Thus if I say to
> someone, "You acted wrongly in stealing that money," I am not stat-
> ing anything more than if I had simply said, "You stole that money."
> In adding that the action is wrong, I am not making any further state-
> ment about it.[6]

The argument of both quotations is essentially this:

1. A sentence is cognitively meaningful if and only if it can be verified.
2. Moral sentences cannot be verified.
3. Therefore moral sentences are not meaningful.

Moral statements are a type of nonsense, albeit a useful type. Even though they cannot be said to be true or false, they express our emotions. "Murder is evil" is really only a shorthand way of expressing our dislike for acts of murder. Saying "Murder is morally wrong" is equivalent to say-ing "Murder—Boo!," and saying "Helping people is morally good" is like saying "Helping people—hoorah!" The only other function ethical state-ments have is to persuade others to take the same attitude toward the activity in question: "Murder—Boo! Don't you agree?" The functions of ethical statements thus take two forms:

(1) "Good" = df expressive of positive emotion (Ayer's version)

or

(2) "X is good" = df I approve of X; do so as well (Stevenson's version)

So the emotivist notes three things about moral language:

1. Moral language is subjective: It is expressive of emotions or feelings. Such sentences are useful, like barking is useful to dogs—providing a release of feelings. But such sentences are not to be confused with the view of subjective relativism, which says that the truth or falsity of a moral judgment depends on the agent holding that judgment. For the emotivist there is no truth or falsity. The difference is the difference between saying "I have a headache" and holding your head while grimacing and groaning: In the first case (analogous to subjectivism) the statement is either true or false, but in the second case (analogous to emotivism) the actions are either sincere or insincere.

2. Moral language is imperative: It commands ("Cheating is wrong" means "Don't cheat, please!"). It is not at all descriptive.

3. Moral language aims at persuading: It has a magnetic force, aiming at influencing another person's actions. According to Stevenson, "This is right" means "I approve of this; do so as well."

Because moral statements are said to be without truth-value (are neither true nor false), they could be said to be without cognitive content. The term *noncognitivism* was used to designate them, separating them from ethical theories that held that moral statements did have truth-value, designated *cognitivism* (held by naturalists, nonnaturalists, and intuitionists).

In "The Emotive Meaning of Ethical Terms" (1937) and *Ethics and Language* (1944), Stevenson gives us a more sophisticated version of emotivism. He does not deny that moral language has meaning, as Ayer does. It is just that it has a different sort of meaning: emotive meaning rather than descriptive meaning. Stevenson provides a careful analysis of the term *good,* arguing that any adequate analysis must meet three criteria: We must be able to disagree about whether something is good; "goodness" must possess a magnetism, a tendency to act in its favor; and it must not be discoverable solely through scientific investigation. He then argues that naturalist theories fail for one reason or another to satisfy these criteria, but that emotivism, which emphasizes the difference between descriptive and emotive meaning, does satisfy all the criteria in the following ways.

Disagreement over whether something is good, Stevenson argues, is simply disagreement in attitude. If you say stealing is bad and I say that it is good, we simply are manifesting different attitudes toward stealing. This "attitude theory" emphasizes that it is precisely the magnetic aspect of the term *good* that is important, that the term has laudatory meaning. And, finally, emotivism recognizes that fundamental disagreements (those not rooted in mere disagreement in beliefs about some nonmoral facts) will not be resolved by empirical methods; if I have a pro-stealing attitude and have considered all the facts relevant to that activity, reason and science are impotent to effect a change in me.

A Critique of Emotivism

Several objections against emotivism were soon forthcoming. First of all, the verification theory of meaning, upon which Ayer's emotivism was founded, was discovered to be problematic. Specifically, it didn't pass its own test; that is, the principle either couldn't be verified or couldn't describe its method of verification, and so, on its own terms, it was meaningless. There is no reason to confine meaningfulness to empirical observation statements.

Second, if the emotivist theory of meaning is correct, one cannot easily distinguish between the effects and the meaning of a value term. The term *good* may cause others to approve, but it is doubtful whether this causal power is part of the meaning of *good*. The term *evil* attached to a noun—as in "that evil man"—may repel us and cause us to avoid the person in question, but the effect is not part of the meaning of the term *evil*. There is a difference between *giving reasons* why someone should do something and *getting* him to do something.

Third, if ethical disagreement is fundamentally a disagreement in attitude (as the emotivist alleges), then a good reason is one that causally resolves a disagreement in attitude. But we think that our reasons for action are separable from the causes that change our attitudes. For example, manipulating some neurons in my temporal lobe may cause a change in attitude toward cheating, but that would not be the same as giving me reasons to believe that the good accomplished by certain instances of cheating would far outweigh the bad effects. It is difficult to separate reasons from persuasive manipulation on the emotivist account, for on that account, the two come to the same thing. According to Alasdair MacIntyre, emotivism obliterates the distinction between manipulative and nonmanipulative behavior in social relations.[7]

Fourth, morality seems deeper than mere emotions or acting on feelings or attitudes. Morality is based on reasons (as we alleged in the third objection), but moral judgments are universalizable: If it is wrong for Jill to steal, then it is wrong for anyone relevantly similar to Jill to steal. That is, morals are not simply isolated emotive ejaculations or attitudes, but principles that guide actions.

Finally, not only does emotivism fail to note the universality of moral principles by treating moral statements as isolated, atomic, verbal ejaculations; it also fails to note that this feature enables us to argue about moral judgments. As universal action-guides, moral principles form the basis of reasoning about morality. So we indeed can argue (and not merely emote) about right and wrong. These last two points are emphasized in the next metaethical theory we'll discuss: prescriptivism.

PRESCRIPTIVISM

Emotivism is not the only kind of noncognitivism. Another version, which was first set forth by R. M. Hare (1919–) in *The Language of Morals* (henceforth *LM*) and called prescriptivism,[8] accepts Moore's open-question argument against naturalism along with the emotivists' radical separation of facts from values. Although he agrees with the emotivists that we cannot ascribe truth or falsity to moral statements and that moral judgments are attitudinal, Hare changes the emphasis regarding moral terms from feelings of approval (or disapproval) to certain types of judgment that include a universalizability feature and a prescriptive element.[9]

According to Hare there are "three most important truths about moral judgments." Moral judgments (1) are prescriptive judgments that (2) exhibit logical relations—that is, involve a rational procedure based on the fact that there are logical relations between prescriptive judgments, and (3) are distinguished from other prescriptions in that they are universalizable.[10] All of this presupposes a fourth, even more fundamental notion—that moral judgments involve principles that in turn call for the weighting of principles in cases of conflict in order to arrive at an overriding principle. Let us examine each of these four metaethical theses.

Prescriptivity

We have already noted that moral judgments seem to do more than simply describe states of affairs. The statement that "Jill should not cheat" is not primarily a description of behavior but rather a prescription for behavior. Moral judgments are given in order to guide actions—to answer questions of the form "What shall I do?"

Moral judgments are a species of value judgments (which include aesthetic evaluations and are centered in the idea of the Good). Following Hume, Hare believes that there is a logical distinction between a statement's descriptive element and its evaluative element. In a sense, value judgments are something extra or superfluous ("supervenient" is the word in fashion) beyond the plain description. For example, when I say of a particular automobile that it is a good car, I mean that it has certain characteristics: It doesn't often break down, it isn't rusted, it will go over 50 mph, it goes at least 30 miles per gallon of gasoline, it serves its owner well for several years, and so forth. But I need not call all of this *good*. I could just as well describe my car item by item. Putting the adjective *good* next to the noun *car* simply means that I, like most people, would commend such an automobile. But Hot-Rod Harry, who has a passion for fast cars and is a skilled mechanic (so that he doesn't mind frequent breakdowns), might not agree with my evaluation. He might agree with my description of a given car and yet not agree that it was a good car. To me my 1979 Chevy is a good car, but to Harry it is a bad car and he wouldn't be seen dead in it:

Description: Car C has features a, b, c, . . . , n

Evaluation: *Good* is always an attribution relative to some standard.

Hot-Rod Harry and I differ in calling car C *good* because we have different standards of reference. We can choose whatever standard of reference we like; any such standard is not intrinsic to the nature of cars.

The point is that the descriptive meaning of *good* does not exhaust its meaning. There is something added—something "supervenient"—that is, the value factor. And this value aspect, the commending nature of *good,* is a matter of choice. "When we commend or condemn anything, it is always in order, at least indirectly, to guide choices, our own or other people's, now or in the future" (*LM,* p. 127).

Now, if I know that someone needs a car and has similar needs and values as mine, I can commend a used Chevy sedan like mine to him. "It's a good car," I might say. Or "If you want a good used car, get a Chevy sedan" or "You ought to buy an inexpensive second-hand Chevy like mine." All of these speech acts have the same logical force. The first sentence is an indicative value statement; the second is a hypothetical imperative (of the form, "If you want X, do A"); the third is an indicative sentence, containing the prescriptive verb *ought.*

Value judgments cannot be equated with imperatives; but they do have something in common with them: Both are prescriptive. A moral judgment entails an imperative. "You ought not to cheat" is just another way of saying "Don't cheat, please!" When I accept the judgment that cheating is wrong—that people ought not to cheat—I am committing myself to live by that prescription myself. My moral judgment that you ought not to do X is meant to "guide" your action, not in the sense that it necessarily moves you to do X, but in the sense that your accepting my judgment commits you to doing X, and your not doing X implies that you have rejected my judgment.

The Logic of Moral Reasoning

A particular feature of Hare's theory that advances the program of noncognitivism is the idea that there is a logic to prescriptive judgments. Although moral judgments do not have truth-value, they do have a logical form. We can argue about particular judgments and use arguments to reach particular prescriptions.

Hare holds two theses about the distinction between *is* and *ought*—between descriptive and prescriptive statements as they pertain to logical form:

I. No indicative conclusion can be validly drawn from a set of premises that cannot be validly drawn from the indicatives among them alone.

and

II. No imperative conclusion can be validly drawn from a set of premises that does not contain at least one imperative.

Because the first thesis is controversial, we would do well to focus on the second one. A case of arguing from an indicative premise to an imperative would be:

A. 1. This is a box.

    2. Therefore, take this box to the railroad station.

Something is clearly missing. We must add a major premise in the form of an imperative:

1. Take all the boxes to the railroad station.

As a result, the argument becomes:

B. 1. Take all the boxes to the railroad station.

    2. This is a box.

    3. Therefore, take this to the railroad station.

When we recall that *ought* judgments are a type of imperative, and then apply thesis II to moral judgments, we see that a valid moral argument must contain at least one *ought* (imperatival) premise in order to reach a moral conclusion:

C. 1. Students ought not to cheat on tests. (imperative form: Never cheat, please!)

   2. Jill is taking a philosophy test. (indicative statement)

   3. Therefore, Jill ought not to cheat on her test. (imperative form: Therefore, don't cheat, Jill!)

The form of a moral argument is an example of an Aristotelian practical syllogism which has the form:

D. 1. Always do X! (A universal imperative)

   2. This A is a case of X. (singular indicative)

   3. Conclusion: Do A! (singular imperative)

or

E. 1. Never do X!

   2. This A is a case of X.

   3. Conclusion: Don't do A!

Universalizability

This is the most important feature of Hare's moral theory, for it gives the theory a formal structure. There is no special content to Hare's system, but there is a method. The method is essentially Kantian, similar to the categorical imperative: Act in such a way as to be able to will that the principle of your action could be a universal law. What distinguishes Kant's theory from Hare's is Kant's belief that the categorical imperative will generate substantive universal principles.

According to Hare's principle of universalizability, it is a necessary and sufficient condition of any moral judgment that one would impartially enjoin the same principle in any case of the same kind as the one in question. In making a moral judgment one has to say that one would make the same judgment in all similar cases. A judgment is not moral unless the agent is prepared to universalize his or her principle. "To ask whether I ought to do A in these circumstances is to ask whether or not I will that doing A in such circumstances should become a universal law" (*LM,* p. 70).

For example, the statement "You ought not to steal from your boss" entails, via the principle of universalizability, that the speaker believes that no one should steal in relevantly similar circumstances. Furthermore, for you to say that I should not steal is for you to commit yourself to a principle of forbidding stealing, and it is from that commitment that you are *prescribing* that others live that way also. Universalizability is the recognition that "what is sauce for the goose is sauce for the gander." It constrains our choices to the extent that it warns us that by whatever judgment we judge we too shall be judged.

Is Hare correct? Is universalizability both a necessary and a sufficient condition for moral principles? A strong intuitive case can be made for viewing universalizability as a necessary condition, for if you say that object X has a certain property F and point out that object Y is exactly similar to X, then we would expect that Y would also have property F. If this cube of sugar is sweet and the one next to it is exactly similar in every relevant way, we should have to conclude that it is also sweet.

Some moral philosophers, however, argue that there are counterexamples to the principle of universalizability. The Old Testament's Abraham may have felt that he had an obligation to sacrifice his son Isaac but that no other father had a similar obligation, or I may believe that I have a special duty to give all my money to the poor without believing that everyone has a similar duty.

But I don't think that this analysis is correct. What these examples indicate is that the principle of universalizability must be carefully applied to relevant characteristics and that it is sometimes difficult to specify just what the relevant characteristic is. If Abraham had a special duty to sacrifice Isaac, it is because God demanded this and God had a right to demand this. If this is so, God has a right to demand of anyone relevantly similar to Abraham (and in a similar situation as Abraham's) that he sacrifice his child. Likewise, there must be some reason why I in particular ought to give all my money to the poor. For example, perhaps I simply feel an overwhelming pity for them, which causes me to believe that I have a duty to give my money to the poor. But if I reflect on this, don't I have to believe that anyone relevantly similar to me who feels a similar overwhelming pity for the poor must also have such an obligation?

It seems at least plausible to assert that universalizability is a necessary condition for moral judgment, but it is not as obvious that universalizability is a sufficient condition for moral judgments. Universalizability merely grants moral judgments formal consistency.

Principles

One of the most insightful aspects of Hare's work is his recognition of the centrality of principles in moral reasoning. As already noted, they serve as major premises in arguments that guide our actions. In order to get a better look at this feature, let us contrast principle-centered systems with a non-principled system. One such type of ethics is situational ethics, especially as advocated by Joseph Fletcher in his book *Situation Ethics* (Westminister Press, 1966). Fletcher relates the following story to illustrate his thesis that principles are unnecessary for moral living: During the 1964 election campaign a friend of Fletcher's was riding in a taxi and happened to ask the taxi driver about his political views. The driver said, "I and my father and grandfather...and their fathers, have always been straight-ticket Republicans." "Ah," said the friend, who is himself a Republican, "I take it that means you will vote for Senator Goldwater." "No," said the driver, "There are times when a man has to push his principles aside and do the right thing." The taxi driver is the hero of Fletcher's book, and his attitude is that we can jolly well do without principles.

But Hare would point out that in Fletcher's mind there is a confusion between viewing principles as rigid absolutes and as reasons that are necessary to inform our deliberations. If Fletcher's friend had pressed the taxi driver a bit further, he no doubt would have gotten him to give some reasons for switching his vote (for example, he might have argued that Senator Goldwater wanted to escalate the war in Vietnam and such an escalation would both be unjust and lead to terrible consequences).

Indeed, Hare argues that all moral reasoning involves principles and that without principles most teaching would be impossible, for we usually teach not particular items but a set of action-guiding principles. That is, we don't learn isolated individual acts, but classes of acts in classes of situations.

> In learning to drive, I learn, not to change gear *now*, but to change gear when the engine makes a certain kind of noise. If this were not so, instruction would be of no use at all; for if all an instructor could do were to tell us to change gear now, he would have to sit beside us most of the rest of our lives in order to tell us just when, on each occasion, to change gear.

> (*LM*, pp. 60 f)

After we have basic principles, we next learn when to use them and when to subordinate them to suit a complex situation. In driving we first learn to draw to the side of the road before stopping. Later we learn that this does not apply when stopping before making a left-hand turn onto a side road, for then we must stop near the middle of the road until it is possible to turn. Still later we learn that in this maneuver it is not necessary to stop at all if it is an uncontrolled junction, and we can see that there is no traffic which we will obstruct by turning. And so the process of modifying our driving principles goes on.

The good driver is one whose actions are so exactly governed by principles which have become a habit with him, that he normally does not have to think just what to do. But road conditions are exceedingly various, and therefore it is unwise to let all one's driving become a matter of habit. . . . The good driver constantly attends to his habits, to see whether they might not be improved; he never stops learning.

(LM, p. 63)

Now, often a dilemma occurs when two accepted principles conflict. Suppose that you are hurrying to make an appointment with your teacher, whom you have promised to meet at 3 P.M. in his office. On the way there you come upon an accident and see a woman in need of your attention. If you stop to help her, you will miss your appointment and so be guilty of breaking your promise. But you sense that you also have an obligation to help the woman, which you will not be meeting if you do not stop. You cannot meet both obligations, so you need to find out which obligation overrides the other. Whenever two of our principles conflict, we must decide which principle overrides the other.

But how do we decide which obligation is the greater? Here Hare becomes an existentialist in a way reminiscent of Jean-Paul Sartre's description of the student who must choose between staying with his mother and going abroad to fight with the Free French Army against the German occupiers of his country. Just as Sartre argues that there is no "true" answer to this question, Hare argues that there are no objectively right or wrong things—absolutes given for all time and place, independent of our choosings. One is free to choose one's own principles, but having chosen, one must commit oneself to the principle, thus universalizing it; your being willing to commit yourself to that prescription is a necessary and sufficient condition for the justification of that principle. Hare wrote that

a complete justification of a decision would consist of a complete account of its effects, together with a complete account of the principles which it observed, and the effects of observing those principles. . . .
If pressed to justify a decision completely, we have to give a complete specification of the way of life of which it is a part. This complete specification it is impossible in practice to give; the nearest attempts are those given by the great religions. . . . If the inquirer still goes on asking "But why *should* I live like that?" then there is no further answer to give him, because we have already, *ex hypothesi,* said everything that could be included in this further answer. We can only ask him to

make up his own mind which way he ought to live; for in the end everything rests upon such a decision of principle.

(LM, p. 69)

Hare believes that by using the imagination and putting oneself "in the shoes" of other people, we will be able to arrive at a group of common principles. For although Hare's system, like Ayer's and Stevenson's, seems relativistic, he believes (unlike these emotivists) that if all normal people use his approach, they will in fact end up with a common normative moral theory—some form of utilitarianism. This conclusion has been hotly contested.

At this point it may be useful to provide a diagram[11] (Figure 3) of the positions we have surveyed.

A Critique of Prescriptivism

The first sustained criticism of Hare's strong fact/value dichotomy is Philippa Foot's "Moral Beliefs,"[12] which was delivered at the Aristotelian Society in 1958. It represents the first clear critique of the whole formalist enterprise of the noncognitivists. She argues that the noncognitivists have separated the evaluative meaning from the descriptive meaning of *good* in an implausible way. There are limits to what we can reasonably prescribe as a moral judgment and there are some so-called descriptive concepts that include moral or valuational overtones: "dangerous," "courage," "injury," and "justice." Foot is not a naturalist, or at least not a straightforward naturalist, for she doesn't believe that value terms can be defined by factual statements. But she does try to show that there is not a complete logical gap between facts and values (as all of the other ethicists in this section have maintained in their adherence to the naturalistic fallacy). Certain facts logically entail values. Foot's compromise position was labeled "descriptivism" or "neonaturalism."[13]

Let's look more closely at the kinds of criticisms leveled at Hare's prescriptivism by Foot and others. Essentially, three kinds of criticisms are aimed at the radical formal dimension of the theory. Prescriptivism is charged with (1) being too broad, (2) permitting the trivial, and (3) allowing the moral substance in life to slip away from ethical theory. We shall examine each of these charges. Then I'll add a fourth criticism of my own.

1. Prescriptivism is too broad: It allows terribly immoral agents and acts to count as moral. Hare himself was the first to point this out in Chapter 6 of *Freedom and Reason* (1962). He admitted that the fanatic who prescribed that all people of a certain race should be exterminated could,

FIGURE 3 Fact-Value Positions

	Problems of Meaning	**Problems of Justification**
Cognitivism [Ethical claims have truth-value and it is possible to know what it is.]		
A. Naturalism	Ethical terms are defined in factual terms; they refer to natural properties.	Ethical judgments are disguised assertations of some kind of fact and thus can be justified empirically.
1. Subjective	Their truth originates in individual or social decision.	
2. Objective	Their truth is independent of individual or social decision.	
B. Nonnaturalism	Ethical terms cannot be defined in factual terms; they refer to nonnatural properties.	Ethical conclusions cannot be derived from empirically confirmed propositions.
1. Intuitionism		Intuition alone provides confirmation.
2. Religious revelation		Some form of divine revelation provides confirmation.
Noncognitivism [Ethical claims do not have truth-value.]		
A. Emotivism	Ethical terms do not ascribe properties, and their meaning is not factual but, rather, emotive.	Ethical judgments are not factually, rationally, or intuitively justifiable.
B. Prescriptivism	Ethical terms do not ascribe properties, and their meaning is not factual but, rather, signifies universal prescriptions.	Ethical judgments are not factually, intuitively, or rationally justifiable, but are existentially justified.

on his account, be considered as moral judged by his theory. A convinced Nazi could validly use argument A:

A. 1   All Jews ought to be exterminated.

  2.   David is a Jew.

  3.   Therefore, David should be exterminated.

And a MacCarthyite or right-wing fanatic could reason:

B. 1.   No socialist should be allowed to teach in an American university.

  2.   Herbert Aptheker is a socialist.

  3.   Therefore, Herbert Aptheker should not be allowed to teach in an American university.

The only constraint on choosing moral principles is that one should use one's sympathetic imagination and put oneself "into the other person's shoes" before making the judgment. But this doesn't hinder the fanatic, who reasons, "If I were ever to become a socialist (or found to be a Jew), I would deserve the same treatment as I am prescribing." Many of us would argue that there is no way to justify these principles. Perhaps the fanatic has been misinformed on the dangers of Jews or socialists, but there is no reason to accept his or her principles as legitimate. There must be something wrong with a theory that is so broad as to allow heinous acts to count as moral. Such a theory seems subject to the same criticisms as subjective relativism (cf. Chapter 2).

2. Prescriptivism allows the most trivial considerations to count as moral judgments: Consider the following arguments:

C. 1. Everyone ought to rub his or her tummy on Tuesday mornings.

2. Today is Tuesday and it is morning.

3. Therefore, you and I ought to rub our tummies.

D. 1. Everyone ought to tie one's right shoe before one's left.

2. You are about to tie your shoes.

3. Therefore, you have a moral duty to tie your right shoe before your left shoe.

It would seem that any noncontradictory principle or judgment whatsoever could become a moral principle or judgment simply by being chosen (that is, prescriptively universalized by some agent). Morality has no special subject matter, no core content.

3. Prescriptivism misses the point of morality: Not only does it allow too much to be counted as moral, it allows too much to slip through the moral net. We generally think that we have some moral obligations whether we are fully aware of them or not and whether we like it or not. We think it wrong in general to lie or cheat or kill innocent people or harm others without good reason, and any moral theory worth its salt would have to recognize these minimal principles as part of its theory. But there is no necessity to recognize these principles in Hare's theory; the principle "Killing innocent people is wrong" (or "One ought not to kill innocent people") is not a necessary principle in prescriptivism. One may choose the very opposite of that principle if one so wished: "One ought to kill innocent people." So when mass-murderer Mike comes before the judge after being accused of killing forty-seven children, he may rightly say, "Your Honor, I protest your sentencing me to life-imprisonment. Yes, I broke the law, but morality is higher than the law, and I was only doing what was morally right— killing innocent people. Mine were acts of civil disobedience." A judge who was a prescriptivist would have to agree and reply, "Yes, I can see

that you have a different set of moral principles than most of us and that there is no objectively valid way of deciding the issue. But one of my moral principles (indeed, I make my living by it) is to carry out the mandate of the law. So I am sentencing you to life-imprisonment."

Perhaps we could imagine that a conversation like this might actually occur, but there is something counterintuitive about it. We think that morality is (or should be) about important aspects of human existence. Its principles are not something we *invent,* but something we *discover* by reflection.

A fourth criticism—one that I have not seen mentioned in the litera- ture—is that not only are there no limits on what may count as a moral principle but, equally troublesome, there are no logical constraints on altering one's principles or the hierarchy of one's principles as one feels inclined. Hare admits that our moral principles are revisable, but he doesn't seem to notice how damaging this is for a stable moral system. Suppose when you are rich and I am poor, I universalize the principle that "The rich ought to help the poor in every way possible," and suppose also that I convince you to act on this principle. But suppose now that our situations have reversed—I am rich and you are poor—and you notice that I am no longer acting on this principle, and you accuse me of hypocrisy. I can reply that I am not at all a hypocrite, (which implies not living by one's principles); on the contrary, I am living by my principles— only they are altered principles! I have decided to live by the principle that "No one has a duty to help the poor." Of course, if I should become poor again, I might very well change my principles again. You may object that this is insincere. But why should I universalize the principle of uni- versal consistency over time? I am sincere about living by my current principles, and that is all that Hare's moral theory requires. Perhaps this shows a lack of character, but then Hare's theory doesn't give us any objective standards for character. Perhaps I choose to universalize the principle that one may change one's character to suit one's principles. The point here is that there are no nonarbitrary constraints on when and why I may change my moral principles.

THE RENAISSANCE OF NATURALISM

It is the third criticism—that of missing the point of morality—that has been most often hurled against Hare's prescriptivism, and this criticism was first given a sustained form by Geoffrey Warnock. Warnock claims that the formalist nature of noncognitivist moral philosophy is barren and misses the point of morality; that is, morality has a *content,* which, he claims, is to ameliorate the human predicament, which has a tendency to get worse. We can call this claim the entropy principle of social relations. Because of limitations in resources, intelligence, knowledge, rationality and sympathy, the social fabric tends to come apart, which as a result threatens to produce a Hobbesian state of nature in which chaos reigns. Morality is antientropic. It counters the set of limitations, especially by concentrating on expanding our sympathies, and thus it contributes to "the betterment—or non-deterioration of the human predicament."[14]

Warnock's work paved the way for a new, more sophisticated naturalism. Many philosophers, going back to Aristotle, Hobbes, Kant, and Mill, sought to reinstate a version of naturalistic cognitivism. They endeavored to answer Moore's open-question argument by showing that on reflection a natural property is what we mean by *moral goodness.*

Moore might ask the naturalist, who identifies goodness with some property F, "X has F, but is it good?" and the naturalist would answer, "Yes." When Moore points out that this substitution leads to a tautology ("X is good, but is it good?"), the naturalist might point out that this difference in meaning doesn't affect the essential referent. Consider again the illustrations given earlier in this chapter:

D. 1. This is Venus, but is it the Morning Star?

by Moorean substitution:

D. 2. This is Venus, but is it Venus?

or

E. 1. This is the 42nd President of the United States, but is it Bill Clinton?

by Moorean substitution:

E. 2. This is Clinton, but is it Clinton?

In both cases adequate information convinces that the answer to both questions is "yes," even though the statements 1 and 2 in each case may not mean the same thing. Likewise, we might remain or become naturalists and have an answer to the open-question argument. For example, we might say that *good* means or includes as part of meaning "the flourishing of rational (or sentient) beings."

The analogous form would look like this:

F. 1. This act promotes the flourishing of rational beings, but is it good?

by substitution:

F. 2. This act promotes the flourishing of rational beings, but does it promote the flourishing of rational beings?

The naturalist answers that, on reflection, we would answer the question in the affirmative. Promoting human flourishing is what we deeply mean by *moral goodness*. Whether the noncognitivist or the nonnaturalist can show that this sort of answer is illegitimate is a matter that is currently a subject of keen debate.

In fact, it seems to me like Moore's question is itself a problem, for it seems to presuppose a Platonic answer; that is, Moore seems to have reified a concept, treating an idea as though it were a thing. This error is sometimes called the fallacy of hypostatization. Consider this conversation in Lewis Carroll's *Through the Looking Glass:*

> "Just look along the road, and tell me if you can see either of the messengers," said the King.
>
> "I can see nobody on the road," said Alice.
>
> "I only wish *I* had such eyes," the King remarked in a fretful tone. "To be able to see Nobody! And at that distance too! Why, it's as much as *I* can do to see real people, by this light."
>
> [The messenger arrives] "Who did you pass on the road?" the King went on, holding out his hand to the Messenger for some more hay.
>
> "Nobody," said the Messenger.
>
> "Quite right," said the King; "this young lady saw him too. So of course Nobody walks slower than you."
>
> "I do my best," the Messenger said in a sullen tone. "I'm sure nobody walks much faster than I do!"
>
> "He can't do that," said the King, "or else he'd have been here first."[15]

The King makes the ludicrous mistake of treating an indefinite, functional pronoun as a proper noun. In like manner, Platonists and Mooreans treat functional common nouns as proper nouns; they seem to treat functional terms like *good* as though they were things, just as gold and water are things. This seems wrong.

Consider the way we use *good* in sentences.

1. "The weather is good today."
2. "That was a good catch" (of a football tight end who has leaped high into the air to snag a pass).
3. "It's good to increase the GNP."
4. "Telling the truth is a good thing to do, though sometimes it's the wrong thing to do."

It's difficult to give a satisfactory definition of *good*. Perhaps the closest ones are "the most general term of commendation" and "satisfying some requirement." When the weather suits our aesthetic or prudential desires, we call it "good"—although it is relative to the speaker, for the sunbather and the farmer have different frames of reference. When the tight end behaves in a manner befitting his function, we commend his execution. When a nation's productivity is increased, giving promise of a higher standard of living, we express our approval with the adjective "good." Attributing goodness to an activity or artifact represents our approval of that activity or artifact—our judgment that it meets an appropriate standard.

Likewise in ethical discussion, *good* serves as a term of commendation, expressing the perception that such and such a behavior meets our standards of fitting behavior or contributes to goals we deem positive. When we say that telling the truth is a good thing to do, we do not mean that there is an independently existing form of the Good that truth-telling somehow represents or is "plugged into." If we are reflective, we generally mean that there is something proper or valuable (either intrinsically or extrinsically) about truth-telling. Furthermore, we generally do not judge that the goodness attached to truth-telling is absolute, for it can be overridden in some cases by other considerations. For example, we judge it to be a bad thing to tell the truth to criminals who will use the information given to murder an innocent person.

We have a notion of good ends that morality serves. Even if we are deontologists, we still think that there is a point to morality, and that point generally has to do with producing better outcomes—truth-telling generally produces better outcomes than lying. These ends can be put into nonmoral language in terms of happiness, flourishing, welfare, equality and the like; that is, at least part of our notion of moral goodness is predicated on a notion of nonmoral goodness. A certain logic pertains in what can be called morally good, depending on these nonmoral values.

If this analysis is correct, then it doesn't make much sense to treat the notion of *good* like a thing (for example, gold or water) and define it in the realist language, any more than it makes sense to treat *tallness* and *spectacularity* and *equality* as things. As my teacher, Gilbert Ryle, used to say, It's a category mistake to treat a functional term as though it were a thing.

Conclusion

In Warnock's work we have come full circle from the naturalism of Hume, Bentham, and Mill to which the nonnaturalists reacted in the first place some seventy years earlier. If a new naturalism seems more plausible than noncognitivist theories, it has profited importantly from their efforts. Naturalism is different now—almost beyond recognition as a variation of the earlier naturalisms.

One way to see what divides the new cognitivists, such as Warnock, Kurt Baier, William Frankena, and Kai Nielsen, from their noncognitivist predecessors is to note the point where reason and value come into the various theories. For Ayer, Stevenson, and Hare we begin with value—we feel an emotion or have an attitude or choose a principle; that is, the *oughtness* (the evaluative element) comes in at the outset and solves the *is/ought* problem. On the other hand, for the cognitivist, the Good or the Right—the proper set of moral principles—is discovered, existing, as it were, independent of any particular agent's choice. But a question that never rightly arises for the noncognitivist soon arises for the cognitivist, namely, "Why should I be moral?"

Put another way, reason enters the naturalist's domain right at the start in order to pick out the right principles, but then there is an additional problem of choosing the moral point of view. For the noncognitivist (for example, Hare's prescriptivist), the moral point of view is whatever the agent chooses to live by. Reason, then, plays a secondary and formal role in assuring consistency of judgment—that is, in universalizing the principles.

The debate between cognitivism and noncognitivism and between the various renditions of naturalism and nonnaturalism is still going on, mainly under the realism/antirealism controversy. Realists, such as Nicholas Sturgeon, David Brink, and Peter Railton, contend that moral judgments have truth value. For example, the judgment that murder is always wrong is either true or false (they would say it's true). Antirealists, such as J. L. Mackie, Gilbert Harman, and R. M. Hare, deny that moral judgments have truth value. The realism debate is complicated by the fact that the antirealist is not necessarily a moral relativism. Indeed, Warnock's position is consistent with antirealism. One can be an objectivist and an antirealist at the same time, though as a matter of fact most antirealists, such as Mackie and Harman, but not Hare (in his later writings), tend to deny the objective validity of ethical principles. The key point is whether moral judgments correspond to facts about the world. Moral realists assert, but antirealists deny, that such correspondence obtains. But objectivists like Hare argue that moral judgments are like imperatives—not truths about the world, but judgments about how we *ought* to make the world. So the *is/ought* problem is still with us, only in a more complicated and refined manner.[16]

I hope that this chapter helps you understand the major aspects of the *is/ought* debate, and I hope that you have enough information to make an informed judgment on the merits of the case.

NOTES

1. G. E. Moore, *Principia Ethica* (Cambridge University Press, 1903). All quotes from Moore in this chapter refer to this work.

2. The naturalist fallacy (according to Moore) involves breaking Hume's *is/ought* law by making an invalid inference from a descriptive *is* statement to a prescriptive *ought* statement. The open-question argument is used to show that all forms of naturalism are false. For a good discussion of the possibility of annulling the *is/ought* problem, see the articles in W. D. Hudson, ed, *The Is/Ought Problem* (St. Martin's Press, 1969).

3. Moore's Platonism is nicely brought out in a quote from John Maynard Keynes' memoir, *My Early Beliefs:*

   The New Testament is a handbook for politicians compared with the unworldliness of Moore's chapter on the Ideal. I know no equal to it in literature since Plato. And it is better than Plato because it is quite free from *fancy.* It conveys the beauty of the literalness of Moore's mind, the pure and passionate intensity of his vision, unfanciful and undressed up. Moore had a nightmare once in which he could not distinguish propositions from tables. But even when awake, he could not distinguish love and beauty and truth from the furniture. They took on the same definition of outline, the same stable, solid objective qualities and common sense reality. I see no reason to shift from the fundamental intuitions of *Principia Ethica;* though they are much too few and too narrow to fit actual experience. That they furnish a justification of experience wholly independent of outside events has become an added comfort, even though one cannot live today secure in the undisturbed individualism which was the extraordinary achievement of the early Edwardian days. [Quoted in Mary Warnock's *Ethics Since 1900* (Oxford University Press, 1960), p. 54f]

4. See C. L. Stevenson, *Ethics and Language* (Yale University Press, 1944) and "The Emotive Meaning of Ethical Terms," *Mind* 46 (1937): 14–31.

5. I. A. Richards and C. K. Ogden, *The Meaning of Meaning* (Harcourt Brace Jovanovich, 1923), p. 125.

6. A. J. Ayer, *Language, Truth, and Logic,* 2nd ed. (Dover, 1946), p. 107.

7. Alasdair MacIntyre, *After Virtue* (University of Notre Dame Press, 1981), Chapter 1.

8. An interesting fact of Hare's theory is that his ideas were influenced by his experiences in Japanese prison camps in Singapore and Thailand during the Second World War. It was in these

"grim and barren prison compounds" that the first draft of his book *The Language of Morals* (Oxford University Press, 1952) was written (Ved Mehtha, "The Bewitchment of the Intellect" *The New Yorker,* Dec. 9, 1961).

9. Here is how Hare states the difference between himself and the emotivists:

The process of *telling* someone to do something, and *getting* him to do it, are quite distinct, logically, from each other. The distinction may be elucidated by considering a parallel one in the case of statements. To tell someone that something is the case is logically distinct from getting (or trying to get) him to believe it. Having told someone that something is the case we may, if he is not disposed to believe what we say, start on a quite different process of trying to get him to believe it (trying to persuade or convince him that what we have said is true). No one, in seeking to explain the function of indicative sentences, would say that they were attempts to persuade someone that something is the case. And there is no more reason for saying that commands are attempts to persuade or get someone to do something; here, too, we first tell someone what he is to do, and then, if he is not disposed to do what we say, we may start on the wholly different process of trying to get him to do it." (*Language of Morals,* pp. 13–14)

Here we see Hare's fundamental disagreement with emotivists like Stevenson on the nature of moral judgments: They are meant not merely to persuade, for if they were,

there would be no difference between reasoning and propaganda.

10. R. M. Hare, *Freedom and Reason* (Oxford University Press, 1963), pp. 4f.

11. This diagram is modeled on one by Tom L. Beauchamp, *Philosophical Ethics* (New York: McGraw-Hill, 1982), p. 359.

12. Philippa Foot, "Moral Beliefs," in her *Virtues and Vices* (Blackwell's, 1978).

13. If we define a *naturalist* as one who holds that factual claims entail (or are entailed by) fundamental ethical claims, then we would call Foot a naturalist. In that case we would need to amend our chart to include a form of naturalism which was not definitional (that is, did not define ethical terms by natural ones) but instead was broadly logical.

14. Geoffrey Warnock, *The Object of Morality* (Methuen, 1971), p. 26.

15. Lewis Carroll, *Through the Looking Glass* (Pan Books, 1947), pp. 232f. Compare this passage to the hypostatization of *time* in Carroll's *Alice's Adventures in Wonderland* (Pan Books, 1947), p. 54.

16. For a good discussion of the moral realism debate see the readings in Part IX of my *Ethical Theory: Classical and Contemporary Readings* (Wadsworth, 1995). See also David McNaughton, *Moral Vision* (Blackwell, 1988) and Michael Smith, "Realism" in Peter Singer, ed., *A Companion to Ethics* (Blackwell, 1991), pp. 399–410. R. M. Hare's later thought is found in *Moral Thinking* (Oxford University Press, 1981).

FOR FURTHER REFLECTION

1. Review this chapter in order to make sure that you understand the major positions of naturalism, nonnaturalism, noncognitivism, and prescriptivism.

Which, if any, seem to capture the truth about moral judgments?

2. P. H. Nowell-Smith, as a noncognitivist, suggests that value words are

multifunctional: They are used to express tastes and preferences, to express decisions and choices, to criticize, grade and evaluate, to advise, admonish, warn, persuade, and dissuade, to praise, encourage and reprove, to promulgate and draw attention to rules; and doubtless for other purposes also. [*Ethics.* Penguin Books, 1954, p. 98]

He believes that moral language is used primarily for choosing actions and advising others. Does this description of noncognitivism make the theory more plausible?

3. In a classic article on the subject of the *is/ought* problem "How to Derive 'Ought' from 'Is'" *The Philosophical Review* (1964), John Searle sets forth the following argument which he claims shows that we can derive a "fact statement" from a "value statement." He argues as follows:

1. John says, "I promise to pay you (Mary) the $10 you have just loaned me."

2. John promised to pay Mary $10 (description of 1 above).

3. John has put himself under an obligation to pay Mary $10.

4. John has an obligation to pay Mary $10.

5. John ought to pay Mary $10.

According to Searle we have gone from an *is* to an *ought* statement without committing any logical mistake. Is he correct? What does this tell us about the *is/ought* problem?

4. At the outset of this book we said that morality served four purposes: to keep society from falling apart, the promotion of human flourishing, the amelioration of suffering, and the just resolution of conflicts of interest. How would each of the theories studied in this chapter respond to those purposes? Would they argue over whether those were, indeed, the correct purposes in the first place? Would they question whether there was any definite set of purposes that morality played? What are the purposes of morality suggested by each of these theories?

FOR FURTHER READING

Blum, Lawrence A. *Friendship, Altruism and Morality.* Routledge & Kegan Paul, 1980. Contains a sustained critique on some aspects of rule-governed ethics such as the principles of universalizability and impartiality.

Foot, Philippa. *Virtues and Vices.* Blackwell's, 1978. See especially her essay, "Moral Beliefs."

Goodpaster, K. E., ed., *Perspectives on Morality: Essays by William K. Frankena.* University of Notre Dame, 1976. Contains important essays on the subject matter of this chapter.

Hancock, Roger. *Twentieth Century Ethics.* Columbia University Press, 1974.

Hare, R. M. *The Language of Morals.* Oxford University Press, 1952.

Hare, R. M. *Freedom and Reason.* Oxford University Press, 1963.

Hudson, W. D., ed. *The Is/Ought Question.* St. Martin's Press, 1969.

Hudson, W. D. *Modern Moral Philosophy,* 2nd ed. Macmillan, 1983. A clear, comprehensive survey of the issues discussed in this chapter.

Moore, G. E. *Principia Ethica.* Cambridge University Press, 1903. The book that started the major discussion of metaethics in the 20th century.

Nowell-Smith, Patrick. *Ethics.* Penguin Books, 1954.

Pritchard, H. A. *Moral Obligation.* Oxford University Press, 1968.

Ross, David W. *The Right and the Good.* Oxford University Press, 1930.

Searle, John. "How to Derive 'Ought' from 'Is'." *The Philosophical Review,* 73 (1964).

Sellars, Wilfred, and John Hospers, eds. *Readings in Ethical Theory,* 2nd ed. Prentice-Hall, 1970. The largest collection of essays on the problems discussed in this section.

Stevenson, C. L. *Ethics and Language.* Yale University Press, 1944.

Urmson, J. O. *The Emotive Theory of Ethics.* Hutchinson, 1968.

Warnock, G. J. *The Object of Morality.* Methuen, 1971. The book that signaled the revival of ethical naturalism.

Warnock, Mary. *Ethics Since 1900.* Oxford University Press, 1960. A short, clear exposition of the history of ethics in the 20th century.

12

Moral Realism
and the
Challenge of Skepticism

Take any action allowed to be vicious; willful murder, for instance. Examine it in all lights and see if you can find that matter of fact...which you call vice. *In whichever way you take it, you only find certain passions, motives, volitions and thoughts.... The vice entirely escapes you, as long as you consider the object. You can never find it till you turn your reflection into your own breast, and find a sentiment of disapprobation, which arises in you, towards that action*

DAVID HUME *A TREATISE OF HUMAN NATURE*

We ended the last chapter with an analysis of Geoffrey Warnock's return to objectivist-naturalism. This brought the debate over morality full circle from the beginning of this century, when utilitarian naturalism dominated the Anglo-American philosophical world. But shortly after Warnock's work, new challenges to objectivism arose that centered on the question of whether moral principles could be considered to have truth value. This question is called the problem of *moral realism versus moral antirealism* or *moral skepticism*. A moral realist holds that moral facts exist and that they exist independently of whether we believe them. Typically, realists are *cognitivists,* holding that we can know these truths, but they could be *skeptics,* who believe that such truths cannot be known. Realism about morality includes naturalism, nonnaturalism (intuitionism), and supernaturalism (the

FIGURE 4 Cognitivism versus Noncognitivism

Cognitivism		Noncognitivism
Realism	Error Theory	Antirealism
Naturalism	Moral Skepticism	Emotivism
Nonnaturalism		Prescriptivism
Supernaturalism		Projectivism[2]

Cognitivism: Moral principles (or judgments) have truth values (they are propositions that are true or false).

Realism: Moral facts or properties exist, hence moral principles (or judgments) are propositional and true—part of the fabric of the universe. Examples of realism are naturalism, nonnaturalism, and supernaturalism.

Error theory: Realism is the correct analysis of moral principles, but we are in error about them. There are no moral truths. This is a form of moral nihilism.

Moral skepticism: There may or may not be moral truths, but even if they exist, we cannot know them.

Noncognitivism: Moral principles (or judgments) do not have truth values (they are pro attitudes or con attitudes, not essentially propositional).

Antirealism: Moral principles (or judgments) do not have truth values. There are no moral facts. Examples of antirealism are emotivism, prescriptivism, and projectivism (the view that, in making moral judgments, we project our attitudes or emotions onto the world).

thesis that God creates or sustains moral truths). Opposed to the realists are the antirealists, among whom are noncognitivists but also moral skeptics. One need not have a positive theory about morality in order to deny what the realist asserts. One might reject both traditional cognitivism and noncognitivism in different ways. That is, a philosopher may reject noncognitivism as an adequate account of morality, believing instead that cognitivism is the correct account of moral claims, but he or she may hold that in fact none of our moral theories is true. Spinoza said that good and evil are "nothing more but modes in which the imagination is affected in different ways, and, nevertheless, they are regarded by the ignorant as being special attributes of things."[1] Figure 4 compares cognitivism with noncognitivism.

In 1977, the Oxford philosopher J. L. Mackie in his *Ethics: Inventing Right and Wrong* set forth a Spinozist interpretation of morality. Mackie accepts the cognitivist's analysis of morality as presupposing moral facts, but he denies that there are any. "The denial of objective values will have to be put forward...as an 'error theory,' a theory that although most people in making moral judgments implicitly claim, among other things, to be pointing to something objectively prescriptive, these claims are all false."[3] Moral skeptics, then, doubt or deny that any of our moral theories or judgments are true.

Mackie acknowledges the importance of the realist's claims in holding to objective values but offers two arguments against such views: the *argument from relativity* (or disagreement) and the *argument from queerness.* The argument from relativity points out that there is no universal moral code that all people everywhere adhere to, which seems to indicate that morality is culturally dependent. The argument from queerness aims at showing the implausibility of supposing that such things as values have an independent existence. Hence, according to the *principle of simplicity* (do not multiply kinds of objects beyond necessity), we should conclude that moral facts do not exist.

Two years after Mackie's tidal wave rocked the seas of moral philosophy, a second work, Gilbert Harman's *The Nature of Morality* (1979) created, if anything, even greater shock waves, as he defended a radical *moral nihilism.*[4] Harman argues that an asymmetry exists between scientific theories (which require observation to confirm them) and moral theories (which don't seem to be confirmed in the same way). Scientific theories are tested against the world, so that, if a predicted observation occurs, then it confirms our theory, but if it doesn't occur, then we feel strong pressure to alter or reject our theory. With regard to moral theories, we do not identify "rightness" or "wrongness" in acts in the same way that we identify a vapor trail in a cloud chamber as evidence of a proton's behavior:

> Scientific hypotheses can . . . be tested in real experiments, out in the world. Can moral principles be tested in the same way, out in the world? You can observe someone do something, but can you ever perceive the rightness or wrongness of what he does? If you round a corner and see a group of young hoodlums pour gasoline on a cat and ignite it, you do not need to *conclude* that what they are doing is wrong; you can *see* that it is wrong. But is your reaction due to the actual wrongness of what you see or is it simply a reflection of your moral "sense," a "sense" that you have acquired perhaps as a result of your moral upbringing? (p. 4)

Harman thinks the answer to his question is that moral insights occur because of our upbringing, not because of the way the world is. Hence, we may conclude that moral facts do not exist in the way that scientific facts do. Hence, we may conclude, moral nihilism is true.

While doing so in different ways, the antirealists Mackie and Harman attack both the notion of objective moral principles and their truth value. They go beyond mere noncognitivism. A noncognitivist prescriptivist like Hare would agree that there are no moral propositions, since propositions are *descriptions,* characterizations of the way the world is, whereas moral principles are *prescriptions,* imperatives that guide our actions. That is, there is an opposing direction of fit in propositions and prescriptions. A proposition (e.g., "snow is white") is true if it corresponds to the facts (i.e., snow really is white). The direction of fit is *word to world.* If the world is the way the words in the sentence say it is, then the sentence is true. If the world doesn't correspond to the words in the sentence, then the sentence is false. The direction of fit in moral judgments, however, is *world to word.* In moral activity, we endeavor to make the world correspond to our ideals and norms. We hold that promise-keeping is (prima facie) obligatory, so we prescribe that you honor your wedding vow to remain faithful to your spouse. We do not say that moral principles are true, but that moral principles are universally binding or valid. They are action-guiding word to world judgments.[5]

First we will examine Mackie's error theory of morality and then turn to Harman's moral nihilism. In the process, we will consider some realist responses.

MACKIE'S ERROR THEORY OF MORALITY

Mackie opens his book with the sentence, "There are no objective values." He elaborates by saying:

> The claim that values are not objective, are not part of the fabric of the world, is meant to include not only moral goodness, which might be most naturally equated with moral value, but also other things that could be more loosely called moral values or disvalues—rightness and wrongness, duty, obligation, an action's being rotten and contemptible, and so on. It also includes non-moral values, notably aesthetic ones, beauty and various kinds of artistic merit. (p. 15)

He distinguishes his view from a moral subjectivism in which the statement "This action is right" *means* "I approve of this action." His view is not about *meaning* but about *facts,* about whether there are any right or good actions. His answer is a skeptical one—we have no good reason to believe that moral facts exist. An example of a theory holding to moral facts is Plato's theory of the forms, and in particular the form of the good, which are eternal realities, "a very central part of the universe." If God exists, then there likewise might be moral truths in God or truths that God created. But Mackie, as an atheist, rejects this possibility. Other notions of objectivity might be the intuitionist notions of moral principles being discoverable by an inner sense or the naturalist notions of objective qualities, such as happiness, being "intrinsically desirable." Certainly, we feel as though certain actions are objectively right or wrong and that happiness is better than misery, but these are just our subjective preferences— even if others agree, intersubjective agreement is still subjective. When we apply a philosophical microscope to our judgments, we are forced to conclude that commonsense morality-qua-objectivity is simply false. However nice it would be to have an infallible or imposing moral authority, there is no reason to believe it exists. There are no moral truths. Nothing is morally wrong.

In explaining the tendency to objectify morality, Mackie refers to Hume, who pointed out in *Treatise of Human Nature* (1739) that when we perceive a murder we do not perceive the *vice* in it, nor can we infer it from what we do perceive by any valid principles of inference (see the quotation at the beginning of this chapter). Hume speaks of our mind's "propensity to spread itself on external objects." Mackie calls this the *pathetic fallacy,* "our tendency to read our feelings into their objects. If a fungus, say, fills us with disgust, we may be inclined to ascribe to the fungus itself a non-natural quality of foulness." The difference between this and morality is that, with regard to morality, society influences what we find repulsive or good.

Let us further examine Mackie's two arguments for his error theory. First is his *argument from relativity.* It is an anthropological truism that the content of moral codes varies enormously from culture to culture. Some cultures promote monogamy, whereas others promote polygamy. Some cultures practice euthanasia, and others proscribe it. Our moral beliefs seem largely a product of our cultural upbringing. We tend to internalize the mores of our group. The argument from relativity holds that the best explanation for actual moral diversity is the absence of universal moral truths, rather than the distorted perceptions of objective principles.

We can neutralize this argument from relativity by considering whether the description of the moral life and its constitutive principles can find an independent justification. The fact of cultural diversity doesn't constitute a very strong argument against an objective core morality any more than disagreement about economics is good evidence against the thesis that some theories are better than others. Disagreement about morals could be due to ignorance, immaturity, moral insensitivity, superstition, or irrational authority. A criminal I once knew, whom I will call Sam, was accused of attempted rape. Asked to compare the significance of rape with other actions, he replied, "It's like choosing between chocolate and vanilla ice cream." Why should I allow Sam's perception to undermine my confidence in the principle, "Rape is immoral"? Just as there can be physical blindness or partial blindness, can't there be gross moral blindness? Can't I conclude that something is wrong with Sam—rather than concluding "Oh, well, different strokes for different folks" or "Different morals for different cultures"? I have already dealt with this issue in Chapters 1 through 3. In any case, Mackie acknowledges that his argument from relativity is indecisive, although, if we allow it, it adds weight to his crucial second argument.

The second argument is his *argument from queerness.* If there were objective values, then they would have to be "of a very strange sort, utterly different from anything else in the universe." Mackie thinks that all forms of moral realism boil down to intuitionism and that moral intuitionism requires "a special sort of intuition." The burden of proof seems to rest with the intuitionist to explain why we should espouse this unexplained, extra mechanism—this strange "moral sense." The principle of simplicity favors the simpler explanation that moral principles are merely subjective judgments.

The argument from queerness holds that moral facts, if they existed, would be strange objects, which would require a strange faculty to perceive. What evidence there is suggests that no such strange faculty exists. Rather, there are simpler explanations for our moral beliefs. Hence, we should reject the thesis that moral facts exist. Hence, there is nothing wrong (or right).

We could reject Mackie's characterization, as some have done, by pointing out that moral facts are not independent objects as such, but rather they *supervene* on natural properties or social practices. The concept of *supervenience* is important here. For example, our perception of the color red is a supervenient effect of the reflection of certain light waves off surfaces as communicated to our retinas. The color red supervenes on the noncolored properties of these surfaces. The color is not in the objects themselves, but there is a causal relationship between the light rays and our perceptions. Likewise, moral expressions, such as right and wrong or good and bad, may be supervenient on natural properties, such as happiness or suffering. In this book, especially Chapters 1–3, I have treated moral properties as *functional,* standing for practices that tend to fulfill the purpose of morality (the *right*) or tend to thwart it (the *wrong*). Morality's purpose is to promote human flourishing and ameliorate suffering and so forth, so *moral truths* are practices that satisfy the conditions for fulfilling that purpose.

We must note one further problem with Mackie's error theory: It seems to dissolve moral discourse altogether. Mackie actually wants to assert that some things really are wrong. He says, for instance, "As the world is, wars and revolutions cannot be ruled to be morally completely out of the question. The death penalty, I believe, can."[6] I confess to being dumbfounded. If nothing is wrong, then how can the death penalty be wrong? This seems a contradiction. Perhaps all Mackie means is "Death penalty—boo!" as an emotivist might exclaim. In that case, his opponents' "Death penalty—hurrah!" is no less valid.

If nothing is morally wrong, then isn't everything morally permissible (morally right)? If rape is not morally wrong, then doesn't that make it morally permissible? Mackie seems to want to say that both wrongness and permissibility are category mistakes. Neither exists. But if this really were so, then does it really matter what we do? Morality doesn't exist at all. We have not merely moral skepticism, but moral *nihilism* (which I will discuss in the next section). But if this is so, don't we need something else to guide our behavior—practical reason to prohibit certain practices (e.g., rape and killing innocent people) and promote others (e.g., cooperation and promise-keeping)? It seems so. But if we use practical reason to coordinate our practices, then aren't some of these practices *better* than others from the standpoint of optimizing our wants and interests? Cooperation and promise-keeping and respecting others will promote the interests of members of a society more than rape and the killing of innocents. But if the former are more optimific, then aren't they the ones we will advise other societies to follow? Hence, we can judge Hindu Indian society immoral for practicing suttee—the burning of widows—and we can condemn Nazi society for exterminating Jews, and we can judge certain West African societies as wrong for performing clitorectomies on young girls. But given these considerations, it would seem that we can use objective moral language, just so long as we recognize the point of moral discourse. We will pursue this line of thought further in the next section.

Mackie holds that morality is an invention, not a discovery. What could this mean? The Greek philosopher Xenophon (570–478 B.C.) said that religion is an invention, the making of God in the image of one's own group:

> The Ethiopian make their gods black and snub-nosed; the Thracians say theirs have blue eyes and red hair. Yes, and if oxen and horses or lions had hands, and could paint with their hands, and produce works of art as men do, horses would paint the forms of the gods like horses, and oxen like oxen, and make their bodies in the image of their several kinds.[7]

Is this how we create morality—in our own images and according to our own desires, giving it authority in the process? Does Mackie mean that we consciously invent morality, principles, and sanctions to achieve social control? It seems so, for he writes,

We need morality to regulate interpersonal relations, to control some of the ways in which people behave towards one another, often in opposition to contrary inclinations. We therefore want our moral judgements to be authoritative for other agents as well as for ourselves: objective validity would give them the authority required. (p. 43)

Suppose that Mackie is correct, and we do invent these practices and institutions. We find ourselves cooperating, then we notice the wonderful benefits it brings, and thus reinforced, the behavior tends to be repeated and promoted. We notice that truth-telling is indispensable for achieving our goals, so we invent sanctions to encourage it. But even if we did create all our moral practices *ab initio* in the way Mackie seems to suppose, still it would be an objective matter—a matter of *discovery*—to determine whether they really work! Suppose we decide to invent the practice of respecting property. We then discover that it really enhances the freedom and meaning of our lives. Just as the Ethiopian invention of black gods doesn't make it true that gods are black, our invention of moral practices doesn't make these practices true or valid or successful in meeting the relevant conditions. We don't *invent* the fact that respect for property brings us freedom and mean-ing. It either does or it doesn't. There is a fact of the matter.

HARMAN'S MORAL NIHILISM

Gilbert Harman asks: Can moral principles be tested in the same way that scientific hypotheses can be tested—by experiment and observation? He asks us to consider cases of scientific and moral observation. Consider first a scientific observation. A physicist makes an observation to test a scientific theory. Seeing a vapor trail in a cloud chamber, he or she thinks, "There goes a proton." If the observation is relevant to the theory, then the obser-vation confirms the existence of the proton. The best explanation of the vapor trail is the scientific fact—a proton. On the other hand, consider a moral observation. You see some children pouring gasoline on a cat and setting the cat on fire. You don't see "moral wrongness," nor do you infer it as the best explanation of the event. The wrongness is something you impose on the observation. Generalizing from this comparison, Harman argues that there is a disanalogy between scientific observation of some-thing (which leads us to posit scientific entities as the best explanation) and so-called moral observation (which does not lead us to posit special *moral facts* as the best explanation). The explanation of a scientific observation is in the world (external to the observer), whereas the explanation of a moral observation is in the observer's psychological state (internal to the observer). Hence, we should conclude that there are no moral facts. Harman calls this position moral nihilism. He writes:

> We have seen that observational evidence plays a role in science and mathematics it does not seem to play in ethics. Moral hypotheses do not help explain why people observe what they observe. So ethics is problematic and nihilism must be taken seriously. Nihilism is the doctrine that there are no moral facts, no moral truths, and no moral knowledge. This doctrine can account for why reference to moral facts does not seem to help explain observations, on the grounds that what does not exist cannot explain anything.
>
> An extreme version of nihilism holds that morality is simply an illusion: nothing is ever right or wrong, just or unjust, good or bad. In this version, we should abandon morality, just as an atheist abandons religion after he has decided that religious facts cannot help explain observations. Some extreme nihilists have even suggested that morality is merely a superstitious remnant of religion.[8]

Extreme nihilism is hard to swallow, as we noted earlier. It would say there is nothing wrong with murdering your mother or exterminating twelve million people in Nazi concentration camps. Dostoevsky thought that either God exists or moral nihilism does—this is a good reason to believe in God, or at least to get others to do so. But this won't help agnostics or atheists.

Moderate nihilism holds that, although no moral truths exist, moral discourse is expressive—roughly emotivist (see Chapter 11). In this way, since morality is noncognitive, it is not undermined by the observation requirement. Morality allows us to express our feelings and attempt to get others to feel the way we do, but, at bottom, it is no more objective than extreme nihilism. Morality is merely a functionally useful way of projecting our feelings onto the world.

Harman contends that we cannot know by observation (or by any other way) that setting a cat on fire is immoral. How would we counter his contention? Perhaps we could set up the following argument:

1. It is wrong to cause unnecessary suffering.

2. Burning a cat causes unnecessary suffering.

3. Therefore, it is wrong to burn the cat.

Well, suppose we have to justify the first premise. Intuitionists might argue that this is self-evident—either immediately obvious or self-evident on reflection by any rational person. The wrongness of causing unnecessary suffering, they would hold, is as apparent upon reflection as the truth that two plus two equals four or that other minds exist. Although added justification might help, it is not necessary, since the justification would be no more certain (to a rational person upon adequate reflection) than the original judgment itself is. Anyone who doesn't *see* this is just morally blind—as blind as someone who doesn't see the redness of apples or the greenness of grass. This answer agrees with Harman's argument that scientific and moral principles are tested differently but says that the difference doesn't matter. Each principle is true in its own sphere. This argument may be correct, but it is unsatisfactory for distinguishing valid intuitions from invalid ones. Anyone can play the intuitionist game and claim that some activity X is wrong or right. For example, an American might say, "It's just obvious that the American way of life is superior," or a Nazi might say, "It's just obvious that Jews should be exterminated." A racist may think its intuitively obvious that people of other races are subhuman, even evil. Superstitions are often justified in this way. How do we distinguish superstitions from valid moral principles? We seem to need something more than mere intuitions.

Similarly, religionists might appeal to the laws of God. We must refrain from harming sentient beings for the fun of it, because God has so commanded us or because God informs us of the wrongness of such actions. Perhaps this is so, but how do we know that God exists or that this particular command is really authentic? The appeal to religion just shifts the discussion to an equally difficult topic—justifying religion.

More importantly, suppose we are naturalists like Harman. How can we justify the first premise? We can theorize about sentience, holding that sentient beings desire happiness or pleasure and avoid pain or suffering. Moral principles are guides to action that, among other things, promote happiness and ameliorate suffering.[9] If Principle P promotes happiness or ameliorates suffering, then P qualifies as a moral principle. It follows from the nature of principles that it is right to do P and to refrain from acting against P—that is, refrain from anything that would diminish another's happiness or increase another's suffering. Perhaps we could link moral principles with promoting the interests of sentient beings. Or perhaps, for some reason, you are not sure about including animals in the circle of morally considerable beings. Then instead of premise 2 we could use premise 2′:

2′. Burning Jews in gas ovens causes unnecessary suffering.

Or instead of premise 2′ we could use premise 2*:

2★. Burning little children causes unnecessary suffering.

This argument assumes that morality is a functional institution that concerns promoting happiness and ameliorating suffering. I think this assumption is correct. Why can't we characterize morality as having these features? If someone objects that this is begging the question about the definition of *morality,* my reaction is to say, "OK. I'll give you the word *morality.* Call this feature *lorality* and say that it consists of practices that, among other things, promote (human) happiness and ameliorate suffering." But I see no need to use lorality, for we already have a well-established commonsense notion of morality with a long history in Eastern and Western thought connecting this notion with promoting happiness, ameliorating suffering, striving for justice, and ensuring the survival of society. Hence, the pretenses of moral nihilists or moral skeptics needn't intimidate us.

Richard Werner and Nicholas Sturgeon, among others, have argued that, even if we accept Harman's observation requirement, we should conclude that moral facts exist.[10] There is no strong disanalogy between scientific and moral observation. The most reasonable explanation for many scientific observations is a scientific entity (e.g., the proton in a cloud chamber). Likewise, the most reasonable explanation for a moral observation is a moral entity (e.g., the wrongness of causing unnecessary suffering). One may argue that, just as one needs background knowledge to recognize that vapor in a cloud chamber is evidence of a subatomic particle, one needs background evidence about animal sentience and the properties of fire to infer that burning a cat is torturous and hence causes unnecessary suffering. Even if the children were ignorant of that evidence and burned the cat out of curiosity, we would still judge the act to be wrong—though we would judge the children to be guiltless. We would instruct them, "Don't you realize that cats feel extreme pain in being burned?" If the children know of the pain caused by extreme heat, then they will realize that burning hurts the cat and will realize that it is a bad thing to do, inasmuch as causing pain is a bad thing to do.

However, according to Harman, this argument still entails a disanalogy between scientific and moral reasoning. Werner illustrates Harman's *disanalogy thesis* by comparative diagrams as shown in Figures 5 and 6.

In Figure 5, principle SP is derivable from ST, whereas SO and RSO are derivable from SP together with some observation (the trail in the cloud chamber). SO tends to verify SP, which in turn verifies ST. So the entities posited in ST and SP must exist in order to be observed in SO.

FIGURE 5 Scientific Explanatory Model

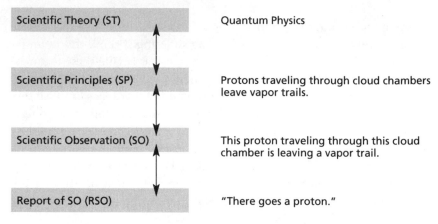

Scientific Theory (ST) — Quantum Physics

Scientific Principles (SP) — Protons traveling through cloud chambers leave vapor trails.

Scientific Observation (SO) — This proton traveling through this cloud chamber is leaving a vapor trail.

Report of SO (RSO) — "There goes a proton."

FIGURE 6 Moral Explanatory Model

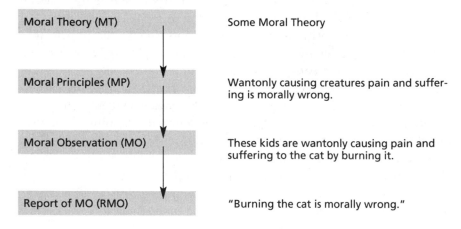

Moral Theory (MT) — Some Moral Theory

Moral Principles (MP) — Wantonly causing creatures pain and suffering is morally wrong.

Moral Observation (MO) — These kids are wantonly causing pain and suffering to the cat by burning it.

Report of MO (RMO) — "Burning the cat is morally wrong."

In Figure 6, principle MP is derivable from MT, whereas MO and RMO are derivable from MP together with some observation (the wanton burning of the cat). MO does not tend to verify MT, since the most reasonable explanation of RMO depends on the observer's psychological set and does not require the positing of moral facts. So there is a disanalogy between scientific and moral reasoning.[11]

Werner thinks that the diagram in Figure 6 is incomplete, and so do I. We could construct a set of upward-pointing arrows, saying that the best explanation for our moral observations is the truth of our moral principles and theory. Suppose our moral theory includes the principle that it is wrong to inflict unnecessary suffering on beings. The background conditions will include the fact that we socialize children to feel guilt about inflicting such cruelty on others. A second criterion will be that this socialization process must survive rational scrutiny (that is, we would have confidence in this process under conditions of impartiality and wide knowledge). We will appeal to the children's own experience of pain and suffering to confirm that pain is intrinsically bad. This would be hard to teach if, as rarely happens, the children cannot feel physical pain. But they could still comprehend psychological pain. Let us assume this connection between the idea that pain is intrinsically bad and the observation that we feel guilt if we cause cruelty or moral indignation at the sight of others causing cruelty, that is, unnecessary suffering. We can then say that our judging of the children as doing something wrong confirms the thesis that it is indeed wrong to cause unnecessary suffering. If this is correct, then Harman's disanalogy evaporates, and we can say that moral judgments are derivable from moral principles and theories and that they tend to confirm those principles and theories.

If this is correct, then we can conclude that moral realism, with its thesis that there are moral facts, is correct. So is moral cognitivism, the thesis that we can have moral knowledge. But note, even if we are unclear about the strength of the argument for moral realism, even if we remain skeptical about cognitivism, we could still adhere to a weaker type of moral objectivism. Suppose we are impressed with the world to word direction of fit and conclude that moral principles are imperatives—they are prescriptions and not descriptions—that aim at matching world to word, hence they lack truth value. I think this is a tempting position, one I held for many years and one that R. M. Hare holds.[12] We would be noncognitivists, but we could still be objectivists, as I was. We could still hold that, from an ideal perspective, a specific set of principles (such as those described in Chapter 3 on objective morality) is necessary for human flourishing. We would speak of these prescriptive principles as being *valid* or *adequate to our purposes,* rather than *true,* but we would still preserve the universality and objectivity of morality. So while cognitivism and realism seem surer paths to moral objectivism, noncognitivism is compatible with it.

Conclusion

Are there moral facts? The main arguments against this thesis are (1) the principle of simplicity—that we should not multiply properties or things beyond necessity—and (2) the world to word direction of fit—that moral principles are more like prescriptions or imperatives, not descriptions of the world. We have countered the first argument in terms of the explanatory power of moral properties. Our response to the second argument is as follows. Just as we can say of a medical prescription, "Taking an aspirin a day is the correct prescription if you want to prevent a heart attack," we can also correctly say, "Promoting human flourishing by deeds of kindness and love is the way to make this a better world." Both statements are true—or if they aren't, then their opposites are true. So moral principles do entail truth claims in this broad sort of way.

But the moral realist wants to say more than this. He or she is making a metaphysical claim about the fabric of the universe. Philosophers like Harman and Hare are correct to point out that moral principles cannot be tested by observation in the same way that empirical theories can. But they may be tested. Cultures that fail to instantiate moral principles such as truth-telling, promise-keeping, cooperating, and not killing innocent members of the community will probably not survive, or if they do, their members will not be very happy or prosperous. To me, thought experiments (such as Golding's *Lord of the Flies*) as well as anthropological and sociological data (such as studies of the Ik culture and the Mafia subcultures) seem to confirm the need for morality as much as vapor trails in a cloud chamber confirm the existence of protons. So, in a way, our reflective moral judgments, those surviving critical scrutiny, do roughly confirm our moral theories. But even as our scientific theories are open to revision and qualification, so our moral theories are open to revision in the light of better evidence and reflection.

One other consideration accommodates the view that moral principles have truth value and that they do make up the fabric of the universe. This is the thesis that not all truths about the universe are empirical ones. *Not all facts are empirical ones.* The laws of logic are not empirical, yet I believe as strongly as I believe anything that the law of noncontradiction is true of all possible worlds. Furthermore, I suspect that there are universals and not just particulars. There is a universal property "red" that all red things have in common, a universal horse aspect that all horses have in common, a universal idea of pain that all experiences of pain have in common, a universal concept of belief that all beliefs have in common. There is a universal property of being a prime number that empiricism does not even bear on. There are two-placed relations, such as the relationship of being to the left of something (e.g., aRb, where "R" stands for the relation, and "a" and "b" stand for the objects) that characterize objects in space and relations in time (e.g., a occurred before b). If universals are admitted as part of the fabric of the universe, then I see no reason to withhold moral properties from this class of entities. There seem to be moral properties, and if so, then there are moral truths, whether or not anyone acknowledges them and whether or not we discover them.

Although I have generally supported a naturalist account of morality, holding that moral properties supervene on natural ones (e.g., the property "goodness" is consequent upon the experience of being happy or loving), I have not ruled out intuitionism, the thesis that moral properties are non-natural, that they are self-evident truths discovered upon reflection. I have also allowed for the possibility that moral properties are rooted in a transcendent reality. The naturalism that I have defended is a functional naturalism, not a metaphysical one. The common thesis of these theories is that universal moral truths exist. If so, we have objective guidelines for our actions, by which we should live and structure our societies.[13]

NOTES

1. Baruch Spinoza, *Ethics,* (Haffner Press, 1949), p. 77.

2. Projectivism or expressivism is a non-cognitivist theory set forth by Simon Blackburn. It holds that to make a moral claim is to perform an action with functions such as

   "to set oneself for or against something, to invite others to share this orientation, to prescribe courses of action, to lay down boundaries and give warning against trespass, or to smile encouragingly on conformity. It is to take up an attitude or stance, and centrally it involves making an emotional response to contemplated events and states of affairs....It enables us to share our stances with others, to shape our sensibilities in light of the opinions of others, and to hear and voice assent and dissent." [Blackburn, "Securing the Nots: Moral Epistemology for the Quasi-Realist," in W. Sinnott-Armstrong, and M. Timmons, eds., *Moral Knowledge* (Oxford University Press, 1996)].

3. J. L. Mackie, *Ethics: Inventing Right and Wrong,* (Penguin, 1977), p. 35.

4. Gilbert Harman, *The Nature of Morality* (Oxford University Press, 1979). It

is not clear that Harman accepts moral nihilism. Sometimes he seems to accept an internal ethical relativism.

5. Of course, one can embed principles in propositions. For example, "It is true that promise-keeping is a prima facie moral principle." This is trivially true (if we assume that it is true at all). The moral realist has a more robust notion of moral truth. Moral truths are part of the structure of the universe as much as tables and chairs, atoms and molecules.

6. Jonathan Harrison in his "Mackie's Moral 'Sceptisim'" in *Philosophy* 57 (1982) drew my attention to this point. Harrison's article deeply influenced my analysis of Mackie's thought.

7. Quoted in Wallace Matson, *A New History of Philosophy* (Harcourt Brace Jovanovich, 1987), vol. I.

8. Harman, *The Nature of Morality,* p. 11.

9. I distinguish between pain and suffering. Pain is typically physiological or at least phenomenological, as in "I'm pained by his betrayal of his family." Suffering, as I define it, is more objective and encompasses pain but is broader in scope. I may be suffering from incurable cancer but not be

..re of it, let alone be in pain. Both indicate harm to the agent, but pain is consciously experienced, whereas suffering need not be.

10. Richard Werner, "Ethical Realism," *Ethics* 93 (1983), pp. 653–79; Nicholas Sturgeon "Moral Explanations," in L. Pojman, ed., *Ethical Theory* (Wadsworth, 1998). See the readings in Geoffrey Sayre-McCord, ed., *Essays in Moral Realism* (Cornell University Press, 1990). See also David Brink, *Moral Realism and the Foundations of Ethics* (Cambridge University Press, 1989), and Michael Smith, *The Moral Problem* (Blackwell, 1994).

11. Werner, "Ethical Realism," p. 655.

12. R. M. Hare, *Moral Thinking* (Oxford University Press, 1981). See also his "Prescriptivism: The Structure of Ethics and Morals," in L. Pojman, ed., *Ethical Theory.*

13. My thanks to Jonathan Harrison and Robert Audi, who constructively critiqued an earlier version of this chapter. Audi reminded me that intuitionism is a viable alternative to naturalism. See his "Intuitionism, Pluralism and the Foundations of Ethics" in W. Sinnott-Armstrong and M. Timmons, eds. *Moral Knowledge* (Oxford University Press, 1996). Strictly speaking, I have also allowed for a noncognitivist or antirealist *objectivism,* which posits universal, contingent principles as prescriptions but denies that they have truth value. Whether this position can remain distinct from relativism is a difficult issue, one that is on the cutting edge of contemporary metaethics.

FOR FURTHER READING

Brink, David O. *Moral Realism and the Foundations of Ethics.* University of Indiana Press, 1989.

Butchvarov, P. *Skepticism in Ethics.* University of Indiana Press, 1989.

Darwall, Stephen, Allan Gibbard and Peter Railton, eds. *Moral Discourse and Practice.* Oxford University Press, 1997. Contains the best set of readings on the debate over moral realism, especially the editors' opening summary essay on ethics in the twentieth century.

Fumerton, R. *Reason and Morality.* Cornell University Press, 1990.

Harman, Gilbert. *The Nature of Morality.* Oxford University Press, 1979.

Mackie, J. L.. *Ethics: Inventing Right and Wrong.* Penguin, 1977.

Pojman, Louis, ed. *Ethical Theory: Classical and Contemporary Readings.* Wadsworth, 1998. Section IX contains several readings on this subject, including ones by Brink, Sturgeon and Russell.

Sinnott-Armstrong, Walter and Mark Timmons, eds. *Moral Knowledge.* Oxford University Press, 1996. An excellent collection on moral epistemology. Sinnot-Armstrong's probing opening essay sets the pace and is followed by some first-rate papers by Robert Audi, Richard Brandt, David Copp, and others.

Smith, Michael. *The Moral Problem.* Blackwell's, 1994. Perhaps the most comprehensive defense of internalist moral realism.

A Concluding Reflection:

Minimal Morality, Virtue Ethics, and the Development of Character

Can anything be better for a commonwealth than to produce men and women of the best type?

PLATO, *THE REPUBLIC*

In Chapter 8 we discussed the relationship between action-centered ethics and virtue-based ethics. Due to the length of that chapter I was unable to deal with the importance of virtue ethics for moral character. I would like to close this work with reflections on this topic.

In a seminal article, David Norton has argued for a fundamental distinction between traditional action-centered ethics and classical virtue ethics (or *eudaimonist ethics,* which Richard Taylor has more appropriately labeled the ethics of aspiration).[1] Traditional rule-governed ethics—such as Hobbesian contractualism (including its present-day expressions in the formulations of Gilbert Harman and David Gauthier), Mill's weak form of utilitarianism, and most forms of deontological ethics—tends to be minimalist, calling on us to adhere to a core of necessary rules (e.g., do not steal, harm, murder, or lie) in order for society to function. The accent is on *social control:* Morality is largely preventive, safeguarding rights and moral space where people may carry out their projects unhindered by the intrusions of others. Norton exempts from this characterization strong utilitarianism such as that found in Peter Singer's work, but he argues that strong utilitarianism misses the point of the incremental nature of moral responsibility. I will discuss this in a moment.

Daniel Callahan characterizes such a *moral minimalist* ethic this way:

> It has been one that stressed the transcendence of the individual over the community, the need to tolerate all moral viewpoints, the autonomy of the self as the highest human good, the informed consent contract as the model of human relationships. We are obliged under the most generous reading of a minimalist ethic only to honor our voluntarily undertaken family obligations, to keep our promises, and to respect contracts freely entered into with other freely consenting adults. Beyond those minimal standards, we are free to do as we like, guided by nothing other than our private standards of good and evil.[2]

Moral minimalism has the advantage that it appeals to minimal common sense and so can easily be universalized; its injunctions apply to all rational agents. Its claims are exceedingly modest, since it permits most of life to go on without the scrutiny of morality. As Mill says, "Ninety-nine hundredths of all our actions are done from other [than moral] motives, and rightly so done if the rule of duty does not condemn them."[3] The major portion of life comes not under the domain of moral obligation but under the domain of the permissible. We are given a generous portion of morally free space in which to develop our personality and talents as we see fit—just as long as we do not break out of the broad confines of moral constraints. The morally free zone is sometimes identified with what is prudent or what pertains to our self-interest.

Classical eudaimonist ethics, going back to Socrates, Plato, and Aristotle, presupposes two theses absent in minimalist ethics: First of all, "morality is coterminus with human life and unrestrictedly pervasive within it."[4] There is no separate moral-free zone, and prudence cannot be separated from morality, at least not to the extent that minimalism separates it. The Good is good for you. Second, nonminimalist ethics supposes a duty of moral development or growth, so that while not everyone is called on to be a saint or hero, if we develop properly, we may all develop moral sensitivities and abilities in ways that approximate those of the saints and heroes. A hero is one who accomplishes good deeds when the average person would be prevented by fear, terror, or a drive of self-interest. A saint is one who acts for good when inclination, desire, or self-interest would prevent most people from so acting.

The sort of view that Norton has in mind is illustrated by Plato's rhetorical remark on the function of government: "Can anything be better for a commonwealth than to produce in it men and women of the best type?"[5] It is also found in Mill: "The most important point of excellence which any form of government can possess is to promote the virtue and intelligence of the people themselves."[6] And John Dewey said, "Democracy has many meanings, but if it has a moral meaning, it is found in resolving that the supreme test of all political institutions and industrial arrangements shall be the contribution they make to the all-around growth of every member of society."[7]

The crucial factor in classical aspiration ethics is the *duty* to grow as a moral person, so that one may be able to take on greater moral responsibility. With increased responsibility comes increased competence in making moral choices and increased exhilaration at scaling moral mountain peaks. Consider Reinhold Messner's description of his state of being while climbing in the Himalayan mountains: "Striding along, my body becomes so highly-charged it would be quite impossible for me to stop. It feels as if something wants to break free, to burst from my breast. It is a surge of longing that carries me forward as if I were possessed."[8] Every saint and moral hero must have similar sensations. The deeply moral person can experience joys and hardships unknown to the "flatlands" minimal moralist who has not developed his or her moral-climbing abilities.

In this regard Norton allows that strong utilitarianism, such as Peter Singer's theory, is more sensitive to the demands of eudaimonism. Singer's principle is: "If it is in our power to prevent something bad from happening, without thereby sacrificing anything of comparable moral importance, we ought, morally, to do it."[9] A moment's reflection on the implications of this principle should convince you of its radicalness. If we were to follow it, we would all be left just slightly better off than the worst-off people in the world (who would be somewhat better off). People would have to turn in their second cars and second homes and share the ones they already have. America—which has less than 4.5 percent of the world's population but which uses something like 35 percent of the world's resources and 25 percent of its nonrenewable energy, consumes 33 percent of its food, and produces 36 percent of its pollution—would have to put up with a greatly lowered standard of living.

However, Norton argues, Singer misses the point by universalizing this principle to become everyone's duty, thus missing the incremental nature of morality. We do not all have the same kinds of duties, just as we cannot all scale difficult mountains. "But how can it be other than futile to present a mountaineering demand to flatland-dwellers without reckoning with the problem that they are devoid of climbing skills?"[10]

Just as an intellectual or scholar experiences bliss over ideas in a manner unavailable to one who gets stimulation from watching mud-wrestling matches or football games on television, so the saint or moral hero experiences a sense of aesthetic ecstasy at accomplishing moral deeds that are out of the realm of possibility for the average moral person. There is *elitism* in morality. There are even moral experts: the saints and moral heroes. What may appear an act of supererogation to a moral neophyte may be an everyday feat to a moral hero. We do not all have the same responsibilities, but we all have a general duty to develop our moral capacities to the point where we can experience greater happiness and greater responsibility in the moral domain, to the point where many more of us could perform heroic and saintly acts.

Norton has identified a crucial problem in contemporary moral theory: It is not enough to get people to adhere to a minimal morality. We must come to realize that not only do we have a duty to obey core moral injunctions but we also have a responsibility to develop our moral sensitivities and abilities to the point where we can live life on a higher moral plane, both enjoying the exhilaration of high and challenging places and bearing burdens unknown to fledglings in moral climbing.

If this argument is correct, moral learning never stops, and moral education from childhood onward is one of the most important things we can engage in, both for society's sake (for it is in our interest to have deeply moral citizens) and for our own sake (it is in our interest to be deeply moral people).

NOTES

1. David L. Norton, "Moral Minimalism and the Development of Moral Character," in Peter A. French, Theodore E. Uehling, and Howard K. Wettstein, eds., *Midwest Studies in Philosophy,* Vol. XIII (University of Minnesota, 1988), pp. 180–195. Richard Taylor, *Ethics, Faith and Reason* (Prentice-Hall, 1985), p. 5.

2. Daniel Callahan, "Minimal Ethics: On the Pacification of Morality," *Hastings Center Report* 11 (Oct 1981), pp. 19–25.

3. John Stuart Mill, *Utilitariansim,* (Bobbs–Merrill, 1957) p. 23.

4. Norton, *"Moral Minimalism"* p. 187.

5. Plato, *The Republic,* trans. F. M. Cornford (Oxford University Press, 1947), p. 154.

6. John Stuart Mill, *Considerations on Representative Government* (London, 1861), p. 25.

7. John Dewey, *Reconstruction in Philosophy* (New American Library, 1920), p. 186.

8. Reinhold Messner and Alessandro Gonga, *K-2: Mountain of Mountains* (1980), p. 78; quoted in Norton, "Moral Minimalism."

9. Peter Singer, "Famine, Affluence and Morality," in Joel Feinberg, ed., *Reason and Responsibility* (Wadsworth, 1985), p. 523; quoted in Norton, "Moral Minimalism," p. 193.

10. Norton, "Moral Minimalism," p. 193.

Appendix 1

An Analysis of the Modified Divine Command Theory

In Chapter 10 I argued that the Divine Command Theory (DCT) had severe problems that made it unacceptable as a moral theory. Since many religious people, theologians, and philosophers hold to something like this theory, and might suspect that I did not examine its most sophisticated form, it is necessary that I look at what, to my knowledge, is the most plausible version of the theory.

Sophisticated divine command theorists seek to answer two criticisms—the "redundancy" and the "arbitrary" objections—without giving up the essential insights of the DCT. One example of such a modified version of the DCT is that of Robert Adams.[1] Adams is moved by the objection that the DCT allows for the possibility that God could command acts that are patently vicious. For example, he could command me "to make it my chief end in life to inflict suffering on other human beings, for no other reason than that He commanded it" (p. 526). This will not do. Accordingly, Adams suggests a modification of the DCT:

> According to the modified divine command theory [MDCT], when I say "It is wrong to do X" [at least part of] what I mean is that it is contrary to God's command to do X. "It is wrong to do X" *implies* "It is contrary to God's commands to do X." But "It is contrary to God's

commands to do X" implies "It is wrong to do X" only if certain conditions are assumed—namely, only if it is assumed that God has the character which I believe Him to have, of loving His human creatures. If God were really to command us to make cruelty our goal, then He would not have that character of loving us, and I would not say it would be wrong to disobey Him. (p. 527)

By the MDCT, God's command is a necessary but not sufficient condition for full ethical validity. The command must also be issued from the motive of love or, at least, be consistent with the character of love. Since we have other values (our secular "ethical" values), it would not be "wrong" for us to disobey a command of God to make gratuitous suffering the goal of life. If God did command this, "my concept of ethical wrongness (and my concept of ethical permittedness) would 'break down.'" Although this is logically possible, it is "unthinkable that God should do so" (p. 528).

If I understand Adams, his argument boils down to this:

1. Necessarily, for any person S and for all acts A, if A is forbidden (required) of S, then God commands that not-A (A) for S. Likewise, if A is permitted for S, then God has commanded neither A nor not-A for S. That is, God's command defines our ethical duties, as the divine command theory affirms.

2. It is logically possible for God to issue command C: S must engage in gratuitous cruelty.

3. If C, S would be permitted (nonmorally) to disobey God (since S has other values besides ethical ones). In this case ethics would break down for S.

4. Since God is love, it is unthinkable for God to command C.

A fully ethical act is defined in this way:

5. Necessarily, for any person S and for all acts A, A is forbidden (required) of S, if and only if God commands that not-A (A) for S and the command is issued in a state of love. Likewise, A is permitted for S, if and only if God, in a state of love, has commanded neither A nor not-A for S.

A complete moral command is so if and only if it fulfills two necessary and jointly sufficient conditions: God commanded it, and he did so in a state of love. There seem to be two levels of meaning to the words *wrong, permitted,* and *right*—an ethical one and a nonethical one that actually may override the ethical use. Although Adams refers to the second type of use as "nonmoral," it has all the features of a moral obligation or permission: It overrides other duties. So let us call this type of duty our "secular ethical duty," since it refers to those values we arrive at through reason. On the one hand, God's command makes something an ethical duty; but on the other hand, we may not be required to obey the command if it is not made in love.

Adams states rather mystically that the believer will have a Platonic/Moorean view of ethical goodness. It is an unanalyzable, nonnatural property residing in God, and our attribution of the term *good* to God suggests that "God has some important set of qualities which one regards as virtuous in human beings" (p. 534). Adams argues that it makes no sense to say that God has duties, for that implies that there must be some higher/outside authority whence come commands, which is logically impossible.

A CRITIQUE OF THE MODIFIED DIVINE COMMAND THEORY

A critic may challenge Adams' ingenious reformulation of the divine command theory and argue that his version of the MDCT is not a divine command theory at all, but merely a modified version of the autonomy thesis. It is an example of *act agapism,* the theory that one has a duty to act out of love and never to act against what is the loving thing to do. Agapism is suggested by certain passages in the New Testament, such as: "God is love" (1 John 4:8) together with "Love is patient and kind....Love does not insist on its own way....it does not rejoice in wrong but rejoices in the right....Make love your aim." (1 Cor. 13:4–6; 14:1).

Love turns out to be the criterion of highest value, and a command is not a fully ethical command unless it is done in love. God can—but must not—act out of character. Here is how we might reconstruct the MDCT as offered by Adams in terms of Euthyphro's dilemma:

1. God doesn't command the right (in the sense of require) because it is right; rather, the right is right because God commands it (DCT). That is, God's command is what makes an act *formally ethical.*

2. But God must properly command what is (consistent with) loving. Otherwise, the command is not an ethical command we must obey (one that overrides all other duties). That is, although an unloving command might be formally right, we would be permitted to disobey

it. In other words, the secular ethic may override the formally ethical obligation.

3. But love is defined as being benevolently concerned for the good of its object. It has to do with human flourishing. So even God cannot make something ethically good that does not conform to what is good for his creatures.

4. So God can properly command only what is good. His love connects the right to the good, so that he commands us to do what is right independent of his commands.

5. There is a contradiction between premises 1 and 4. Therefore, one of the premises must be rejected.

If we prefer the MDCT to the DCT, then we must say that the DCT is false, and the MDCT becomes equivalent to the autonomy thesis: God commands the Good (or right) because it is good (or right), and the Good (right) is not good (right) simply because God commands it. Furthermore, if this is correct, then we can discover our ethical duties through reason, independent of God's command. For what is good for his creatures is so objectively, (e.g., being tortured gratuitously is not good for them, and being happy and wise is good for them). We do not need God to tell us that it is bad to cause unnecessary suffering or that it is good to ameliorate suffering; reason can do that. It begins to look like the true version of ethics is what we called "secular ethics."

Adams might reply that this argument doesn't represent his position, for he distinguishes the Good from the right. It is God's command that defines the right, but other values (e.g., love) may define the Good, so that the right and the Good may not be in harmony. When the *right* defies the *good,* the *good* may override the *right.* As Adams says, it would not be wrong to disobey God when he commanded something that was heinous from the point of view of our deepest notion of the Good. The believer's "positive valuation of doing whatever God may command is not clearly greater than his independent negative valuation of cruelty"—even if God should command it. But normally, we think of morality as being that which overrides all other duties, our highest duty. Indeed, isn't that part of the motivation of the divine command theory in the first place, to link God to our highest moral duty? By bifurcating our value system in this way, Adams leaves us with a dual value system, which seems to create more problems than it solves.

If my revisionist interpretation of Adams' argument is correct, then by making love a necessary condition for God's proper command, Adams' modification of the DCT transforms the DCT into its opposite, the autonomy thesis. He does not seem to recognize that love serves MDCT ethics in exactly the same way that the Good serves autonomous ethics. Even as an act is right (at least in teleological systems) only if it serves the Good, so likewise with the MDCT—an act is right only if it issues from love. Proponents of the autonomy thesis typically make goodness a necessary condition for rightness, whereas the MDCT makes love a necessary condition; and love, it turns out, is simply a functional term for the Good.

Of course, Adams would probably reply that, at most, what this shows is that the autonomy thesis is part of the MDCT but not the whole. It is goodness plus God's command that determines what is right. But, the question arises, what does God add to rightness that is not there simply with goodness? It is not simply that God *knows* more outcomes than we, for the autonomy thesis would gladly grant that. If love or goodness prescribes act A, what does A gain by being commanded by God? Materially, nothing at all.

In a later article, "Divine Command Metaethics Modified Again" (see Note 1), Adams seeks to make a distinction that might answer the objection just made. He tries to distinguish two senses of ethics: the real one and the functionally equivalent one. Both the DCT and autonomous ethics might result in the same principles, but they are nonetheless not the same. He refers to Saul Kripke's thesis of natural kinds, which goes something like this: Suppose that on some other planet (or someplace on our planet) there is a substance W that seems functionally equivalent to what we call water. Would W be water? No, Kripke says. Water is necessarily H_2O, and anything that is functionally equivalent to water but not H_2O would not be water, no matter how similar in taste, touch, and physiological effects. Likewise, avers Adams, although ethical principles that do not arise from God may be functionally equivalent to those that do, they are nonetheless not really *ethical* principles; they are simply look-alikes.

How valid is this analogy between water and ethics? It seems to be a distinction without a difference. For if both ethics (MDCT) and secular ethics have human (or sentient beings') flourishing as the goal, what difference should it make whether the very same principle issues from a special personal authority (God) or from the authority of reason? After all, don't we need to use reason even to adjudicate revelatory claims to divine authority? Otherwise, how could we distinguish the devil's commands from God's?

If we reject this position, and with it the Divine Command Theory itself, we need to consider the implications of the second horn of Euthyphro's dilemma—that which posits God as commanding the Good because it is good.

At this point it must be asked whether there is any need for theists to go to such enormous pains in order to save the Divine Command Theory. Why should they be threatened by the autonomy thesis? If there is an inherent logic to goodness that precludes God's inventing right and wrong, why should that bother religious people? It is widely recognized that God's omnipotence isn't threatened by the fact that the laws of logic exist independent of him. Why should the fact that there is a logic to ethics be troubling to the notion of God's sovereignty or omnipotence? Couldn't it be that God's sovereignty comes in, not at the point of inventing morality once creation is in place, but at the point of deciding what kinds of beings to create?

Suppose that God creates people on two planets in the universe: our Earth and Planet X. His creative will allows him to construct two admirable but different systems. We have some idea of how things work on Earth. On Planet X God created humanoids, beings like us but with exometallic skeletons and limbs that replace themselves like our fingernails do, and who reproduce by spontaneously cloning their cells rather than by sexual intercourse. In fact, Xians are never tempted to fornicate or commit adultery (though disloyalty is a problem). Likewise, since they feel very little pain, torture is not a possibility (though suffering is).

On both Earth and X there are rules designed to ameliorate suffering and promote the survival and flourishing of rational beings. There are many rules in common—for example, ones prescribing truth-telling and beneficence and proscribing disloyalty and the killing of innocents. But X does not have a rule against adultery or torture or dismembering humanoids.

God, who loves variety, could have created us like Xians, but he didn't. Had he done so, we would have had some different moral rules than we do. Instead he chose to make us the way we are, so that certain rules of conduct are necessary for our survival and well-being. They are necessary since even God can't change them now that he has made us the way we are. Moral right and wrong are solid facts, just as solid as those of arithmetic or logic or chemistry.

If this is correct, then morality has an independent rationale. It may indirectly depend on God, assuming he exists, in that he could have created us with a different nature. But once God creates rational beings like us, the moral law took on a life of its own that even God must respect.

Of course, the question that takes precedence here is whether there is a God and whether he is totally benevolent. But this gets us into metaphysics and the philosophy of religion, subjects outside the perimeter of this work.

NOTE

1. Robert M. Adams, "A Modified Divine Command Theory of Ethical Wrongness," in Gene Outka and John P. Reeder, eds., *Religion and Morality: A Collection of Essays* (Anchor, 1973). I have not been able to respond to all of the richness of this challenging article. The major portion of the essay is reprinted in Louis Pojman, ed., *Philosophy of Religion* (Wadsworth, 1987), pp. 525-537. For convenience, the page numbers in the text refer to this anthology. Adams' "Divine Command Metaethics Modified Again," *Journal of Religious Ethics* 7 (1979). Philip Quinn's *Divine Commands and Moral Requirements* (Oxford University Press, 1978) is a closely argued defense of a position very similar to Adams'.

Appendix 2

How to Read and Write a Philosophy Paper

Nothing worthwhile was ever accomplished without great difficulty.

PLATO, THE REPUBLIC

Just about everyone who comes to philosophy—usually in college—feels a sinking sensation in their stomach when first encountering this very strange material, involving a different sort of style and method from anything else they have ever dealt with. It was certainly my first reaction as a student. Lured by questions such as "Is there a God? What can I truly know? What is the meaning of life? How shall I live my life?" I began to read philosophy on my own. My first book was Bertrand Russell's *History of Western Philosophy,* which is much more than a history of the subject, being also Russell's own analysis and evaluation of major themes in the history of Western philosophy. Although it is not a terribly difficult text, most of the ideas and arguments were new to me. Since he opposed many of the beliefs that I had been brought up with, I felt angry with him. But since he seemed to argue so persuasively, my anger gave way to confusion and then to a sense of defeat and despair. Yet I felt compelled to go on with this

Adapted from Louis P. Pojman, ed., *Introduction to Philosophy: Classicial and Contemporary Readings* (Wadsworth, 1991), pp. 617-620.

"forbidden fruit," finishing Russell's long work and going on to read Plato's *Republic*, René Descartes' *Meditations*, David Hume's *Dialogues on Natural Religion*, selected writings of Immanuel Kant, William James' *Will to Believe*, and finally contemporary readings by Antony Flew, R. M. Hare, John Hick, and Ludwig Wittgenstein. Gradually, I became aware that on every issue on which I disagreed with Hume or Russell, Kant or Hick, someone else had a plausible counterargument. Eventually, I struggled to the place where I could see weaknesses in arguments (sometimes in the arguments of those figures with whom I had agreed), and finally I came to the point where I could write out arguments of my own. The pain of the process slowly gave way to joy—almost addictive joy, let me warn you—so that I decided to go to graduate school to get an advanced degree in philosophy.

As I mentioned earlier, it was a gnawing worry about fundamental questions of existence that drew me to philosophy. Is there a God? What can I know for sure? Do I have a soul that will live forever? Am I truly free, or simply determined by my heredity and environment? What is it to live a moral life: If you have asked these questions and pondered alternative responses, most of the discussions in this book will make sense to you. But if you haven't spent a lot of time thinking about this sort of subject matter, you might ask yourself whether or not these questions are important, and you might outline you own present responses to them. For unless you've asked the question, the proposed answers may sound like only one end of a telephone conversation.

This textbook is meant to suggest responses in order to stimulate you to work out your own position on the questions addressed herein. This text, offering arguments on alternative sides of each issue, along with a teacher to serve as guide—and, I hope, some fellow students with whom to discuss the material—should challenge you to begin to work out your own moral philosophy.

However, neither the textbook nor the teacher will be sufficient to save you from a sense of disorientation and uncertainty in reading and writing about philosophy, so let me offer a few tips from my experience as a student and as a teacher of philosophy.

SUGGESTIONS FOR READING
A PHILOSOPHY TEXT

The styles and methods of philosophy are different from those of other subjects with which you have been acquainted since grammar school:

English, history, psychology, and science. Of course, there are many methods. And some writings—for example, those of the existentialists: Søren Kierkegaard, Friedrich Nietzsche, Albert Camus, and Jean-Paul Sartre—resemble more what we encounter in literature than they do more typical essays in philosophical analysis. In some ways philosophy resembles mathematics, since it usually strives to develop a deductive argument much like a mathematical proof, only the premises of the argument are usually in need of a lot of discussion and objections need to be considered. Sometimes I think of arguing about a philosophical problem as a kind of legal reasoning before a civil court: Each side presents its evidence and gives reasons for accepting its conclusion rather than the opponent's. For example, suppose you believe in freedom of the will and I believe in determinism. We each set forth the best reasons we have for accepting our respective conclusions. The difference between philosophical argument and the court case is that we are also the jury. We can change our minds on hearing the evidence and even change sides by hearing our opponent make a persuasive case.

SUGGESTIONS FOR WRITING A
PHILOSOPHY PAPER

Talking about philosophy and writing philosophy are excellent ways to improve your understanding of the content and process of the subject as well as to improve your philosophical reasoning skill. Writing an essay on a philosophical issue focuses your mind and forces you to concentrate on the essential arguments connected with the issue. The process is hard, but it's amazing how much progress you can make—some of us faster than others, but in my experience some of those who have the hardest time at first end up doing the deepest, most through work.

First of all, identify a *problem* you want to shed light on or solve or a *thesis* you want to defend. Be sure that you have read at least a few good articles on different sides of the issue and can put the arguments in your own words—or minimally can explain them in your own words.

Now you are ready to begin to write. Here are some suggestions that may help you.

1. Identify the problem you want to analyze. For example, you might want to show that utilitarianism is a tenable (or untenable) theory.

2. As clearly as possible, state the problem and what you intend to show. For example: "I intend to analyze the arguments for and against

act–utilitarianism and show how utilitarianism can meet the main objections to it."

3. Set forth your arguments in logical order, and support your premises with reasons. It helps to illustrate your points with examples or to point out counterexamples to opposing points of view.

4. Consider alternative points of view as well as objections to your own position. Try to meet these charges and show why your position is more plausible.

5. Apply the principle of charity to your opponent's reasoning. That is, give his or her case the strongest interpretation possible, for unless you can meet the strongest objections to your own position, you cannot be confident that your position is the best. I should add that applying the principle of charity is one of the hardest practices in philosophical discussion. Even otherwise very good philosophers have an inclination to caricature or settle for a weak version of their opponent's arguments.

6. End your paper with a summary and a conclusion. That is, succinctly review your arguments and state what you think you've demonstrated. In the conclusion it is always helpful to show the implications of your conclusion for other issues. Answer the question "Why does it matter?"

7. Be prepared to write at least two drafts before you have a working copy. It helps to have another philosophy student go over the pre-liminary draft before you write a final draft. Make sure that your arguments are well constructed and that your paper as a whole is coherent.

8. Regarding style: write *clearly*, and in an active voice. Avoid ambiguous expressions, double negatives, and jargon. Put other people's ideas in your own words as much as possible, and give credit in the text and in bibliographical notes whenever you have used someone else's idea or quoted someone. Knowing just when to credit another person is an exercise in good judgment. While academics are rightly indignant with students who fail to refer to their sources, some students are fastidious to a fault, even documenting where they heard common knowledge. There is a middle way that common sense should be able to discover.

9. Include a bibliography at the end of your paper. In it list all the sources you used in writing your paper.

10. Put the paper aside for a day, then read it afresh. Chances are you will find things to change.

When you have a serious problem, do not hesitate to contact your teacher. That is what he or she is there for: to help you progress in your philosophical reasoning. Your teacher should have reasonable office hours in which he or she is available to discuss the work of students.

Good luck! I hope you come to enjoy philosophical inquiry—and especially moral philosophy—as much as I have.

Glossary

Absolute A principle that is universally binding and may never be overridden by another principle. Utilitarianism is a type of system that has only one absolute principle: "Do the action that maximizes utility." Kant's system has several absolutes, whereas other deontological systems may have only a few broad absolutes, such as "Never cause unnecessary harm."

Absolutism or **Ethical Absolutism** The notion that there is only one correct answer to every moral problem. A completely absolutist ethic consists of absolute principles that provide an answer for every possible situation in life, regardless of culture. Diametrically opposed to ethical absolutism is **Ethical Relativism**, which says that the validity of ethical principles depends on social acceptance. In between these polar opposites is *ethical objectivism*. See **Objectivism; Relativism.**

Agapism (from the Greek *agape,* altrustic love) An ethical theory based on the principle of love. Sometimes this is based on the New Testament injunctions to love (Matt. 22:37-40, 1 Cor. 13). *Act-agapism* holds that one ought always do whatever is the most loving thing to do; this has been called "situational ethics." *Rule-agapism* holds that one ought to follow the most love-embodying set of rules. See page 262.

Altruism Unselfish regard or concern for others; disinterested, other–regarding action. See Chapter 4; see also **Egoism.**

Antirealism (sometimes called irrealism) A metaethical theory denying the assertions of moral realism, which holds that moral facts exist.

Aretaic Ethics   (from the Greek *arete,* virtue) The theory, first presented by Aristotle, that the basis of ethical assessment is character. Rather than seeing the heart of ethics in actions or duties, it focuses on the character and dispositions of the agent. Whereas *deontological* and *teleological* ethical systems emphasize *doing,* aretaic (or virtue) ethics emphasizes *being*—that is, being a certain type of person who will no doubt manifest his or her being in appropriate actions. See Chapter 8.

Autonomy   (from the Greek for "self-rule") Self-directed freedom. The autonomous individual arrives at his or her moral judgments through reason rather than simple acceptance of authority. The *autonomy thesis* states that ethical truths can be known and justified on the basis of human reason without divine revelation. See Chapters 7 and 11; see also **Heteronomy.**

Categorical Imperative (CI) A command to perform actions that are necessary of themselves without reference to other ends. It contrasts with *Hypothetical Imperatives,* which command actions not for their own sake but for some other good. For Kant, moral duties command categorically; they represent the injunctions of reason, which endows them with universal validity and objective necessity. See Chapter 7; see also **Hypothetical Imperative.**

Cognitivism   A theory claiming that moral judgments have truth value. That is, such statements as "Lying is morally wrong" do not simply express negative feelings toward lying but express an objective truth about lying, namely that it has a wrong-making quality (e. g., it is bad). Such judgments are made true or false by reference to properties, either natural (e. g., an object of desire or pleasure) or nonnatural (e. g., Moore's simple, unanalyzable property discovered by intuition). If the right property is present, then the judgment is true; if the right property is absent, then the judgment is false. See Chapter 9; see also **Noncognitivism.**

Cultural Relativism   The theory that different cultures have different moral rules. It makes no judgment of the validity of those rules and is thus neutral between ethical *objectivism* and *Ethical Relativism.* Sometimes a culture's moral systems are called *positive morality:* any existing moral code as distinguished from an adequate or justified moral code. For example, Nazi morality is a moral code, but most objectivists would deny that it is an adequate or justified moral code. It contains invalid principles such as "Always kill Jews, gypsies, and Poles." See Chapter 2; see also **Objectivism** and **Ethical Relativism.**

Deontic (from the Greek *deon,* duty or obligation) Refers to action-based ethical systems, such as deontological and teleological systems, and the type of judgment (i. e., evaluations of actions) that proceed from these systems, as opposed to judgments of motivation and character that proceed from aretaic systems. See Chapter 8; see also **Aretaic Ethics.**

Deontological Ethics (from the Greek *deon,* duty or obligation) Ethical systems that consider certain features in the moral act itself to have intrinsic value. These contrast with *teleological ethics*, which holds that the ultimate criterion of morality lies in some nonmoral value that results from actions. For example, for the deontologist, there is something right about truth-telling, even when it may cause pain or harm, and there is something wrong about lying, even when it may produce good consequences. See Chapters 6 and 7; see also **Teleological Ethics.**

Divine Command Theory (DCT) The theory that holds that moral principles are defined in terms of God's commands or that moral duties are logically dependent on God's commands. See Chapter 11 and Appendix 1.

Egoism *Psychological egoism* is a *descriptive* theory about human motivation, holding that people always act to satisfy their perceived best interests. *Ethical egoism* is a *prescriptive* or normative theory about how people *ought* to act; they ought to act according to their perceived best interests. See Chapter 4.

Emotivism A version of **Noncognitivism** holding that moral judgments do not have truth values but are expressions of our attitudes; these judgements express our feelings and help us persuade others to act as we desire. According to A. J. Ayer, a prominent emotivist, the moral judgment that murder is wrong reduces to the emotional expression "Murder—Boo!" See Chapter 9.

Error Theory The thesis that, if moral principles are objectively valid, then there must be moral facts (or properties). But there are no moral facts (or properties). Hence there are no moral truths, and we are in error if we think there are. See the discussion of J. L. Mackie's work in Chapter 12.

Ethical Relativism Holds that the validity of moral judgments depends on cultural acceptance. It is opposed to **Objectivism** and **Absolutism**. See Chapter 2.

Euthyphro's Dilemma The puzzle set forth in Plato's dialogue *Euthyphro,* in which Socrates asks whether God loves the pious because it is pious or whether the pious is pious because God loves it. It is associated with the **Divine Command Theory** and the *autonomy thesis.* See Chapter 11.

Hedon (from the Greek *hedone,* pleasure) Possessing a pleasurable or painful quality. Sometimes "hedon" stands for a quantity of pleasure.

Hedonism *Psychological hedonism* is the theory that motivation must be explained exclusively through desire for pleasure and aversion of pain. *Ethical hedonism* is the theory that pleasure is the only intrinsic positive value and that pain or "unpleasant consciousness" is the only negative intrinsic value (or intrinsic disvalue). All other values derive from these two. See Chapter 5.

Heteronomy Kant's term for the determination of the will on nonrational grounds. It contrasts with *autonomy of the will,* in which the will is guided by reason.

Hypothetical Imperative A command that enjoins actions because they help attain some end that one desires. Ethicists who regard moral duties as dependent on consequences would view moral principles as hypothetical imperatives. They have the form: "If you want X, do action A" (e. g., "If you want to live in peace, do all in your power to prevent violence"). This contrasts with the **Categorical Imperative**. See Chapter 7.

Intuitionism The ethical theory that the good or the right thing to do can be known directly via the intuition. G. E. Moore (Chapter 9) and W. D. Ross (Chapter 7) hold different versions of this view. Moore is an intuitionist about the Good, defining it as a simple, unanalyzable property; Ross is an intuitionist about what is right.

Metaethics The theoretical study that inquires into semantic, logical, and epistemological issues in ethics. It investigates the meaning of ethical terms, the nature of value judgments, and the justification of ethical theories and judgments. A central metaethical issue is the relation of facts to values (see Chapter 11). Metaethics contrasts with *normative ethics,* which constructs ethical theories and makes moral judgments from within various theoretical frameworks.

Natural Law The theory that an eternal, absolute moral law can be discovered by reason. First set forth by the Stoics but developed by Thomas Aquinas in the 13th century. See Chapter 3.

Naturalism The theory that ethical terms are defined through factual terms, in that ethical terms refer to natural properties. *Ethical hedonism* is one version of ethical naturalism, for it states that the Good, which is at the basis of all ethical judgment, refers to the experience of pleasure. Naturalists such as Geoffrey Warnock speak of the content of morality in terms of promoting human flourishing or ameliorating the human predicament. See Chapter 9.

Noncognitivism   The theory that ethical judgments have no truth value but rather express attitudes or prescriptions. See Chapter 11; see also **Cognitivism; Emotivism; Prescriptivism.**

Nonnaturalism The theory that moral facts exist but are not natural. They are discovered by intuition. See Chapter 11.

Objectivism (or **Ethical Objectivism**)   The view that moral principles have objective validity whether or not people recognize them as such; that is, moral rightness or wrongness does not depend on social approval, but on such independent considerations as whether the act or principle promotes human flourishing or ameliorates human suffering. Objectivism differs from *absolutism* in allowing that all or many of our principles are overridable in given situations. See Chapters 2 and 3; see also **Ethical Relativism; Absolutism.**

Paradox of Hedonism   The apparent contradiction that arises between two hedonistic theses: (1) pleasure is the only thing worth seeking and, whenever one seeks pleasure, it is not found; and (2) pleasure normally accompanies the satisfaction of desire whenever one reaches a goal. See Chapter 4.

Prescriptivism   The noncognitivist theory set forth by R. M. Hare (Chapter 11) claiming that, although moral judgments do not have truth values, they are more than mere expressions of attitudes; moral judgments are universal prescriptions. For example, the judgment that Mary should have an abortion implies that *anyone* in circumstances relevantly similar to Mary's should have an abortion.

Prima Facie   Latin for "at first glance." It signifies an initial status of an idea or principle. In ethics, beginning with W. D. Ross, it stands for a duty that has a presumption in its favor but may be overridden by another duty. *Prima facie* duties contrast with *actual duties* or *all-things-considered duties.* See Chapters 3 and 7.

Realism The metaethical thesis that moral facts exist and are independent of our beliefs and attitudes about them. The opposite of antirealism. See Chapter 12.

Relativism Cultural relativism is a descriptive thesis stating that moral beliefs vary enormously across cultures; it is neutral about whether this is the way things ought to be. **Ethical relativism**, on the other hand, is an evaluative thesis stating that the truth of a moral judgment depends on whether a culture recognizes the principle in question. See Chapter 2.

Skepticism   The view that we can have no knowledge. *Universal skepticism* holds that we cannot know anything at all, whereas *local* or *particular skepticism* holds that we are ignorant in important realms (e. g., see Hume on metaphysics). *Moral skepticism* holds that we cannot know whether any moral truth exists.

Slippery Slope Fallacy Objecting to a proposition on the erroneous grounds that accepting the proposition will lead to a chain of other propositions that will eventually result in an absurdity. For example, I might object in the following manner to the statement that some people are rich: "You will agree that owning only one cent does not make someone rich and that adding one cent to whatever someone owns will not in itself make him or her rich. So imagine that I have only one cent and then imagine giving me an additional cent. I still am not rich. You can give me as many pennies as you like, but at no point will you change my status from being poor to being rich. Even though I might eventually end up with a million dollars' worth of pennies, there is no point at which the transition from poverty to wealth takes place. Therefore, neither I nor anyone else can be rich. This conclusion, of course, is false.

Solipsism A person's view that only he or she exists; everyone else merely exists in that person's mind. *Moral solipsism* is a person's view that only he or she is worthy of moral consideration; it is an extreme form of egoism. See Chapter 4.

Supererogatory   (from the Latin *supererogatus,* beyond the call of duty) An act that is not required by moral principles but contains enormous value; it is beyond the call of duty, such as risking one's life to save a stranger. Although most moral systems allow for the possibility of supererogatory acts, some theories (most versions of classical utilitarianism) deny that such acts are possible.

Supervenience A dependency relationship between properties or facts of one type with properties or facts of another type. For example, if we hold that a car satisfies the purpose of a car, then we commend the car, that is, we attribute *goodness* to it. Any car having exactly the same properties as this car would necessarily be good. In metaethics, supervenience is the idea that moral properties supervene or emerge out of natural ones. For example, *badness* is an emergent or supervenient property of pain, as *goodness* is of happiness. *Rightness* is supervenient of truth-telling and promise-keeping, and *wrongness* is

supervenient of doing unnecessary harm. The doctrine of supervenience is a strategy for getting around Hume's fork of the fact–value
distinction. See Chapters 11 and 12.

Teleological Ethics This places the ultimate criterion of morality in
some nonmoral value (e. g., happiness or welfare) that results from
acts. Whereas **Deontological Ethics** ascribes intrinsic value to features of the acts themselves, teleological ethics sees only instrumental
value in the acts but intrinsic value in their consequences. Both ethical egoism and **Utilitarianism** are teleological theories. See Chapters
4 and 6.

Universalizability Found explicitly in Kant's and R. M. Hare's philosophy and implicitly in most ethicists' work, this principle states that, if
some act is right (or wrong) for one person in a situation, then it is
right (or wrong) for any relevantly similar person in that kind of situation. It is a principle of consistency that aims to eliminate irrelevant
considerations from ethical assessment. See Chapters 7 and 11; see
also **Prescriptivism.**

Utilitarianism The theory that the right action is one that maximizes
utility. Sometimes *utility* is defined in terms of *pleasure* (Jeremy Bentham), *happiness* (J. S. Mill), *ideals* (G. E. Moore and H. Rashdall), or
interests (R. B. Perry). Its motto, which characterizes one version of
utilitarianism, is "The greatest happiness for the greatest number."
Utilitarians further divide into *act-* and *rule-utilitarians.* Act-utilitarians
hold that the right act in a situation is one that results (or is most
likely to result) in the best consequences, whereas rule–utilitarians
hold that the right act is one that conforms to the set of rules that in
turn will result in the best consequences (as compared with other sets
of rules). See Chapter 6.

Index